ABOUT THIS PUBLICATION

FOR SERVICE ASSISTANCE

Please call Customer Service Department At:
1.704.898.0770

North Carolina General Statues is published by The Muliti-Media Group of Greater Charlotte in Charlotte, North Carolina. Copyright 2015 by the Multi-Media Group of Greater Charlotte. This book or parts thereof may not be reproduced in any form, stored in a retrieval system, or transmitted in any form by any means—electronic, mechanical, photocopy, recording or otherwise—without prior written permission of the publisher, except as provided by United States of America copyright law.

The records required by U.S. Code 2257(a) through (c) and the pertinent regulations 28 C.F.R. Cli. 1, Part 75 with respect to this publication and all materials associated with such records are maintained by The Multi-Media Group of Greater Charlotte, Publisher and available for review by Attorney General.

www.visionbooks.org

Copyright © 2015 by MMGGC
All rights reserved!

TID: 5061460
ISBN (10) digit: 1502913313
ISBN (13) digit: 978-1502913319

123-4-56789-01239-Paperback
123-4-56789-01239-Hardback

First Edition

090520140547

Printed in the United States of America

2015 EDITION

North Carolina Criminal Law And Procedure-Pamphlet # 35

Printed In conjunction with the Administration of the Courts

North Carolina Criminal Law and Procedure
Pamphlet Reference Guide

Chapters	Pamphlet
Chapter 1 Civil Procedure	1
Chapter 1 Civil Procedure (Continue)	2
Chapter 1A Rules of Civil Procedure	2
Chapter 1B Contribution.	2
Chapter 1C Enforcement of Judgments.	2
Chapter 1D Punitive Damages.	2
Chapter 1E Eastern Band of Cherokee Indians.	2
Chapter 1F North Carolina Uniform Interstate Depositions and Discovery Act.	2
Chapter 2 - Clerk of Superior Court [Repealed and Transferred.]	3
Chapter 3 - Commissioners of Affidavits and Deeds [Repealed.]	3
Chapter 4 - Common Law	3
Chapter 5 - Contempt [Repealed.]	3
Chapter 5A - Contempt	3
Chapter 6 - Liability for Court Costs	3
Chapter 7 - Courts [Repealed and Transferred.]	3
Chapter 7A – Judicial Department	3
Chapter 7A – Continuation (Judicial Department)	4
Chapter 7A – Continuation (Judicial Department)	5
Chapter 7B - Juvenile Code	5
Chapter 8 - Evidence	6
Chapter 8A - Interpreters for Deaf Persons [Recodified.]	6
Chapter 8B - Interpreters for Deaf Persons	6
Chapter 8C - Evidence Code	6
Chapter 9 - Jurors	6
Chapter 10 - Notaries [Repealed.]	6
Chapter 10A - Notaries [Recodified.]	6
Chapter 10B - Notaries	6
Chapter 11 - Oaths	6
Chapter 12 - Statutory Construction	6
Chapter 13 - Citizenship Restored	6
Chapter 14 - Criminal Law	7
Chapter 14 –Criminal Law (Continuation)	8
Chapter 15 - Criminal Procedure	9
Chapter 15A - Criminal Procedure Act (Continuation)	10
Chapter 15A - Criminal Procedure Act (Continuation)	11
Chapter 15B - Victims Compensation	11
Chapter 15C - Address Confidentiality Program	11
Chapter 16 - Gaming Contracts and Futures	11
Chapter 17 - Habeas Corpus	11

4

Chapter 17A - Law-Enforcement Officers [Recodified.]	11
Chapter 17B - North Carolina Criminal Justice Education and Training System [Recodified.] Chapter 17C - North Carolina Criminal Justice Education and Training Standards Commission	11 11
Chapter 17D - North Carolina Justice Academy	11
Chapter 17E - North Carolina Sheriffs' Education and Training Standards Commission	11
Chapter 18 - Regulation of Intoxicating Liquors [Repealed.]	12
Chapter 18A - Regulation of Intoxicating Liquors [Repealed.]	12
Chapter 18B - Regulation of Alcoholic Beverages	12
Chapter 18C - North Carolina State Lottery	12
Chapter 19 - Offenses against Public Morals	12
Chapter 19A - Protection of Animals	12
Chapter 20 - Motor Vehicles	13
Chapter 20 - Motor Vehicles (Continuation)	14
Chapter 20 - Motor Vehicles (Continuation)	15
Chapter 20 - Motor Vehicles (Continuation)	16
Chapter 21 - Bills of Lading	17
Chapter 22 - Contracts Requiring Writing	17
Chapter 22A - Signatures	17
Chapter 22B - Contracts Against Public Policy	17
Chapter 22C - Payments to Subcontractors	17
Chapter 23 - Debtor and Creditor. r 24 - Interest	17
Chapter 24 – Interest	17
Chapter 25 – Uniform Commercial Code	18
Chapter 25 – Uniform Commercial Code (Continuation)	19
Chapter 25A – Retail Installment Sales Act	20
Chapter 25B - Credit	20
Chapter 25C - Sales of Artwork	20
Chapter 26 - Suretyship	20
Chapter 27 - Warehouse Receipts [Repealed.]	20
Chapter 28 - Administration [Repealed.]	20
Chapter 28A - Administration of Decedents' Estates	20
Chapter 28B - Estates of Absentees in Military Service	20
Chapter 28C - Estates of Missing Persons	20
Chapter 29 - Intestate Succession	21
Chapter 30 - Surviving Spouses	21
Chapter 31 - Wills	21
Chapter 31A - Acts Barring Property Rights	21
Chapter 31B - Renunciation of Property and Renunciation of Fiduciary Powers Act	21
Chapter 31C - Uniform Disposition of Community Property Rights at Death Act	21
Chapter 32 - Fiduciaries	21
Chapter 32A - Powers of Attorney	21
Chapter 33 - Guardian and Ward [Repealed and Recodified.]	21

Chapter 33A - North Carolina Uniform Transfers to Minors Act	21
Chapter 33B - North Carolina Uniform Custodial Trust Act	21
Chapter 34 - Veterans' Guardianship Act	22
Chapter 35 - Sterilization Procedures	22
Chapter 35A - Incompetency and Guardianship	22
Chapter 36 - Trusts and Trustees [Repealed.]	22
Chapter 36A - Trusts and Trustees	22
Chapter 36B - Uniform Management of Institutional Funds Act [Repealed.]	22
Chapter 36C - North Carolina Uniform Trust Code	22
Chapter 36D - North Carolina Community Third Party Trusts, Pooled Trusts	23
Chapter 36E - Uniform Prudent Management of Institutional Funds Act	23
Chapter 37 - Allocation of Principal and Income [Repealed.]	23
Chapter 37A - Uniform Principal and Income Act	23
Chapter 38 - Boundaries	23
Chapter 38A - Landowner Liability	23
Chapter 39 - Conveyances	23
Chapter 39A - Transfer Fee Covenants Prohibited	23
Chapter 40 - Eminent Domain [Repealed.]	23
Chapter 40A - Eminent Domain	23
Chapter 41 - Estates	23
Chapter 41A - State Fair Housing Act	23
Chapter 42 - Landlord and Tenant	23
Chapter 42A - Vacation Rental Act	23
Chapter 43 - Land Registration	23
Chapter 44 - Liens	24
Chapter 44A - Statutory Liens and Charges	24
Chapter 45 - Mortgages and Deeds of Trust	24
Chapter 45A - Good Funds Settlement Act	24
Chapter 46 - Partition	24
Chapter 47 - Probate and Registration	25
Chapter 47A - Unit Ownership	25
Chapter 47B - Real Property Marketable Title Act	25
Chapter 47C - North Carolina Condominium Act	25
Chapter 47D - Notice of Settlement Act [Expired.]	25
Chapter 47E - Residential Property Disclosure Act	25
Chapter 47F - North Carolina Planned Community Act	25
Chapter 47G - Option to Purchase Contracts	25
Chapter 47H - Contracts for Deed	25
Chapter 48 - Adoptions +	26
Chapter 48A - Minors	26
Chapter 49 - Bastardy	26
Chapter 49A - Rights of Children	26
Chapter 50 - Divorce and Alimony	26
Chapter 50A - Uniform Child-Custody Jurisdiction and	

Enforcement Act	26
Chapter 50B - Domestic Violence	26
Chapter 50C - Civil No-Contact Orders	26
Chapter 51 - Marriage	26
Chapter 52 - Powers and Liabilities of Married Persons	27
Chapter 52A - Uniform Reciprocal Enforcement of Support Act [Repealed.]	27
Chapter 52B - Uniform Premarital Agreement Act	27
Chapter 52C - Uniform Interstate Family Support Act	27
Chapter 53 - Banks	27
Chapter 53A - Business Development Corporations and North Carolina Capital Resource Corporations	28
Chapter 53B - Financial Privacy Act	28
Chapter 54 - Cooperative Organizations	28
Chapter 54A - Capital Stock Savings and Loan Associations [Repealed.]	28
Chapter 54B - Savings and Loan Associations	29
Chapter 54C - Savings Banks	29
Chapter 55 - North Carolina Business Corporation Act	30
Chapter 55A - North Carolina Nonprofit Corporation Act	31
Chapter 55B - Professional Corporation Act	31
Chapter 55C - Foreign Trade Zones	31
Chapter 55D - Filings, Names, and Registered Agents for Corporations, Nonprofit Corporations, and Partnerships	31
Chapter 56 - Electric, Telegraph and Power Companies [Repealed.]	31
Chapter 57 - Hospital, Medical and Dental Service Corporations [Recodified.]	31
Chapter 57A - Health Maintenance Organization Act [Recodified.]	31
Chapter 57B - Health Maintenance Organization Act [Recodified.]	31
Chapter 57C - North Carolina Limited Liability Company Act.	31
Chapter 58 - Insurance.	32
Chapter 58 - Insurance (Continuation)	33
Chapter 58 - Insurance (Continuation)	34
Chapter 58 - Insurance (Continuation)	35
Chapter 58 - Insurance (Continuation)	36
Chapter 58 - Insurance (Continuation)	37
Chapter 58 - Insurance (Continuation)	38
Chapter 58A - North Carolina Health Insurance Trust Commission [Recodified.]	38
Chapter 59 - Partnership.	39
Chapter 59B - Uniform Unincorporated Nonprofit Association Act.	39
Chapter 60 - Railroads and Other Carriers [Repealed and Transferred.]	39
Chapter 61 - Religious Societies	39
Chapter 62 - Public Utilities	39

Chapter 62 - Public Utilities (Continuation)	40
Chapter 62A - Public Safety Telephone Service And Wireless Telephone Service	40
Chapter 63 - Aeronautics	40
Chapter 63A - North Carolina Global TransPark Authority	40
Chapter 64 - Aliens	40
Chapter 65 – Cemeteries	40
Chapter 66 - Commerce and Business	41
Chapter 67 - Dogs	41
Chapter 68 - Fences and Stock Law	41
Chapter 69 - Fire Protection	41
Chapter 70 - Indian Antiquities, Archaeological Resources and Unmarked Human Skeletal Remains Protection	42
Chapter 71 - Indians [Repealed.]	42
Chapter 71A - Indians	42
Chapter 72 - Inns, Hotels and Restaurants	42
Chapter 73 - Mills	42
Chapter 74 - Mines and Quarries	42
Chapter 74A - Company Police [Repealed.]	42
Chapter 74B - Private Protective Services Act [Repealed.]	42
Chapter 74C - Private Protective Services	42
Chapter 74D - Alarm Systems	42
Chapter 74E - Company Police Act	42
Chapter 74F - Locksmith Licensing Act	42
Chapter 74G - Campus Police Act	42
Chapter 75 - Monopolies, Trusts and Consumer Protection	42
Chapter 75A - Boating and Water Safety	43
Chapter 75B - Discrimination in Business	43
Chapter 75C - Motion Picture Fair Competition Act	43
Chapter 75D - Racketeer Influenced and Corrupt Organizations	43
Chapter 75E - Unlawful Activities in Connection With Certain Corporate Transactions	43
Chapter 76 - Navigation	43
Chapter 76A - Navigation and Pilotage Commissions	43
Chapter 77 - Rivers, Creeks, and Coastal Waters	43
Chapter 78 - Securities Law [Repealed.]	43
Chapter 78A - North Carolina Securities Act	43
Chapter 78B - Tender Offer Disclosure Act [Repealed.]	43
Chapter 78C - Investment Advisers	43
Chapter 78D - Commodities Act	43
Chapter 79 - Strays [Repealed.]	43
Chapter 80 - Trademarks, Brands, etc.	44
Chapter 81 - Weights and Measures [Recodified.]	44
Chapter 81A - Weights and Measures Act of 1975.	44
Chapter 82 - Wrecks [Repealed.]	44
Chapter 83 - Architects [Recodified.]	44

Chapter 83A - Architects	44
Chapter 84 - Attorneys-at-Law	44
Chapter 84A - Foreign Legal Consultants	44
Chapter 85 - Auctions and Auctioneers [Repealed.]	44
Chapter 85A - Bail Bondsmen and Runners [Recodified.]	44
Chapter 85B - Auctions and Auctioneers	44
Chapter 85C - Bail Bondsmen and Runners [Recodified.]	44
Chapter 86 - Barbers [Recodified.]	44
Chapter 86A - Barbers	44
Chapter 87 - Contractors	44
Chapter 88 - Cosmetic Art [Repealed.]	44
Chapter 88A - Electrolysis Practice Act	44
Chapter 88B - Cosmetic Art	45
Chapter 89 - Engineering and Land Surveying [Recodified.]	45
Chapter 89A - Landscape Architects	45
Chapter 89B - Foresters	45
Chapter 89C - Engineering and Land Surveying	45
Chapter 89D - Landscape Contractors	45
Chapter 89E - Geologists Licensing Act	45
Chapter 89F - North Carolina Soil Scientist Licensing Act	45
Chapter 89G - Irrigation Contractors	45
Chapter 90 - Medicine and Allied Occupations	45
Chapter 90 - Medicine and Allied Occupations (Continuation)	46
Chapter 90 - Medicine and Allied Occupations (Continuation)	47
Chapter 90 - Medicine and Allied Occupations (Continuation)	48
Chapter 90A - Sanitarians and Water and Wastewater Treatment Facility Operators	48
Chapter 90B - Social Worker Certification and Licensure Act	48
Chapter 90C - North Carolina Recreational Therapy Licensure Act	48
Chapter 90D - Interpreters and Transliterators	48
Chapter 91 - Pawnbrokers [Repealed.]	48
Chapter 91A - Pawnbrokers Modernization Act of 1989	48
Chapter 92 - Photographers [Deleted.]	48
Chapter 93 - Certified Public Accountants	48
Chapter 93A - Real Estate License Law	49
Chapter 93B - Occupational Licensing Boards	49
Chapter 93C - Watchmakers [Repealed.]	49
Chapter 93D - North Carolina State Hearing Aid Dealers and Fitters Board.	49
Chapter 93E - North Carolina Appraisers Act	49
Chapter 94 - Apprenticeship	49
Chapter 95 - Department of Labor and Labor Regulations	49
Chapter 95 - Department of Labor and Labor Regulations (Continuation)	50
Chapter 96 - Employment Security	50
Chapter 97 - Workers' Compensation Act	50
Chapter 97 - Workers' Compensation Act (Continuation)	51

Chapter 98 - Burnt and Lost Records	51
Chapter 99 - Libel and Slander	51
Chapter 99A - Civil Remedies for Criminal Actions	51
Chapter 99B - Products Liability	51
Chapter 99C - Actions Relating to Winter Sports Safety and Accidents	51
Chapter 99D - Civil Rights	51
Chapter 99E - Special Liability Provisions	51
Chapter 100 - Monuments, Memorials and Parks	51
Chapter 101 - Names of Persons	51
Chapter 102 - Official Survey Base	51
Chapter 103 - Sundays, Holidays and Special Days	51
Chapter 104 - United States Lands	51
Chapter 104A - Degrees of Kinship	51
Chapter 104B - Hurricanes or Other Acts of Nature	51
Chapter 104C - Atomic Energy, Radioactivity and Ionizing Radiation [Repealed and Recodified.]	51
Chapter 104D - Southern States Energy Compact	51
Chapter 104E - North Carolina Radiation Protection Act	51
Chapter 104F - Southeast Interstate Low-Level Radioactive Waste Management Compact [Repealed]	51
Chapter 104G - North Carolina Low-Level Radioactive Waste Management Authority Act of 1987 [Repealed]	51
Chapter 105 - Taxation	51
Chapter 105 - Taxation (Continuation)	52
Chapter 105 - Taxation (Continuation)	53
Chapter 105 - Taxation (Continuation)	54
Chapter 105A - Setoff Debt Collection Act	55
Chapter 105B - Defaulted Student Loan Recovery Act	55
Chapter 106 - Agriculture	55
Chapter 106 - Agriculture (Continue)	56
Chapter 106 - Agriculture (Continue)	57
Chapter 107 - Agricultural Development Districts [Repealed.]	57
Chapter 108 - Social Services [Repealed and Recodified.]	57
Chapter 108A - Social Services	57
Chapter 108B - Community Action Programs	58
Chapter 108C Medicaid and Health Choice Provider Requirements.	58
Chapter 108D Medicaid Managed Care for Behavioral Health Services.	58
Chapter 109 - Bonds [Recodified.]	58
Chapter 110 - Child Welfare	58
Chapter 111 - Aid to the Blind	58
Chapter 112 - Confederate Homes and Pensions [Repealed.]	58
Chapter 113 - Conservation and Development	58
Chapter 113 - Conservation and Development (Continuation)	59

Chapter 113A - Pollution Control and Environment	59
Chapter 113A - Pollution Control and Environment (Continuation)	60
Chapter 113B - North Carolina Energy Policy Act of 1975	60
Chapter 114 - Department of Justice	60
Chapter 115 - Elementary and Secondary Education [Repealed.]	60
Chapter 115A - Community Colleges, Technical Institutes, and Industrial Education Centers [Repealed.]	60
Chapter 115B - Tuition and Fee Waivers	60
Chapter 115C - Elementary and Secondary Education	60
Chapter 115C - Elementary and Secondary Education (Continuation)	61
Chapter 115C - Elementary and Secondary Education (Continuation)	62
Chapter 115C - Elementary and Secondary Education (Continuation)	63
Chapter 115D - Community Colleges	63
Chapter 115E - Private Educational Facilities Finance Act [Recodified]	63
Chapter 116 - Higher Education	63
Chapter 116 - Higher Education (Continuation)	63
Chapter 116A - Escheats and Abandoned Property [Repealed.]	64
Chapter 116B - Escheats and Abandoned Property	64
Chapter 116C - Continuum of Education Programs	64
Chapter 116D - Higher Education Bonds	64
Chapter 117 - Electrification	64
Chapter 118 - Firemen's and Rescue Squad Workers' Relief and Pension Funds [Recodified.]	64
Chapter 118A - Firemen's Death Benefit Act [Repealed.]	64
Chapter 118B - Members of a Rescue Squad Death Benefit Act [Repealed.]	64
Chapter 119 - Gasoline and Oil Inspection and Regulation	64
Chapter 120 - General Assembly	65
Chapter 120 - General Assembly (Continuation)	66
Chapter 120 - General Assembly (Continuation)	67
Chapter 120C - Lobbying	67
Chapter 121 - Archives and History	67
Chapter 122 - Hospitals for the Mentally Disordered [Repealed.]	67
Chapter 122A - North Carolina Housing Finance Agency	67
Chapter 122B - North Carolina Agricultural Facilities Finance Act [Repealed.]	67
Chapter 122C - Mental Health, Developmental Disabilities, and Substance Abuse Act of 1985	67
Chapter 122C - Mental Health, Developmental Disabilities, and Substance Abuse Act of 1985 (Continuation)	68
Chapter 122D - North Carolina Agricultural Finance Act	68

Chapter 122E - North Carolina Housing Trust and Oil Overcharge Act	68
Chapter 123 - Impeachment	69
Chapter 123A - Industrial Development [Repealed.]	69
Chapter 124 - Internal Improvements	69
Chapter 125 - Libraries	69
Chapter 126 - State Personnel System	69
Chapter 127 - Militia [Repealed.]	69
Chapter 127A - Militia	69
Chapter 127B - Military Affairs	69
Chapter 127C - Advisory Commission on Military Affairs	69
Chapter 128 - Offices and Public Officers	69
Chapter 128 - Offices and Public Officers (Continuation)	70
Chapter 129 - Public Buildings and Grounds	70
Chapter 130 - Public Health [Repealed.]	70
Chapter 130A - Public Health	70
Chapter 130A - Public Health (Continuation)	71
Chapter 130A - Public Health (Continuation)	72
Chapter 130B - Hazardous Waste Management Commission [Repealed.]	72
Chapter 131 - Public Hospitals [Repealed.]	72
Chapter 131A - Health Care Facilities Finance Act	72
Chapter 131B - Licensing of Ambulatory Surgical Facilities [Repealed.]	72
Chapter 131C - Charitable Solicitation Licensure Act [Repealed.]	72
Chapter 131D - Inspection and Licensing of Facilities	72
Chapter 131E - Health Care Facilities and Services	72
Chapter 131E - Health Care Facilities and Services (Continuation)	73
Chapter 131F - Solicitation of Contributions	73
Chapter 132 - Public Records	73
Chapter 133 - Public Works	74
Chapter 134 - Youth Development [Recodified.]	74
Chapter 134A - Youth Services [Repealed.]	74
Chapter 135 - Retirement System for Teachers and State Employees; Social Security; Health Insurance Program for Children	74
Chapter 135 - Retirement System for Teachers and State Employees; Social Security; Health Insurance Program for Children	75
Chapter 136 - Transportation	75
Chapter 136 - Transportation (Continuation)	76
Chapter 137 - Rural Rehabilitation [Repealed.]	76
Chapter 138 - Salaries, Fees and Allowances	76
Chapter 138A - State Government Ethics Act	76
Chapter 139 - Soil and Water Conservation Districts	76

Chapter 140 - State Art Museum; Symphony and Art Societies	76
Chapter 140A - State Awards System	76
Chapter 141 - State Boundaries	76
Chapter 142 - State Debt	76
Chapter 143 - State Departments, Institutions, and Commissions	77
Chapter 143 - State Departments, Institutions, and Commissions (Continuation)	78
Chapter 143 - State Departments, Institutions, and Commissions (Continuation)	79
Chapter 143 - State Departments, Institutions, and Commissions (Continuation)	80
Chapter 143A - State Government Reorganization	80
Chapter 143B - Executive Organization Act of 1973	80
Chapter 143B - Executive Organization Act of 1973 (Continuation)	81
Chapter 143B - Executive Organization Act of 1973 (Continuation)	82
Chapter 143C - State Budget Act	83
Chapter 143D - The State Governmental Accountability and Internal Control Act	83
Chapter 144 - State Flag, Official Governmental Flags, Motto, and Colors	83
Chapter 145 - State Symbols and Other Official Adoptions.	83
Chapter 146 - State Lands	83
Chapter 147 - State Officers	83
Chapter 148 - State Prison System	84
Chapter 149 - State Song and Toast	84
Chapter 150 - Uniform Revocation of Licenses [Repealed.]	84
Chapter 150A - Administrative Procedure Act [Recodified.]	84
Chapter 150B - Administrative Procedure Act	84
Chapter 151 - Constables [Repealed.]	84
Chapter 152 - Coroners	84
Chapter 152A - County Medical Examiner [Repealed.]	84
Chapter 152A - County Medical Examiner [Repealed.] (Continuation)	85
Chapter 153 - Counties and County Commissioners [Repealed.]	85
Chapter 153A - Counties	85
Chapter 153B - Mountain Resources Planning Act	85
Chapter 153C - Uwharrie Regional Resources Act	85
Chapter 154 - County Surveyor [Repealed.]	85
Chapter 155 - County Treasurer [Repealed.]	85
Chapter 156 - Drainage	85
Chapter 156 – Drainage (Continuation)	86

Chapter 157 - Housing Authorities and Projects	86
Chapter 157A - Historic Properties Commissions [Transferred.]	86
Chapter 158 - Local Development	86
Chapter 159 - Local Government Finance	86
Chapter 159 - Local Government Finance (Continuation)	87
Chapter 159A - Pollution Abatement and Industrial Facilities Financing Act [Unconstitutional.]	87
Chapter 159B - Joint Municipal Electric Power and Energy Act	87
Chapter 159C - Industrial and Pollution Control Facilities Financing Act	87
Chapter 159D - The North Carolina Capital Facilities Financing Act	87
Chapter 159E - Registered Public Obligations Act	87
Chapter 159F - North Carolina Energy Development Authority [Repealed.]	87
Chapter 159G - Water Infrastructure	87
Chapter 159H - [Reserved.]	87
Chapter 159I - Solid Waste Management Loan Program and Local Government Special Obligation Bonds	87
Chapter 160 - Municipal Corporations [Repealed And Transferred.]	87
Chapter 160A - Cities and Towns	88
Chapter 160A - Cities and Towns (Continuation)	89
Chapter 160B - Consolidated City-County Act	89
Chapter 160C - Baseball Park Districts [Repealed.]	90
Chapter 161 - Register of Deeds	90
Chapter 162 - Sheriff	90
Chapter 162A - Water and Sewer Systems	90
Chapter 162B Continuity of Local Government in Emergency.	90
Chapter 163 Elections and Election Laws.	90
Chapter 163 Elections and Election Laws. (Continuation)	91
Chapter 164 Concerning the General Statutes of North Carolina.	92
Chapter 165 Veterans.	92
Chapter 166 Civil Preparedness Agencies [Repealed.]	92
Chapter 166A North Carolina Emergency Management Act.	92
Chapter 167 State Civil Air Patrol [Repealed.]	92
Chapter 168 Persons with Disabilities.	92
Chapter 168A Persons With Disabilities Protection Act.	92

§ 58-33A-45. License denial, nonrenewal, or revocation.

(a) The Commissioner may place on probation, suspend, revoke, or refuse to issue or renew a public adjuster's license or may levy a civil penalty in accordance with G.S. 58-2-70 or any combination of actions for any one or more of the following causes:

(1) Providing incorrect, misleading, incomplete, or materially untrue information in the license application.

(2) Violating any insurance laws or violating any regulation, subpoena, or order of the Commissioner or of another state's insurance regulator.

(3) Obtaining or attempting to obtain a license through misrepresentation or fraud.

(4) Improperly withholding, misappropriating, or converting any monies or properties received in the course of doing insurance business.

(5) Intentionally misrepresenting the terms of an actual or proposed insurance contract or application for insurance.

(6) Having been convicted of a felony or a misdemeanor involving dishonesty or breach of trust.

(7) Having admitted or been found to have committed any insurance unfair trade practice or insurance fraud.

(8) Using fraudulent, coercive, or dishonest practices or demonstrating incompetence, untrustworthiness, or financial irresponsibility in the conduct of business in this State or elsewhere.

(9) Having an insurance license, or its equivalent, denied, suspended, or revoked in any other state, province, district, or territory.

(10) Forging another's name to an application for insurance or to any document related to an insurance transaction.

(11) Cheating, including improperly using notes or any other reference material, to complete an examination for an insurance license.

(12) Knowingly accepting insurance business from an individual who is not licensed but who is required to be licensed by the Commissioner.

(13) Failing to comply with an administrative or court order imposing a child support obligation.

(14) Failing to pay state income tax or comply with any administrative or court order directing payment of state income tax.

(b) If the action by the Commissioner is to deny an application for or not renew a license, the Commissioner shall notify the applicant or licensee and advise, in writing, the applicant or licensee of the reason for the nonrenewal or denial of the applicant's or licensee's license. The applicant or licensee may make written demand upon the Commissioner in accordance with Article 3A of Chapter 150B of the General Statutes for a hearing before the Commissioner to determine the reasonableness of the Commissioner's action. The hearing shall be held pursuant to Article 3A of Chapter 150B of the General Statutes.

(c) The license of a business entity may be suspended, revoked, or refused if the Commissioner finds, after hearing, that an individual licensee's violation was known or should have been known by one or more of the partners, officers, or managers acting on behalf of the business entity and the violation was neither reported to the Commissioner nor corrective action taken.

(d) In addition to or in lieu of any applicable denial, suspension, or revocation of a license, a person may, after hearing, be subject to a civil penalty according to G.S. 58-2-70.

(e) The Commissioner shall retain the authority to enforce the provisions of and impose any penalty or remedy authorized by this Chapter against any person who is under investigation for or charged with a violation of this Chapter, even if the person's license or registration has been surrendered or has lapsed by operation of law. (2009-565, s. 1.)

§ 58-33A-50. Bond or letter of credit.

(a) Before issuance of a license as a public adjuster and for the duration of the license, the applicant shall secure evidence of financial responsibility in a format prescribed by the Commissioner through any of the following instruments:

(1) A bond executed and issued by an insurer authorized to issue bonds in this State which meets all of the following requirements:

a. It shall be in the minimum amount of twenty thousand dollars ($20,000).

b. It shall be in favor of this State and shall specifically authorize recovery by the Commissioner on behalf of any person in this State who sustained damages as the result of erroneous acts, failure to act, conviction of fraud, or conviction of unfair practices in his or her capacity as a public adjuster.

c. It shall not be terminated unless at least 30 days' prior written notice will have been filed with the Commissioner and given to the licensee.

(2) An irrevocable letter of credit issued by a qualified financial institution, which meets all of the following requirements:

a. It shall be in the minimum amount of twenty thousand dollars ($20,000).

b. It shall be to an account to the Commissioner and subject to lawful levy of execution on behalf of any person to whom the public adjuster has been found to be legally liable as the result of erroneous acts, failure to act, fraudulent acts, or unfair practices in his or her capacity as a public adjuster.

c. It shall not be terminated unless at least 30 days' prior written notice will have been filed with the Commissioner and given to the licensee.

(b) The issuer of the evidence of financial responsibility shall notify the Commissioner upon termination of the bond or letter of credit, unless otherwise directed by the Commissioner.

(c) The Commissioner may ask for the evidence of financial responsibility at any time he or she deems relevant.

(d) The authority to act as a public adjuster shall automatically terminate if the evidence of financial responsibility terminates or becomes impaired. (2009-565, s. 1.)

§ 58-33A-55. Continuing education.

(a)   An individual who holds a public adjuster license and who is not exempt under subsection (b) of this section shall satisfactorily complete a minimum of 24 hours of continuing education courses, including ethics, reported on a biennial basis in conjunction with the license renewal cycle.

(b)   This section shall not apply to any of the following:

(1)   Licensees not licensed for one full year before the end of the applicable continuing education biennium.

(2)   Licensees holding nonresident public adjuster licenses who have met the continuing education requirements of their home state and whose home state gives credit to residents of this State on the same basis.

(c)   Only continuing education courses approved by the Commissioner shall be used to satisfy the continuing education requirement of subsection (a) of this section. (2009-565, s. 1.)

§ 58-33A-60. Public adjuster fees.

(a)   A public adjuster shall not pay a commission, service fee, or other valuable consideration to a person for investigating or settling claims in this State if that person is required to be licensed under this Article and is not so licensed.

(b)   A person shall not accept a commission, service fee, or other valuable consideration for investigating or settling claims in this State if that person is required to be licensed under this Article and is not so licensed.

(c)   A public adjuster may pay or assign commission, service fees, or other valuable consideration to persons who do not investigate or settle claims in this State, unless the payment would violate G.S. 58-33-85 or G.S. 58-63-15(8).

(d)   In the event of a catastrophic incident, there shall be limits on catastrophic fees. No public adjuster shall charge, agree to, or accept as compensation or reimbursement any payment, commission, fee, or other thing of value equal to more than ten percent (10%) of any insurance settlement or proceeds. No public adjuster shall require, demand, or accept any fee, retainer, compensation, deposit, or other thing of value before settlement of a claim. (2009-565, s. 1.)

§ 58-33A-65. Contract between public adjuster and insured.

(a) Public adjusters shall ensure that all contracts for their services are in writing and contain all of the following terms:

(1) Legible full name of the adjuster signing the contract, as specified in Department records.

(2) Permanent home state business address and phone number.

(3) Department license number.

(4) Title of "Public Adjuster Contract."

(5) The insured's full name, street address, insurance company name and policy number, if known or upon notification.

(6) A description of the loss and its location, if applicable.

(7) Description of services to be provided to the insured.

(8) Signatures of the public adjuster and the insured.

(9) Date contract was signed by the public adjuster and date the contract was signed by the insured.

(10) Attestation language stating that the public adjuster is fully bonded pursuant to State law.

(11) Full salary, fee, commission, compensation, or other considerations the public adjuster is to receive for services.

(b) The contract may specify that the public adjuster shall be named as a co-payee on an insurer's payment of a claim.

(1)   If the compensation is based on a share of the insurance settlement, the exact percentage shall be specified.

(2)   Initial expenses to be reimbursed to the public adjuster from the proceeds of the claim payment shall be specified by type, with dollar estimates set forth in the contract and with any additional expenses first approved by the insured.

(3)   Compensation provisions in a public adjusting contract shall not be redacted in any copy of the contract provided to the Commissioner. Such a redaction shall constitute an omission of material fact in violation of Article 63 of this Chapter.

(c)   If the insurer, not later than 72 hours after the date on which the loss is reported to the insurer, either pays or commits in writing to pay to the insured the policy limit of the insurance policy, the public adjuster shall comply with all of the following:

(1)   Not receive a commission consisting of a percentage of the total amount paid by an insurer to resolve a claim.

(2)   Inform the insured that loss recovery amount might not be increased by insurer.

(3)   Be entitled only to reasonable compensation from the insured for services provided by the public adjuster on behalf of the insured, based on the time spent on a claim and expenses incurred by the public adjuster, until the claim is paid or the insured receives a written commitment to pay from the insurer.

(d)   A public adjuster shall provide the insured a written disclosure concerning any direct or indirect financial interest that the public adjuster has with any other party who is involved in any aspect of the claim, other than the salary, fee, commission, or other consideration established in the written contract with the insured, including, but not limited to, any ownership of, other than as a minority stockholder, or any compensation expected to be received from any construction firm, salvage firm, building appraisal firm, motor vehicle repair shop, or any other firm that provides estimates for work, or that performs any work, in conjunction with damages caused by the insured loss on which the public adjuster is engaged. The word "firm" shall include any corporation, partnership, association, joint-stock company, or person.

(e) A public adjuster contract may not contain any contract term that includes any of the following terms:

(1) Allows the public adjuster's percentage fee to be collected when money is due from an insurance company but not paid, or that allows a public adjuster to collect the entire fee from the first check issued by an insurance company rather than as a percentage of each check issued by an insurance company.

(2) Requires the insured to authorize an insurance company to issue a check only in the name of the public adjuster.

(3) Imposes collection costs or late fees.

(4) Precludes a public adjuster from pursuing civil remedies.

(f) Before the signing of the contract, the public adjuster shall provide the insured with a separate disclosure document regarding the claim process that states:

(1) Property insurance policies obligate the insured to present a claim to his or her insurance company for consideration. There are three types of adjusters that could be involved in that process. The definitions of the three types are as follows:

a. "Company adjuster" means the insurance adjusters who are employees of an insurance company. They represent the interest of the insurance company and are paid by the insurance company. They will not charge you a fee.

b. "Independent adjuster" means the insurance adjusters who are hired on a contract basis by an insurance company to represent the insurance company's interest in the settlement of the claim. They are paid by your insurance company. They will not charge you a fee.

c. "Public adjuster" means the insurance adjusters who do not work for any insurance company. They work for the insured to assist in the preparation, presentation, and settlement of the claim. The insured hires them by signing a contract agreeing to pay them a fee or commission based on a percentage of the settlement or other method of compensation.

(2) The insured is not required to hire a public adjuster to help the insured meet his or her obligations under the policy but has the right to do so.

(3) The insured has the right to initiate direct communications with the insured's attorney, the insurer, the insurer's adjuster, and the insurer's attorney, or any other person regarding the settlement of the insured's claim.

(4) The public adjuster is not a representative or employee of the insurer.

(5) The salary, fee, commission, or other consideration is the obligation of the insured, not the insurer.

(g) The contracts shall be executed in duplicate to provide an original contract to the public adjuster and an original contract to the insured. The public adjuster's original contract shall be available at all times for inspection without notice by the Commissioner.

(h) The public adjuster shall provide the insurer a notification letter, which has been signed by the insured, authorizing the public adjuster to represent the insured's interest.

(i) The insured has the right to rescind the contract within three business days after the date the contract was signed. The rescission shall be in writing and mailed or delivered to the public adjuster at the address in the contract within the three-business-day period.

(j) If the insured exercises the right to rescind the contract, anything of value given by the insured under the contract will be returned to the insured within 15 business days after the receipt by the public adjuster of the cancellation notice. (2009-565, s. 1; 2013-199, s. 21.)

§ 58-33A-70. Escrow or trust accounts.

A public adjuster who receives, accepts, or holds any funds on behalf of an insured, toward the settlement of a claim for loss or damage, shall deposit the funds in a noninterest-bearing escrow or trust account in a financial institution that is insured by an agency of the federal government in the public adjuster's home state or where the loss occurred. (2009-565, s. 1.)

§ 58-33A-75. Record retention.

(a) A public adjuster shall maintain a complete record of each transaction as a public adjuster. The records required by this section shall include all of the following:

(1) Name of the insured.

(2) Date, location, and amount of the loss.

(3) Copy of the contract between the public adjuster and insured.

(4) Name of the insurer, amount, expiration date and number of each policy carried with respect to the loss.

(5) Itemized statement of the insured's recoveries.

(6) Itemized statement of all compensation received by the public adjuster, from any source whatsoever, in connection with the loss.

(7) A register of all monies received, deposited, disbursed, or withdrawn in connection with a transaction with an insured, including fees, transfers, and disbursements from a trust account and all transactions concerning all interest-bearing accounts.

(8) Name of public adjuster who executed the contract.

(9) Name of the attorney representing the insured, if applicable, and the name of the claims representatives of the insurance company.

(10) Evidence of financial responsibility in a format prescribed by the Commissioner.

(b) Records shall be maintained for at least five years after the termination of the transaction with an insured and shall be open to examination by the Commissioner at all times.

(c)   Records submitted to the Commissioner in accordance with this section that contain information identified in writing as proprietary by the public adjuster shall be treated as confidential by the Commissioner and shall not be subject to Chapter 132 of the General Statutes or G.S. 58-2-100. (2009-565, s. 1.)

§ 58-33A-80. Standards of conduct of public adjusters.

(a)   A public adjuster shall, under his or her license, serve with objectivity and complete loyalty the interest of his or her client alone and render to the insured such information, counsel, and service, as within the knowledge, understanding, and opinion in good faith of the licensee, as will best serve the insured's insurance claim needs and interest.

(b)   A public adjuster shall not solicit, or attempt to solicit, an insured during the progress of a loss-producing occurrence, as defined in the insured's insurance contract.

(c)   A public adjuster shall not permit an unlicensed employee or representative of the public adjuster to conduct business for which a license is required under this Article.

(d)   A public adjuster shall not have a direct or indirect financial interest in any aspect of the claim, other than the salary, fee, commission, or other consideration established in the written contract with the insured, unless full written disclosure has been made to the insured as set forth in G.S. 58-33A-65.

(e)   A public adjuster shall not acquire any interest in salvage of property subject to the contract with the insured unless the public adjuster obtains written permission from the insured after settlement of the claim with the insurer as set forth in G.S. 58-33A-65.

(f)   The public adjuster shall abstain from referring or directing the insured to get needed repairs or services in connection with a loss from any person described by any of the following criteria, unless disclosed to the insured:

(1)   The public adjuster has a financial interest in the person.

(2)   The public adjuster may receive direct or indirect compensation for the referral from the person.

(g) The public adjuster shall disclose to an insured if the public adjuster has any interest or will be compensated by any construction firm, salvage firm, building appraisal firm, motor vehicle repair shop, or any other firm that performs any work in conjunction with damages caused by the insured loss. The word "firm" includes any corporation, partnership, association, joint-stock company, or person.

(h) Any compensation or anything of value in connection with an insured's specific loss that will be received by a public adjuster shall be disclosed by the public adjuster to the insured in writing, including the source and amount of any such compensation.

(i) Public adjusters shall adhere to all of the following general ethical requirements:

(1) A public adjuster shall not undertake the adjustment of any claim if the public adjuster is not competent and knowledgeable as to the terms and conditions of the insurance coverage, or which otherwise exceeds the public adjuster's current expertise.

(2) A public adjuster shall not knowingly make any oral or written material misrepresentations or statements that are false or maliciously critical and intended to injure any person engaged in the business of insurance to any insured client or potential insured client.

(3) No public adjuster, while so licensed by the Department, may represent or act as a company adjuster or independent adjuster on the same claim.

(4) The contract shall not be construed to prevent an insured from pursuing any civil remedy after the three-business-day revocation or cancellation period.

(5) A public adjuster shall not enter into a contract or accept a power of attorney that vests in the public adjuster the effective authority to choose the persons who shall perform repair work.

(6) A public adjuster shall ensure that all contracts for the public adjuster's services are in writing and set forth all terms and conditions of the engagement.

(j) A public adjuster may not agree to any loss settlement without the insured's knowledge and consent.

(k)   Public adjusters shall not solicit a client for employment between the hours of 9:00 P.M. and 9:00 A.M. (2009-565, s. 1.)

§ 58-33A-90. Reporting of actions.

(a)   A public adjuster shall report to the Commissioner any administrative action taken against the public adjuster in another jurisdiction or by another governmental agency in this State within 30 days after the final disposition of the matter. This report shall include a copy of the order, consent order, or other relevant legal documents.

(b)   Within 30 days after the initial pretrial hearing date, the public adjuster shall report to the Commissioner any criminal prosecution of the public adjuster taken in any jurisdiction. The report shall include a copy of the initial complaint filed, the order resulting from the hearing, and any other relevant legal documents. (2009-565, s. 1.)

§ 58-33A-95. Rules.

The Commissioner may, in accordance with Chapter 150B of the General Statutes, adopt rules that are necessary or proper to carry out the purposes of this Article. (2009-565, s. 1.)

Article 34.

Agency and Management Contracts.

§ 58-34-1: Repealed by Session Laws 1991, c. 681, s. 50.

§ 58-34-2. Managing general agents.

(a) As used in this Article:

(1) "Control", including the terms "controlling", "controlled by", and "under common control", means the direct or indirect possession of the power to direct or cause the direction of the management and policies of a person, whether through the ownership of voting securities, by contract other than a commercial contract for goods or nonmanagement services, or otherwise, unless the power is the result of an official position with or corporate office held by the person.

(1a) "Custodial agreement" means any agreement or contract under which any person is delegated authority to safekeep assets of the insurer.

(2) "Insurer" means a domestic insurer but does not mean a reciprocal regulated under Article 15 of this Chapter.

(2a) "Management contract" means any agreement or contract under which any person is delegated management duties or control of an insurer or transfers a substantial part of any major function of an insurer, such as adjustment of losses, production of business, investment of assets, or general servicing of the insurer's business.

(3) "Managing general agent" or "MGA" means any person who manages all or part of the insurance business of an insurer (including the management of a separate division, department, or underwriting office) and acts as an agent for the insurer, whether known as a managing general agent, manager, or other similar term, who, with or without the authority, either separately or together with persons under common control, produces, directly or indirectly, and underwrites an amount of gross direct written premium equal to or more than five percent (5%) of the policyholder surplus as reported in the last annual statement of the insurer in any one quarter or year together with one or more of the following activities related to the business produced: (i) adjusts or pays any claims, or (ii) negotiates reinsurance on behalf of the insurer. "MGA" does not mean an employee of the insurer; an underwriting manager who, pursuant to contract, manages all or part of the insurance operations of the insurer, is under common control with the insurer, is subject to Article 19 of this Chapter, and whose compensation is not based on the volume of premiums written; a person who, under Article 15 of this Chapter, is designated and authorized by subscribers as the attorney-in-fact for a reciprocal having authority to obligate them on reciprocal and other insurance contracts; or a U.S. Manager of the United States branch of an alien insurer.

(4) "Qualified actuary" means a person who meets the standards of a qualified actuary as specified in the NAIC Annual Statement Instructions, as amended or clarified by rule, order, directive, or bulletin of the Department, for the type of insurer for which the MGA is establishing loss reserves.

(5) "Underwrite" means the authority to accept or reject risk on behalf of the insurer.

(b) Control is presumed to exist if any person directly or indirectly owns, controls, holds with the power to vote, or holds proxies representing ten percent (10%) or more of the voting securities of any other person. The Commissioner may determine, after furnishing all persons in interest notice and opportunity to be heard and making specific findings of fact to support the determination, that control exists in fact, notwithstanding the absence of a presumption to that effect. The Commissioner may determine upon application that any person does not or will not upon the taking of some proposed action control another person. The Commissioner may prospectively revoke or modify that determination, after the notice and opportunity to be heard, whenever, in the Commissioner's judgment, revocation, or modification is consistent with this Article.

(c) No person shall act as an MGA with respect to risks located in this State for an insurer unless that person is a licensed agent in this State. No person shall act as an MGA representing an insurer with respect to risks located outside of this State unless that person is licensed as an agent in this State; and the license may be a nonresident license. The Commissioner may require a bond in an amount acceptable to the Commissioner for the protection of the insurer. The Commissioner may require the MGA to maintain an errors and omissions policy.

(d) No person acting as an MGA shall place business with an insurer unless there is in force a written contract between the MGA and the insurer that sets forth the responsibilities of each party and, where both parties share responsibility for a particular function, specifies the division of such responsibilities, and that contains the following minimum provisions:

(1) The insurer may terminate the contract for cause upon written notice to the MGA. The insurer may suspend the underwriting authority of the MGA during the pendency of any dispute regarding the cause for termination.

(2) The MGA will render accounts to the insurer detailing all transactions and remit all funds due under the contract to the insurer on not less than a monthly basis.

(3) All funds collected for the account of an insurer will be held by the MGA in a fiduciary capacity in a bank that is a member of the Federal Reserve System. This account shall be used for all payments on behalf of the insurer. The MGA may retain no more than three months estimated claims payments and allocated loss adjustment expenses.

(4) Separate records of business written by the MGA will be maintained. The insurer shall have access to and right to copy all accounts related to its business in a form usable by the insurer, and the Commissioner shall have access to all books, bank accounts, and records of the MGA in a form usable to the Commissioner. The records shall be retained according to the provisions of 11 NCAC 11C.0105.

(5) The contract may not be assigned in whole or part by the MGA.

(6) Appropriate underwriting guidelines, including: the maximum annual premium volume; the basis of the rates to be charged; the types of risks that may be written; maximum limits of liability; applicable exclusions; territorial limitations; policy cancellation provisions; and the maximum policy period. The insurer shall have the right to cancel or nonrenew any policy of insurance subject to applicable laws and rules.

(7) If the contract permits the MGA to settle claims on behalf of the insurer:

a. All claims must be reported to the insurer in a timely manner.

b. A copy of the claim file will be sent to the insurer at its request or as soon as it becomes known that the claim: has the potential to exceed an amount determined by the insurer and approved by the Commissioner; involves a coverage dispute; may exceed the MGA's claims settlement authority; is open for more than six months; or is closed by payment of an amount set by the insurer and approved by the Commissioner.

c. All claim files will be the joint property of the insurer and MGA. However, upon an order of liquidation of the insurer the files shall become the sole property of the insurer or its estate; the MGA shall have reasonable access to and the right to copy the files on a timely basis.

d. Any settlement authority granted to the MGA may be terminated for cause upon the insurer's written notice to the MGA or upon the termination of the contract. The insurer may suspend the settlement authority during the pendency of any dispute regarding the cause for termination.

(8) Where electronic claims files are in existence, the contract must address the timely transmission of the data.

(9) If the contract provides for a sharing of interim profits by the MGA, and the MGA has the authority to determine the amount of the interim profits by establishing loss reserves, controlling claim payments, or by any other manner, interim profits will not be paid to the MGA until one year after they are earned for property insurance business and five years after they are earned on casualty business and not until the profits have been verified under subsection (f) of this section.

(10) The MGA shall not:

a. Bind reinsurance or retrocessions on behalf of the insurer, except that the MGA may bind facultative reinsurance contracts pursuant to obligatory facultative agreements if the contract with the insurer contains reinsurance underwriting guidelines including, for both reinsurance assumed and ceded, a list of reinsurers with which such automatic agreements are in effect, the coverages and amounts or percentages that may be reinsured, and commission schedules;

b. Commit the insurer to participate in insurance or reinsurance syndicates;

c. Appoint any producer without assuring that the producer is lawfully licensed to transact the type of insurance for which the producer is appointed;

d. Without prior approval of the insurer, pay or commit the insurer to pay a claim over a specified amount, net of reinsurance, which shall not exceed one percent (1%) of the insurer's policyholder's surplus as of the preceding December 31;

e. Collect any payment from a reinsurer or commit the insurer to any claim settlement with a reinsurer, without the insurer's prior approval. If prior approval is given, a report must be promptly forwarded to the insurer;

f.   Permit its subproducer to serve on the insurer's board of directors;

g.   Jointly employ an individual who is employed with the insurer; or

h.   Appoint a sub-MGA.

(e)   An insurer shall have on file by June 1 of each year an audited financial report of each MGA with which it is doing business. The report shall include the opinion of an independent certified public accountant, report the financial position of the MGA as of the most recent year-end and the results of its operations and cash flows, and include appropriate notes to financial statements. The insurer shall provide a copy of the report to the Commissioner within 15 days of receipt by the insurer.

(f)   If an MGA establishes loss reserves, the insurer shall provide with its annual statement, in addition to any other required statement of actuarial opinion, the statement of a qualified actuary attesting to the adequacy of loss reserves established on business produced by the MGA. The statement shall comply in all respects with the NAIC Annual Statement Instructions regarding the Statement of Actuarial Opinion.

(g)   The insurer shall periodically, at least semiannually, conduct an on-site review of the underwriting and claims processing operations of the MGA. The insurer shall prepare and maintain a written report on the review and make it available to the Commissioner upon the Commissioner's request.

(h)   Binding authority for all reinsurance contracts, except those contracts expressly permitted under sub-subdivision (d)(10)a. of this section, or participation in insurance or reinsurance syndicates, shall rest with an officer of the insurer, who shall not be affiliated with the MGA.

(i)   Within 15 days after entering into or termination of a contract with an MGA, the insurer shall provide written notification of the appointment or termination to the Commissioner. Notices of appointment of an MGA shall include a copy of the contract, a statement of duties that the MGA is expected to perform on behalf of the insurer, the lines of insurance for which the MGA is to be authorized to act, whether any affiliation exists between the insurer and the MGA and the basis for the affiliation, NAIC biographical affidavit for each officer, director, and each person who owns ten percent (10%) or more of the outstanding voting stock of the MGA, and any other information the

Commissioner may request. The Commissioner may prescribe the form to be used for notification of the information required by this item.

(j)   The Commissioner shall disapprove any such contract that:

(1)   Does not contain the required contract provisions specified in subsection (d) of this section;

(2)   Subjects the insurer to excessive charges for expenses or commission;

(3)   Vests in the MGA any control over the management of the affairs of the insurer to the exclusion of the board of directors of the insurer;

(4)   Is entered into with any person if the person or its officers and directors are of known bad character or have been affiliated directly or indirectly through ownership, control, management, reinsurance transactions, or other insurance or business relationships with any person known to have been involved in the improper manipulation of assets, accounts, or reinsurance; or

(5)   Is determined by the Commissioner to contain provisions that are not fair and reasonable to the insurer.

Failure of the Commissioner to disapprove any such contract within 30 days after the contract has been filed with the Commissioner constitutes the Commissioner's approval of the contract. An insurer may continue to accept business from the person until the Commissioner disapproves the contract. Any disapproval shall be in writing. The Commissioner may withdraw approval of any contract the Commissioner has previously approved if the Commissioner determines that the basis of the original approval no longer exists or that the contract has, in actual operation, shown itself to be subject to disapproval on any of the grounds in this subsection. If the Commissioner withdraws approval of a contract, the Commissioner shall give the insurer notice of, and written reasons for, the withdrawal of approval. The Commissioner shall grant any party to the contract a hearing upon request.

(k)   An insurer shall review its books and records each quarter to determine if any agent has become an MGA. If the insurer determines that an agent has become an MGA, the insurer shall promptly notify the agent of that determination and the insurer and agent must fully comply with the provisions of this Article within 15 days.

(l) An insurer shall not appoint to its board of directors an officer, director, employee, subagent, or controlling shareholder of its MGAs. This subsection does not apply to relationships governed by Article 19 of this Chapter or, if applicable, G.S. 58-3-165.

(m) The acts of an MGA are considered to be the acts of the insurer on whose behalf it is acting. An MGA may be examined by the Commissioner under G.S. 58-2-131 through G.S. 58-2-134 as if it were an insurer.

(n) If the Commissioner determines that an MGA or any other person has not materially complied with this section or with any rule adopted or order issued under this section, after notice and opportunity to be heard, the Commissioner may order:

(1) For each separate violation, a civil penalty under the procedures in G.S. 58-2-70(d); or

(2) Revocation or suspension of the person's license.

(3) Repealed by Session Laws 1993, c. 452, s. 47.

If the Commissioner finds that because of a material noncompliance that an insurer has suffered any loss or damage, the Commissioner may maintain a civil action brought by or on behalf of the insurer and its policyholders and creditors for recovery of compensatory damages for the benefit of the insurer and its policyholders and creditors or for other appropriate relief.

(o) Nothing in this section affects the Commissioner's right to impose any other penalties provided for in this Chapter. Nothing in this Article limits or restricts the rights of policyholders, claimants, and creditors.

(p) If an order of rehabilitation or liquidation of the insurer has been entered under Article 30 of this Chapter, and the receiver appointed under that order determines that the MGA or any other person has not materially complied with this section, or any regulation or order promulgated thereunder, and the insurer suffered any loss or damage therefrom, the receiver may maintain a civil action for recovery of damages or other appropriate sanctions for the benefit of the insurer. (1991, c. 681, s. 51; 1993, c. 452, ss. 43-48; 1993 (Reg. Sess., 1994), c. 678, s. 19; 1995, c. 193, s. 34; 1999-132, s. 11.6; 2001-223, ss. 20.1, 20.2.)

§ 58-34-5. Retrospective compensation agreements.

(a)   Retrospective compensation agreements for business written under Articles 1 through 64 of this Chapter must be filed with the Commissioner for his approval.

(b)   "Retrospective compensation agreement" means any such arrangement, agreement, or contract having as its purpose the actual or constructive retention by a domestic insurer of a fixed proportion of the gross premiums, with the balance of the premiums, retained actually or constructively by the agent or the producer of the business, who assumes to pay therefrom all losses, all subordinate commissions, loss adjustment expenses and his profit, if any, with other provisions of such arrangement, agreement, or contract auxiliary or incidental to such purpose.

(c)   The standards for approval shall be as set forth under G.S. 58-34-2(d)(5). (1987, c. 752, s. 8; 1989, c. 485, s. 60; 1991, c. 681, s. 52.)

§ 58-34-10. Management contracts.

(a)   Subject to G.S. 58-19-30(b)(4), any domestic insurer that enters into a management contract or custodial agreement must file that contract or agreement with the Commissioner on or before its effective date.

(b)   Any domestic insurer that has a management contract or custodial agreement shall file a statement with the initial filing of that contract that discloses (i) criteria on which charges to the insurer are based for that contract; (ii) whether management personnel or other employees of the insurer are to be performing management functions and receiving any remuneration therefor through that contract in addition to the compensation by way of salary received directly from the insurer for their services; (iii) whether the contract transfers substantial control of the insurer or any of the powers vested in the board of directors, by statute, articles of incorporation, or bylaws, or substantially all of the basic functions of the insurer's management; (iv) biographical information for each officer and director of the management firm; and (v) other information concerning the contract or the management or custodian firm as may be included from time to time in any registration forms adopted or approved by the

Commissioner. The statement shall be filed on a form prescribed by the Commissioner.

(c)   Any domestic insurer that amends or cancels a management contract or custodial agreement filed under subsection (a) of this section shall notify the Commissioner within 15 business days after the amendment or cancellation. If the contract is amended, the notice shall provide a copy of the amended contract and shall disclose if the amendment affects any of the items in subsection (b) of this section. The Commissioner may prescribe a form to be used to provide notice under this subsection.

(d)   Any domestic insurer that has a management contract or custodial agreement shall file a statement on or before March 1 of each year, for the preceding calendar year, disclosing (i) total charges incurred by the insurer under the contract; (ii) any salaries, commissions, or other valuable consideration paid by the insurer directly to any officer, director, or shareholder of the management or custodian firm; and (iii) other information concerning the contract or the management or custodian firm as may be included from time to time in any registration forms adopted or approved by the Commissioner. The Commissioner may prescribe a form to be used to provide the information required by this subsection.

(e)   Any domestic insurer that has a management contract may request an exemption from the filing requirements of this section if the contract is for a group of affiliated insurers on a pooled funds basis or service company management basis, where costs to the individual member insurers are charged on an actually incurred or closely estimated basis. The request for an exemption must be in writing, must explain the basis for the exemption, and must be received by the Commissioner on or before the effective date of the contract. As used in this subsection, "affiliated" has the same meaning as in G.S. 58-19-5(1). Management contracts exempted under this subsection must still be reduced to written form. (1987, c. 752, s. 8; 1989, c. 485, s. 61; 1991, c. 681, s. 53; 1993, c. 452, s. 49; 2001-223, s. 20.3.)

§ 58-34-15. Grounds for disapproval.

(a)   The Commissioner must disapprove any management contract or custodial agreement filed under G.S. 58-34-10 if, at any time, the Commissioner finds:

(1)   That the service or management charges are based upon criteria unrelated either to the managed insurer's profits or to the reasonable customary and usual charges for the services or are based on factors unrelated to the value of the services to the insurer; or

(2)   That management personnel or other employees of the insurer are to be performing management functions and receiving any remuneration for those functions through the management or service contract in addition to the compensation by way of salary received directly from the insurer for their services; or

(3)   That the contract would transfer substantial control of the insurer or any of the powers vested in the board of directors, by statute, articles of incorporation, or bylaws, or substantially all of the basic functions of the insurance company management; or

(4)   That the contract contains provisions that would be clearly detrimental to the best interest of policyholders, stockholders, or members of the insurer; or

(5)   That the officers and directors of the management or custodial firm are of known bad character or have been affiliated, directly or indirectly, through ownership, control, management, reinsurance transactions, or other insurance or business relations with any person known to have been involved in the improper manipulation of assets, accounts, or reinsurance.

(6)   That the custodial agreement is not substantially the same as the form adopted by the Commissioner.

(b)   If the Commissioner disapproves any management contract or custodial agreement, notice of the disapproval shall be given to the insurer stating the reasons for the disapproval in writing. The Commissioner shall grant any party to the contract a hearing if the party requests a hearing. (1987, c. 752, s. 8; 1991, c. 681, s. 54; 1993, c. 452, s. 50; 2001-223, s. 20.4.)

§ 58-34-20: Repealed by Session Laws 1993, c. 452, s. 65.

Article 35.

Insurance Premium Financing.

§ 58-35-1. Definitions.

When used in this Article:

(1) An insurance premium finance company is hereby defined to be:

a. Any person engaged, in whole or in part, in the business of entering into insurance premium finance agreements with insureds; or

b. Any person engaged, in whole or in part, in the business of acquiring insurance premium finance agreements from other insurance premium finance companies.

(2) "Insurance premium finance agreement" means a promissory note or other written agreement by which an insured promises or agrees to pay to, or to the order of, an insurance premium finance company the amount advanced or to be advanced under the agreement to an insurer or to an insurance agent, in payment of premiums on an insurance contract, together with a service charge as authorized and limited by this Article. (1963, c. 1118.)

§ 58-35-5. License required; fees.

(a) No person except an authorized insurer shall engage in the business of an insurance premium finance company without obtaining a license from the Commissioner, as provided in this Article.

(b) Application for license required under this Article shall be in writing, and in the form prescribed by the Commissioner.

(c) When an applicant has more than one office, separate applications for license shall be made for each such office.

(d) At the time of filing an application for a license, the applicant shall pay to the Commissioner the license fee. Upon original application or upon application subsequent to denial of application, or revocation, suspension or surrender of a license, an examination fee may be required.

(e) There shall be two types of licenses issued to an insurance premium finance company:

(1) An "A" type license shall be issued to insurance premium finance companies whose business of insurance premium financing is limited to the financing of insurance premiums of one insurance agent or agency and whose primary function is to finance only the insurance premium of such agent or agency. The license fee for an "A" type license shall be six hundred dollars ($600.00) for each license year or part thereof.

(2) A "B" type license shall be issued to an insurance premium finance company whose business of insurance premium financing is not limited to the financing of insurance premiums of one insurance agent or agency and whose primary function is to finance the insurance premiums of more than one insurance agent or agency. The license fee for a "B" type license shall be two thousand four hundred dollars ($2,400) for each license year or part thereof.

A branch office license may be issued for either an "A" type or "B" type license to the second and any subsequent locations where the company operates an office. The fee for the branch office license shall be one hundred dollars ($100.00) for each license year or part thereof. The examination fee when required by this section shall be two hundred fifty dollars ($250.00) per application. (1963, c. 1118; 1967, c. 1232, s. 1; 1989 (Reg. Sess., 1990), c. 1069, s. 7; 1995, c. 507, s. 11A(c); 2009-451, s. 21.2(a).)

§ 58-35-10. Exceptions to license requirements.

(a) Any person, firm or corporation doing business under the authority of any law of this State or of the United States relating to banks, trust companies, installment paper dealers, auto finance companies, savings and loan associations, cooperative credit unions, agricultural credit corporations or associations, organized under the laws of North Carolina or any person, firm or corporation subject to the provisions of the North Carolina Consumer Finance Act and the North Carolina Motor Vehicle Dealers and Manufacturers Licensing

Law, Article 12, Chapter 20, of the General Statutes of North Carolina are exempt from the provisions of this Article.

(b)   An insurance company duly licensed in this State may make an installment payment charge as set forth in the rate filings and approved by the Commissioner and is thereby exempt from the provisions of this Article.

(c)   A fire and casualty insurance agent or an insurance broker duly licensed in this State who extends credit to and only to his own policyholders may charge and collect finance charges or other fees at a periodic (monthly) rate as provided in G.S. 24-11(a), after said amount has been outstanding for 30 days, and is hereby exempt from the provisions of this Article. Notwithstanding the exceptions set forth in subsections (a), (b) and (c) of this section, when any person, firm, or corporation shall exercise a power of attorney taken in connection with the financing of an insurance premium, such person, firm or corporation shall comply with the requirements of G.S. 58-35-85, as if it were an insurance premium financing company. (1963, c. 1118; 1967, c. 942, s. 1; 1971, c. 1186, ss. 1, 2; 1995 (Reg. Sess., 1996), c. 742, s. 25.)

§ 58-35-15. Issuance or refusal of license; bond; duration of license; renewal; one office per license; display of license; notice of change of location.

(a)   Within 60 days after the filing of an application for a license accompanied by payment of the fees for license and examination, the Commissioner shall issue the license or may refuse to issue the license and so advise the applicant. The applicant shall submit with such application any and all information which the Commissioner may require to assist him in determining the financial condition, business integrity, method of operation and protection to the public offered by the person filing such application. The Commissioner may require a bond not to exceed twenty-five thousand dollars ($25,000) on applications and any renewal thereof. Such license to engage in business in accordance with the provisions of this Article at the location specified in the application shall be executed in duplicate by the Commissioner and he shall transmit one copy to the applicant and retain a copy on file. A person required by this subsection to maintain a bond may, in lieu of that bond, deposit with the Commissioner the equivalent amount in cash, in certificates of deposit issued by banks organized under the laws of the State of North Carolina, or any national bank having its principal office in North Carolina, or securities, which shall be held in accordance with Article 5 of this Chapter. Securities may only be obligations of the United States or of federal agencies listed in G.S. 147-69.1(c)(2) guaranteed by the United States, obligations of the State of North Carolina, or obligations of a city or county of this State. Any proposed deposit of an obligation of a city or county of this State is subject to the prior approval of the Commissioner.

(b)   Whenever the Commissioner denies an initial application for a license, he shall notify the applicant and advise, in writing, the applicant of the reasons for the denial of the license. Within 30 days of receipt of notification the applicant may make written demand upon the Commissioner for a hearing to determine the reasonableness of the Commissioner's action. Such hearing shall be scheduled within 30 days from the date of receipt of the written demand.

(c)   Each license issued hereunder shall remain in full force and effect until the last day of June unless earlier surrendered, suspended, or revoked pursuant to this Article, and may be renewed for the ensuing license year upon the filing of an application and conforming with G.S. 58-35-5, but subject to all of the provisions of this Article. If an application for a renewal of a license is filed with the Commissioner before July 1 of any year, the license sought to be renewed shall be continued in full force and effect either until the issuance by the Commissioner of the renewal license applied for or until five days after the Commissioner refuses to issue such renewal license under the provisions of this Article.

(d)   Only one office may be maintained under each license, but more than one license may be issued to the same licensee pursuant to this Article.

(e)   Such license shall state the name and address of the licensee and shall at all times be prominently displayed in the office of the licensee and shall not be transferable or assignable.

(f)   Before any licensee changes any office of his to another location, he shall give written notice thereof to the Commissioner. (1963, c. 1118; 1965, c. 1039; 1989, c. 485, s. 47; 1991, c. 212, s. 3.)

§ 58-35-20. Grounds for refusal, suspension or revocation of licenses; surrender of licenses; reinstatement.

(a) The Commissioner may forthwith deny, suspend, revoke, or refuse to renew or continue any license hereunder if he shall find that:

(1) The licensee has failed to pay the annual license fee or any sum of money lawfully demanded under authority of any section of this Article or has violated or failed to comply with any demand, ruling, provision or requirement of the Commissioner lawfully made pursuant to or within the authority of this Article.

(2) Any fact or condition exists which, if it had been known to exist at the time of the original application, would have caused the original license to have been refused.

(b) The Commissioner may revoke or suspend only the particular license with respect to which grounds for revocation or suspension may occur or exist; or if he shall find that such grounds for revocation or suspension are of general application to all offices, or to more than one office, operated by such licensee, he shall revoke or suspend all of the licenses issued to such licensee or such number of licenses as such grounds apply to, as the case may be.

(1) Any licensee may surrender any license by delivering to the Commissioner written notice that he thereby surrenders such license, but such surrender shall not affect such licensee's civil or criminal liability for acts committed prior to such surrender.

(2) No revocation or suspension or surrender of any license shall impair or affect the obligation of any insured under any lawful insurance premium finance agreement previously acquired or held by the licensee.

(3) Every license issued hereunder shall remain in force and effect until the same shall have been surrendered, revoked, suspended, or expires in accordance with the provisions of this Article; but the Commissioner shall have authority to reinstate suspended licenses or to issue new licenses to a licensee whose license or licenses shall have been revoked, if no fact or condition then exists which clearly would have warranted the Commissioner in refusing originally to issue such license under this Article. (1963, c. 1118.)

§ 58-35-22. Notification of criminal or administrative actions.

(a) If an individual proprietor, officer, or partner of an insurance premium finance company has been convicted in any court of competent jurisdiction for any crime involving dishonesty or breach of trust, the premium finance company shall notify the Commissioner in writing of the conviction within 10 days after the date of the conviction. As used in this subsection, "conviction" includes an adjudication of guilt, a plea of guilty, or a plea of nolo contendere.

(b) An insurance premium finance company shall report to the Commissioner any administrative action taken against the premium finance company, including any branch office, by another state or by another governmental agency in this State within 30 days after the final disposition of the matter. This report shall include a copy of the order or consent order and other information or documents filed in the proceeding necessary to describe the action. (2009-566, s. 19.)

§ 58-35-25. Investigations; hearings.

For the purpose of conducting investigations and holding hearings on insurance premium finance companies, the Commissioner shall have the same authority as that vested in him by G.S. 58-2-50 and 58-2-70. (1963, c. 1118; 1987, c. 864, s. 3(b).)

§ 58-35-30. Licensee's books and records; reports; refusing to exhibit records; making false statements.

(a) The licensee shall keep and use in his business any books, accounts, and records that will enable the Commissioner to determine whether the licensee is complying with the provisions of this Article and with the rules and regulations lawfully made by the Commissioner hereunder. Every licensee shall preserve such books, accounts, and records, including cards used in a card system, if any, for at least three years after making the final entry in respect to any insurance premium finance agreement recorded therein; provided, however, the preservation of photographic reproductions thereof or records in photographic, imaging, microfilm, or microfiche form shall constitute compliance with this requirement by any licensee. The Commissioner may require of licensees under oath and in the form prescribed by him regular or special reports as he may deem necessary to the proper supervision of licensees under this Article.

(b) Any person who shall refuse, on demand, to exhibit to the Commissioner or to any deputy, or person acting with or for the Commissioner, the books, accounts or records as above provided, or who shall knowingly or willfully make any false statement in regard to the same shall be deemed guilty of a Class 1 misdemeanor. (1963, c. 1118; 1991, c. 720, s. 4; 1993, c. 539, s. 463; 1994, Ex. Sess., c. 24, s. 14(c); 1999-157, s. 1.)

§ 58-35-35. Excessive insurance premium finance charges; penalty.

The knowingly taking, receiving, reserving, [or] charging a greater insurance premium finance charge than that authorized in this Article shall be held and adjudged a forfeiture of the entire insurance premium finance charge which the insurance premium finance agreement carries with it, or which has been agreed to be paid thereon; and if a greater insurance premium finance charge has been paid, the person paying the same or his legal representative may recover from the insurance premium finance company twice the entire amount of the insurance premium finance thus paid if action therefor is brought within two years from the time of such payment. (1963, c. 1118.)

§ 58-35-40. Rebates and inducements prohibited; assignment of insurance premium finance agreements.

(a) No insurance premium finance company shall pay, allow, or offer to pay or allow payment to an insurance agent, and no insurance agent shall accept from a company, a rebate as an inducement to the financing of an insurance policy with the company. No insurance premium finance company shall give or offer to give to an insurance agent, and no insurance agent shall accept from a company, any valuable consideration or inducement of any kind, directly or indirectly, other than an article of merchandise not exceeding one dollar ($1.00) in value which shall have thereon the advertisement of the insurance premium finance company. An insurance premium finance company may purchase or otherwise acquire an insurance premium finance agreement from another insurance premium finance company with recourse against the insurance premium finance company on such terms and conditions as may be mutually agreed upon by the parties, if the agreement complies with the requirements of this Article. The terms and conditions of the agreement shall be subject to the approval of the Commissioner.

(b) No filing of the assignment or notice thereof to the insured shall be necessary to the validity of the written assignment of an insurance premium finance agreement as against creditors or subsequent purchases, pledges, or encumbrancers of the assignor.

(c) As used in this section, the term "insurance premium finance company" includes employees of the company; the term "insurance agent" includes employees of the insurance agent; and the word "company" means an insurance premium finance company. (1963, c. 1118; 1989, c. 485, s. 64; 1991 (Reg. Sess., 1992), c. 837, s. 1; 1999-157, s. 7.)

§ 58-35-45. Filing and approval of forms and service charges.

(a) No insurance premium finance agreement form or related form shall be used in this State unless it has been filed with and written approval given by the Commissioner.

(b) In addition each insurance premium finance company shall file with the Commissioner the service charge rate plan to be used in insurance premium financing including all modifications of service charges to be paid by the insured or others under the insurance premium finance agreement. Such filings shall not be used in this State until written approval has been given by the Commissioner. (1963, c. 1118.)

§ 58-35-50. Form, contents and execution of insurance premium finance agreements.

(a) An insurance premium finance agreement shall be in writing, dated, signed by the insured, and the printed portion thereof shall be in type that is legible, as determined by rule. It shall contain the entire agreement of the parties with respect to the insurance contract, the premiums for which are advanced or to be advanced under it, and the following:

"INSURANCE PREMIUM FINANCE AGREEMENT NOTICE

a. Do not sign this agreement before you read it.

b. You are entitled to a copy of this agreement.

c. Under the law, you have the right to pay off in advance the full amount due and under certain conditions to obtain a partial refund of the service charge."

(b) An insurance premium finance agreement shall:

(1) Contain the following:

a. The name and place of business of the insurance agent or broker negotiating the related insurance contract;

b. The name of the insured and the residence, the place of business, or any other mailing address of the insured as specified by the insured;

c. The name and place of business of the insurance premium finance company to which installments or other payments are to be made;

d. A brief description of the insurance contract;

e. The premiums for which are advanced or to be advanced under the agreement; and

f. The amount of the premiums for such insurance contract; and

(2) Set forth the following items where applicable:

a. The total amount of the premiums;

b. The amount of the down payment;

c. The principal balance, which is the difference between items a and b;

d. The amount of the service charge;

e. The balance payable by the insured, meaning the sum of the amounts stated under items c. and d. of this subdivision.

f. The number of installments required, the amount of each installment expressed in dollars and the due date or period thereof.

(c) The items set forth in subsection (b) of this section need not be stated in the sequence or order in which they appear in that subsection, and additional items may be included to explain the computations made in determining the amount to be paid by the insured.

(d) No insurance premium finance agreement shall be signed by an insured when it contains any blank space to be filled in after it has been signed; however, if the insurance contract, the premiums for which are advanced or to be advanced under the agreement, has not been issued at the time of its signature by the insured and it so provides, the name of the authorized insurer by whom such insurance contract is issued and the policy number and the due date of the first installment may be left blank and later inserted in the original of the agreement after it has been signed by the insured. (1963, c. 1118; 1999-157, s. 2.)

§ 58-35-55. Limitations on service charges; computation; minimum charges.

(a) An insurance premium finance company shall not directly or indirectly except as otherwise provided by law, impose, take, receive from, reserve, contract for, or charge an insured greater service charges than are permitted by this Article. No insurance premium finance company shall be permitted to charge or finance any membership fees, dues, registration fees, or any other charges except the service charges provided for in this Article for financing insurance premiums on policies of insurance lawfully placed in this State.

(b) An insurance premium finance company may, in an insurance premium finance agreement, contract for, charge, receive, and collect a service charge for financing the premiums under the agreement computed as provided in subsection (c).

(c) The service charge provided for in this section shall be computed on the principal balance of the insurance premium finance agreement from the inception date of the insurance contract, the premiums for which are advanced or to be advanced under the agreement unless otherwise provided under rules and regulations prescribed by the Commissioner, to and including the date when the final installment of the insurance premium finance agreement is payable, at a rate not exceeding twelve dollars ($12.00) per one hundred dollars ($100.00) per annum; plus a nonrefundable origination fee which shall not exceed fifteen dollars ($15.00) per premium finance agreement.

(d) The provisions of subsection (c) of this section pertaining to the time from which the service charge is calculated apply if the premiums under only one insurance contract are advanced or are to be advanced under an insurance premium finance agreement. If premiums under more than one insurance contract are advanced or are to be advanced under an insurance premium finance agreement, the service charge shall be computed from the earlier of the following:

(1) The date that the premium is advanced on behalf of the insured.

(2) The inception date of any insurance contract financed on the premium finance agreement.

Only one minimum service charge shall apply to each insurance premium finance agreement.

(e) No insurance agent or insurance premium finance company shall induce an insured to become obligated under more than one insurance premium finance agreement for the purpose of or with the effect of obtaining service charges in excess of those authorized by this Article.

(f) A premium service agreement may provide for the payment by the insured of a delinquency and collection charge on each installment in default for a period of not less than five days in an amount of one dollar ($1.00) or a maximum of five percent (5%) of such installment, whichever is greater, provided that only one such delinquency and collection charge may be collected on any such installment regardless of the period during which it remains in default. (1963, c. 1118; 1967, c. 824; 1979, 2nd Sess., c. 1083, ss. 1, 2; 1981, c. 394, s. 1; 1999-157, s. 3.)

§ 58-35-60. Prohibited provisions in insurance premium finance agreements.

No insurance premium finance agreement shall contain any provisions by which:

(1) In the absence of default of the insured, the insurance premium finance company holding the agreement may, arbitrarily and without reasonable cause, accelerate the maturity of any part or all of the amount owing thereunder;

(2) A power of attorney is given to confess judgment in this State; or

(3) The insured relieves the insurance agent or the insurance premium finance company holding the agreement from liability for any legal rights or remedies which the insured may otherwise have against him. (1963, c. 1118.)

§ 58-35-65. Delivery of copy of insurance premium finance agreement to insured.

Before the due date of the first installment payable under an insurance premium finance agreement, the insurance premium finance company holding the agreement or the insurance agent shall cause to be delivered to the insured, or mail to the insured at the insured's address as shown in the agreement, a copy of the agreement. (1963, c. 1118; 1999-157, s. 4.)

§ 58-35-70. Payments by insured without notice of assignment of agreement.

Unless the insured has notice of actual or intended assignment of the insurance premium finance agreement, payment thereunder by him to the last known holder of the agreement shall be binding upon all subsequent holders or assignees. (1963, c. 1118.)

§ 58-35-75. Statement of account; release on payment in full.

(a) At any time after its execution, but not later than one year after the last payment thereunder, an insurance premium finance company holding an insurance premium finance agreement shall, upon written request of the insured, give or mail to him a written statement of the dates and amounts of payments and the total amount, if any, unpaid thereunder.

(b) After the payment of all sums for which an insured is obligated under an insurance premium finance agreement, and upon his written demand, the insurance premium finance company holding the agreement shall deliver, or mail to the insured at his last known address, such one or more good and sufficient instruments as may be necessary to acknowledge payment in full and to release all interest in or rights to the insurance contracts, the premiums for which were advanced or are to be advanced under the agreement. (1963, c. 1118.)

§ 58-35-80. Credit upon anticipation of payments.

(a) Notwithstanding the provisions of any insurance premium finance agreement to the contrary, any insured may pay it in full at any time before the maturity of the final installment of the balance thereof; and, if he does so and the agreement included an amount for service charge, he shall receive and be entitled to receive for such anticipation a refund credit thereon.

(b) The amount of any such refund credit shall represent at least as great proportion of the service charge, if any, as the sum of the periodic balances after the month in which prepayment is made bears to the sum of all periodic balances under the schedule of installments in the agreement. Where the amount of the refund credit for anticipation of payment is less than one dollar ($1.00), no refund need be made. This section does not relieve the premium finance company of its duty to report and deliver these unrefunded monies to the State Treasurer in accordance with G.S. 116B-29(b). (1963, c. 1118; 1981, c. 394, s. 2; 1999-157, s. 5.)

§ 58-35-85. Procedure for cancellation of insurance contract upon default; return of unearned premiums; collection of cash surrender value.

When an insurance premium finance agreement contains a power of attorney or other authority enabling the insurance premium finance company to cancel any insurance contract or contracts listed in the agreement, the insurance contract or contracts shall not be cancelled unless the cancellation is effectuated in accordance with the following provisions:

(1) Not less than 10 days' written notice is sent by personal delivery, first-class mail, electronic mail, or facsimile transmission to the last known address of the insured or insureds shown on the insurance premium finance agreement of the intent of the insurance premium finance company to cancel his or their insurance contract or contracts unless the defaulted installment payment is received. Notification thereof shall also be provided to the insurance agent.

(2) After expiration of the 10-day period, the insurance premium finance company shall send the insurer a request for cancellation and shall send notice of the requested cancellation to the insured by personal delivery, first-class mail, electronic mail, electronic transmission, or facsimile transmission at his last known address as shown on the records of the insurance premium finance company and to the agent. Upon written request of the insurance company, the premium finance company shall furnish a copy of the power of attorney to the insurance company. The written request shall be sent by mail, personal delivery, electronic mail, or facsimile transmission.

(3) Upon receipt of a copy of the request for cancellation notice by the insurer, the insurance contract shall be cancelled with the same force and effect as if the request for cancellation had been submitted by the insured, without requiring the return of the insurance contract or contracts.

(4) All statutory, regulatory, and contractual restrictions providing that the insured may not cancel the insurance contract unless the insurer first satisfies the restrictions by giving a prescribed notice to a governmental agency, the insurance carrier, an individual, or a person designated to receive the notice for said governmental agency, insurance carrier, or individual shall apply where cancellation is effected under the provisions of this section.

(4a) If an insurer receives notification from an insurance agent or premium finance company that the initial down payment for the premium being financed has been dishonored by a financial institution, or otherwise unpaid, there is no valid contract for insurance and the policy will be voided.

(5) When an insurance contract is cancelled in accordance with this section, the insurer shall promptly return the gross unearned premiums that are due under the contract to the insurance premium finance company effecting the cancellation, for the benefit of the insured or insureds, no later than 30 days

after the effective date of cancellation. When the return premium is more than the amount the insured owes the insurance premium finance company under the agreement, the excess shall be promptly remitted to the order of the insured, as provided in subdivision (8) of this section, subject to the minimum service charge provided for in this Article. If a premium is subject to an audit to determine the final premium amount, the amount to be refunded to the premium finance company shall be calculated upon the deposit premium, and the insurer shall return that amount to the premium finance company no later than 90 days after the effective date of cancellation. This subdivision does not limit any other remedies the insurer may have against the insured for additional premiums.

(6)   The provisions of this section relating to request for cancellation by the insurance premium finance company of an insurance contract and the return by an insurer of unearned premiums to the insurance premium finance company, also apply to the surrender by the insurance premium finance company of an insurance contract providing life insurance and the payment by the insurer of the cash value of the contract to the insurance premium finance company, except that the insurer may require the surrender of the insurance contract.

(7)   The insurer shall not deduct from any return premiums any amount owed to the insurer for any other indebtedness owed to the insurer by the insured on any policy or policies other than those being financed under the premium finance agreement.

(8)   In the event that the crediting of return premiums to the account of the insured results in a surplus over the amount due from the insured, the premium finance company shall refund the excess to the insured as soon as possible, but in no event later than 30 days of receipt of the return premium, provided that no refund shall be required if it is in an amount less than one dollar ($1.00). This subdivision does not relieve the premium finance company of its duty to report and deliver these unrefunded monies to the State Treasurer in accordance with G.S. 116B-29(b).

(9)   In the event that a balance due the premium finance company remains on the account after the cancellation of the agreement, the outstanding balance may earn interest at the rate stated in the agreement until paid in full.

(10)   If a mortgagee or other loss payee is shown on the insurance contract, the insurer shall notify the mortgagee or loss payee of the cancellation. The written notice shall be sent by mail, personal delivery, electronic mail, or facsimile transmission to the designated mortgagee's or loss payee's last known

address. Proof of mailing is sufficient proof of notice. Failure to send this notice to any designated mortgagee or loss payee shall not give rise to any claim on the part of the insured. (1963, c. 1118; 1967, c. 825; 1969, c. 941; 1987, c. 864, s. 22; 1995, c. 121, s. 1; 1999-157, s. 6; 2002-187, s. 6.)

§ 58-35-90. Violations; penalties.

Any person who shall engage in the business referred to in this Article without first receiving a license, or who shall fail to secure a renewal of his license upon the expiration of the license year, or shall engage in the business herein referred to after the license has been suspended or revoked as herein provided, or who shall fail or refuse to furnish the information required of the Commissioner, or who shall willfully and knowingly enter false information on an insurance premium finance agreement, or who shall fail to observe the rules and regulations made by the Commissioner pursuant to this Article, shall be deemed guilty of a Class 1 misdemeanor. (1963, c. 1118; 1965, c. 1040; 1985, c. 666, s. 20; 1993, c. 539, s. 464; 1994, Ex. Sess., c. 24, s. 14(c).)

§ 58-35-95. Disposition of fees.

All fees collected hereunder shall be credited to the account of the Commissioner for the specific purpose of providing the personnel, equipment and supplies necessary to enforce this Article, but the Director of the Budget shall have the right to budget the revenues received in accordance with the requirements of the Commissioner for the purposes herein required, and at the end of the fiscal year, if any sum whatever shall remain to the credit of the Commissioner, derived from the sources herein referred to, the same shall revert to the general treasury of the State to be appropriated as other funds. (1963, c. 1118; 1991, c. 720, s. 5.)

§ 58-35-100. Fees are nonrefundable.

All fees that are imposed and collected under this Article are nonrefundable. (1993 (Reg. Sess., 1994), c. 678, s. 20.)

Article 36.

North Carolina Rate Bureau.

§ 58-36-1. North Carolina Rate Bureau created.

There is hereby created a Bureau to be known as the "North Carolina Rate Bureau," with the following objects and functions:

(1) To assume the functions formerly performed by the North Carolina Fire Insurance Rating Bureau, the North Carolina Automobile Rate Administrative Office, and the Compensation Rating and Inspection Bureau of North Carolina, with regard to the promulgation of rates, for insurance against loss to residential real property with not more than four housing units located in this State and any contents thereof and valuable interest therein and other insurance coverages written in connection with the sale of such property insurance; except as provided in G.S. 58-36-3(a)(6), for theft of and physical damage to nonfleet private passenger motor vehicles; for liability insurance for such motor vehicles, automobile medical payments insurance, uninsured motorists coverage and other insurance coverages written in connection with the sale of such liability insurance; and for workers' compensation and employers' liability insurance written in connection therewith except for insurance excluded from the Bureau's jurisdiction in G.S. 58-36-1(3).

(2) The Bureau shall provide reasonable means to be approved by the Commissioner whereby any person affected by a rate or loss costs made by it may be heard in person or by the person's authorized representative before the governing committee or other proper executive of the Bureau.

(3) The Bureau shall promulgate and propose rates for insurance against loss to residential real property with not more than four housing units located in this State and any contents thereof or valuable interest therein and other insurance coverages written in connection with the sale of such property insurance; for insurance against theft of or physical damage to nonfleet private passenger motor vehicles; for liability insurance for such motor vehicles, automobile medical payments insurance, uninsured and underinsured motorists coverage and other insurance coverages written in connection with the sale of

such liability insurance; and, as provided in G.S. 58-36-100, for loss costs and residual market rate filings for workers' compensation and employers' liability insurance written in connection therewith. This subdivision does not apply to motor vehicles operated under certificates of authority from the Utilities Commission, the Interstate Commerce Commission, or their successor agencies, where insurance or other proof of financial responsibility is required by law or by regulations specifically applicable to such certificated vehicles.

(4) Agreements may be made between or among members with respect to equitable apportionment among them of insurance which may be afforded applicants who are in good faith entitled to but who are unable to procure such insurance through ordinary methods. The members may agree between or among themselves on the use of reasonable rate modifications for such insurance, agreements, and rate modifications to be subject to the approval of the Commissioner.

(5) a. It is the duty of every insurer that writes workers' compensation insurance in this State and is a member of the Bureau, as defined in this section and G.S. 58-36-5 to insure and accept any workers' compensation insurance risk that has been certified to be "difficult to place" by any fire and casualty insurance agent who is licensed in this State. When any such risk is called to the attention of the Bureau by receipt of an application with an estimated or deposit premium payment and it appears that the risk is in good faith entitled to such coverage, the Bureau will bind coverage for 30 days and will designate a member who must issue a standard workers' compensation policy of insurance that contains the usual and customary provisions found in those policies. Multiple coordinated policies, as defined by the Bureau and approved by the Commissioner, may be used for the issuance of coverage under this subdivision for risks involved in employee leasing arrangements. Coverage will be bound at 12:01 A.M. on the first day following the postmark time and date on the envelope in which the application is mailed including the estimated annual or deposit premium, or the expiration of existing coverage, whichever is later. If there should be no postmark, coverage will be effective 12:01 A.M. on the date of receipt by the Bureau unless a later date is requested. Those applications hand delivered to the Bureau will be effective as of 12:01 A.M. of the date following receipt by the Bureau unless a later date is requested. The Bureau will make and adopt such rules as are necessary to carry this section into effect, subject to final approval of the Commissioner. As a prerequisite to the transaction of workers' compensation insurance in this State, every member of the Bureau that writes such insurance must file with the Bureau written authority permitting the Bureau to act in its behalf, as provided in this section, and an

agreement to accept risks that are assigned to the member by the Bureau, as provided in this section.

b. The Bureau shall maintain a compendium of employers refused voluntary coverage, which shall be made available by the Bureau to all insurers, licensed agents, and self-insureds' administrators doing business in this State. It shall be stored and indexed to allow access to information by industry, primary classifications of employees, geography, experience modification, and in any other manner the Bureau determines is commercially useful to facilitate voluntary coverage of listed employers. The Bureau shall be immune from civil liability for erroneous information released by the Bureau pursuant to this section, provided that the Bureau acted in good faith and without malicious or willful intent to harm in releasing the erroneous information.

c. Failure or refusal by any assigned employer risk to make full disclosure to the Bureau, servicing carrier, or insurer writing a policy of information regarding the employer's true ownership, change of ownership, operations, or payroll, or any other failure to disclose fully any records pertaining to workers' compensation insurance shall be sufficient grounds for the termination of the policy of that employer.

(6) The Bureau shall maintain and furnish to the Commissioner on an annual basis the statistics on earnings derived by member companies from the investment of unearned premium, loss, and loss expense reserves on nonfleet private passenger motor vehicle insurance policies written in this State. Whenever the Bureau proposes rates under this Article, it shall prepare a separate exhibit for the experience years in question showing the combined earnings realized from the investment of such reserves on policies written in this State. The amount of earnings may in an equitable manner be included in the ratemaking formula to arrive at a fair and equitable rate. The Commissioner may require further information as to such earnings and may require calculations of the Bureau bearing on such earnings.

(7) Member companies shall furnish, upon request of any person carrying nonfleet private passenger motor vehicle insurance in the State upon whose risk a rate has been promulgated, information as to rating, including the method of calculation. (1977, c. 828, s. 6; 1981, c. 888, ss. 1-3; 1983, c. 416, s. 5; 1985 (Reg. Sess., 1986), c. 1027, s. 5.1; 1991, c. 339, s. 1; 1993, c. 409, s. 27; 1993 (Reg. Sess., 1994), c. 679, s. 8.5; 1995, c. 505, s. 1; c. 517, s. 18; 1999-132, ss. 3.1, 3.2; 1999-219, s. 11; 2001-236, s. 2; 2001-389, ss. 1, 2; 2001-423, s. 3.)

§ 58-36-2. Private passenger motor vehicles; number of nonfleet policies.

Notwithstanding the definition of "nonfleet" in G.S. 58-40-10(2), the Bureau shall adopt rules, subject to the Commissioner's approval, that specify the circumstances under which more than four private passenger motor vehicles may be covered under a nonfleet private passenger motor vehicle policy that is subject to this Article. (1995 (Reg. Sess., 1996), c. 730, s. 2.)

§ 58-36-3. Limitation of scope; motorcycle endorsements allowed; Department of Insurance report.

(a)   The Bureau has no jurisdiction over:

(1)   Excess workers' compensation insurance for employers qualifying as self-insurers as provided in Article 47 of this Chapter or Article 5 of Chapter 97 of the General Statutes.

(2)   Farm buildings, farm dwellings, and their appurtenant structures; farm personal property or other coverages written in connection with farm real or personal property.

(3)   Travel or camper trailers designed to be pulled by private passenger motor vehicles, unless insured under policies covering nonfleet private passenger motor vehicles.

(4)   Mechanical breakdown insurance covering nonfleet private passenger motor vehicles and other incidental coverages written in connection with this insurance, including emergency road service assistance, trip interruption reimbursement, rental car reimbursement, and tire coverage.

(5)   Residential real and personal property insured in multiple line insurance policies covering business activities as the primary insurable interest; and marine, general liability, burglary and theft, glass, and animal collision insurance, except when such coverages are written as an integral part of a multiple line insurance policy for which there is an indivisible premium.

(6) Insurance against theft of or physical damage to motorcycles, as defined in G.S. 20-4.01(27)d.

(7) Personal excess liability or personal "umbrella" insurance.

(b) Member companies writing motorcycle liability insurance under this Article and writing insurance against theft of or physical damage to motorcycles under Article 40 of this Chapter may incorporate motorcycle theft and physical damage coverage as an endorsement to the liability policy issued under this Article.

(c) Beginning on February 1, 2003, and annually thereafter, the Department of Insurance shall report to the President Pro Tempore of the Senate and the Speaker of the House of Representatives on the effectiveness of S.L. 2001-389 in assuring the provision of insurance coverage to motorcyclists at fair and economical rates. (2001-389, ss. 3, 5.1.)

§ 58-36-4. Statistical organizations; licensing; recording and reporting; examination; suspension of license; financial disclosure.

(a) For purposes of this Article:

(1) "Statistical organization" means every person, other than an admitted insurer, whether located within or outside this State, who performs one or more of the following functions:

a. Prepares policy forms or makes underwriting rules incident to, but not including, the making of rates, rating plans, or rating systems.

b. Collects and furnishes to admitted insurers or statistical organizations loss or expense statistics or other statistical information and data and acts in an advisory rather than a rate-making capacity. No duly authorized attorney-at-law acting in the usual course of that person's profession shall be deemed to be a statistical organization.

c. Makes rates, rating plans or rating systems, or develops loss costs. Two or more insurers that act in concert for the purpose of making rates, rating plans or rating systems, or developing loss costs and that do not operate within the specific authorizations contained in this Article shall be deemed to be a statistical organization.

d.   Collects data and statistics from insurers and provides reports from these statistics to the Commissioner for the purpose of fulfilling the statistical reporting obligations of those insurers.

"Statistical organization" shall not mean the North Carolina Rate Bureau, the North Carolina Motor Vehicle Reinsurance Facility, the North Carolina Insurance Underwriting Association, or the North Carolina Joint Underwriting Association.

(2)   "Statistical plan" means the document used by a statistical organization to set forth which data elements are to be reported to the statistical organization and to describe the format in which the data must be reported.

(b)   No statistical organization shall conduct its operations in this State, and no insurer shall utilize the service of that organization for any purpose enumerated in this Article unless the organization has obtained a license from the Commissioner. No statistical organization shall refuse to supply any services for which it is licensed in this State to any insurer admitted to do business in this State and offering to pay the fair and usual compensation for the services. A statistical organization applying for a license shall include with its application:

(1)   A copy of its constitution, charter, articles of organization, agreement, association, or incorporation, and a copy of its bylaws, plan of operation, and any other rules or regulations governing the conduct of its business, all duly certified by the custodian of the originals thereof;

(2)   A list of its members and subscribers;

(3)   The name and address of one or more residents of this State upon whom notices, process affecting it, or orders of the Commissioner may be served;

(4)   A statement showing its technical qualifications for acting in the capacity for which it seeks a license; and

(5)   Any other relevant information and documents that the Commissioner may require.

If the Commissioner determines that the applicant and the natural persons through whom it acts are qualified to provide the services proposed and that all requirements of law are met, the Commissioner shall issue a license specifying the authorized activity of the applicant. The Commissioner shall not issue a license if the proposed activity would tend to create a monopoly or to lessen or to destroy price competition. Licenses issued pursuant to this section shall remain in effect until the licensee withdraws from the State or until the license is suspended or revoked. Any change in or amendment to any document required to be filed under this section shall be promptly filed with the Commissioner. Every statistical organization shall file a statistical plan with the Commissioner for approval for each line of insurance for which the organization requests to be licensed. The Commissioner may, in the Commissioner's discretion, modify the plan to collect additional types of data. No statistical organization shall engage in any unfair or unreasonable practice with respect to its activities.

(c) Statistical organizations licensed pursuant to subsection (b) of this section and admitted insurers are authorized to exchange information and experience data between and among themselves in this State and with statistical organizations and insurers in other states and may consult with them with respect to rate making and the application of rating systems.

(d) The Commissioner shall adopt or approve reasonable rules, including rules providing statistical plans, for use thereafter by all insurers in the recording and reporting of loss and expense experience, in order that the experience of those insurers may be made available to the Commissioner. The Commissioner may designate one or more statistical organizations to assist him or her in gathering and making compilations of the experience. All insurers, for lines of insurance that require data to be reported, shall report their data to one of the designated statistical organizations.

(e) The Commissioner shall, at least once every three years, make or cause to be made an examination of each statistical organization licensed pursuant to subsection (b) of this section. This examination shall relate only to the activities conducted pursuant to this Article and to the organizations licensed under this Article. The officers, manager, agents, and employees of any statistical organization may be examined at any time under oath and shall exhibit all books, records, accounts, documents, or agreements governing its method of operation. In lieu of any examination, the Commissioner may accept the report of an examination made by the insurance advisory official of another state, pursuant to the laws of that state.

(f) Subject to the requirements of this Article and of G.S. 58-2-70, the Commissioner may suspend or revoke the license of any statistical organization or impose a monetary penalty against any statistical organization where (i) the Commissioner has reason to believe that any statistical organization has violated any provision of this Chapter, or (ii) the statistical organization fails to comply with an order of the Commissioner within the time limited by the order, or within any extension thereof that the Commissioner may grant. The Commissioner shall not suspend the license of any statistical organization for failure to comply with an order until the time prescribed for an appeal from the order has expired or, if an appeal has been taken, until the order has been affirmed. The Commissioner may determine when a suspension of a license shall become effective, and the suspension shall remain in effect for the period fixed by the Commissioner unless the Commissioner modifies or rescinds the suspension, or until the order upon which the suspension is based is modified, rescinded, or reversed. No license shall be suspended or revoked, and no monetary penalty shall be imposed except upon a written order of the Commissioner stating the Commissioner's findings, made after a hearing held upon not less than 10 days' written notice to the person or organization, and specifying the alleged violation.

(g) A statistical organization is considered an insurance company for purposes of the applicability of G.S. 58-6-7. (2005-210, s. 18; 2006-264, s. 45(b).)

§ 58-36-5. Membership as a prerequisite for writing insurance; governing committee; rules and regulations; expenses.

(a) Before the Commissioner shall grant permission to any stock, nonstock, or reciprocal insurance company or any other insurance organization to write in this State insurance against loss to residential real property with not more than four housing units located in this State or any contents thereof or valuable interest therein or other insurance coverages written in connection with the sale of such property insurance; or insurance against theft of or physical damage to private passenger (nonfleet) motor vehicles; or liability insurance for such motor vehicles, automobile medical payments insurance, uninsured motorists coverage or other insurance coverage written in connection with the sale of such liability insurance; or workers' compensation and employers' liability insurance written in connection therewith; except for insurance excluded from the Bureau's jurisdiction in G.S. 58-36-1(3); it shall be a requisite that they shall subscribe to and become members of the Bureau.

(b) Each member of the Bureau writing any one or more of the above lines of insurance in North Carolina shall, as a requisite thereto, be represented in the Bureau and shall be entitled to one representative and one vote in the administration of the affairs of the Bureau. They shall, upon organization, elect a governing committee which governing committee shall be composed of equal representation by stock and nonstock members. The governing committee of the Bureau shall also have as nonvoting members two persons who are not employed by or affiliated with any insurance company or the Department and who are appointed by the Governor to serve at his pleasure.

(c) The Bureau, when created, shall adopt such rules and regulations for its orderly procedure as shall be necessary for its maintenance and operation. No such rules and regulations shall discriminate against any type of insurer because of its plan of operation, nor shall any insurer be prevented from returning any unused or unabsorbed premium, deposit, savings or earnings to its policyholders or subscribers. The expense of such Bureau shall be borne by its members by quarterly contributions to be made in advance, such contributions to be made in advance by prorating such expense among the members in accordance with the amount of gross premiums derived from the above lines of insurance in North Carolina during the preceding year and members entering the Bureau since that date to advance an amount to be fixed by the governing committee. After the first fiscal year of operation of the Bureau the necessary expense of the Bureau shall be advanced by the members in accordance with rules and regulations to be established and adopted by the governing committee. The Bureau shall be empowered to subscribe for or purchase any necessary service, and employ and fix the salaries of such personnel and assistants as are necessary.

(d) The Commissioner is hereby authorized to compel the production of all books, data, papers and records and any other data necessary to compile statistics for the purpose of determining the underwriting experience of lines of insurance referred to in this Article, and this information shall be available and for the use of the Bureau for the capitulation and promulgation of rates on lines of insurance as are subject to the ratemaking authority of the Bureau. (1977, c. 828, s. 6; 1981, c. 888, s. 4; 1985 (Reg. Sess., 1986), c. 1027, s. 6; 1991, c. 720, s. 4.)

§ 58-36-10. Method of rate making; factors considered.

The following standards shall apply to the making and use of rates:

(1)   Rates or loss costs shall not be excessive, inadequate or unfairly discriminatory.

(2)   Due consideration shall be given to actual loss and expense experience within this State for the most recent three-year period for which that information is available; to prospective loss and expense experience within this State; to the hazards of conflagration and catastrophe; to a reasonable margin for underwriting profit and to contingencies; to dividends, savings, or unabsorbed premium deposits allowed or returned by insurers to their policyholders, members, or subscribers; to investment income earned or realized by insurers from their unearned premium, loss, and loss expense reserve funds generated from business within this State; to past and prospective expenses specially applicable to this State; and to all other relevant factors within this State: Provided, however, that countrywide expense and loss experience and other countrywide data may be considered only where credible North Carolina experience or data is not available.

(3)   In the case of property insurance rates under this Article, consideration may be given to the experience of property insurance business during the most recent five-year period for which that experience is available. In the case of property insurance rates under this Article, consideration shall be given to the insurance public protection classifications of fire districts established by the Commissioner. The Commissioner shall establish and modify from time to time insurance public protection districts for all rural areas of the State and for cities with populations of 100,000 or fewer, according to the most recent annual population estimates certified by the State Budget Officer. In establishing and modifying these districts, the Commissioner shall use standards at least equivalent to those used by the Insurance Services Office, Inc., or any successor organization. The standards developed by the Commissioner are subject to Article 2A of Chapter 150B of the General Statutes. The insurance public protection classifications established by the Commissioner issued pursuant to the provisions of this Article shall be subject to appeal as provided in G.S. 58-2-75, et seq. The exceptions stated in G.S. 58-2-75(a) do not apply.

(4)   Risks may be grouped by classifications and lines of insurance for establishment of rates, loss costs, and base premiums. Classification rates may

be modified to produce rates for individual risks in accordance with rating plans that establish standards for measuring variations in hazards or expense provisions or both. Those standards may measure any differences among risks that can be demonstrated to have a probable effect upon losses or expenses. The Bureau shall establish and implement a comprehensive classification rating plan for motor vehicle insurance under its jurisdiction. No such classification plans shall base any standard or rating plan for private passenger (nonfleet) motor vehicles, in whole or in part, directly or indirectly, upon the age or gender of the persons insured. The Bureau shall at least once every three years make a complete review of the filed classification rates to determine whether they are proper and supported by statistical evidence, and shall at least once every 10 years make a complete review of the territories for nonfleet private passenger motor vehicle insurance to determine whether they are proper and reasonable.

(5) In the case of workers' compensation insurance and employers' liability insurance written in connection therewith, due consideration shall be given to the past and prospective effects of changes in compensation benefits and in legal and medical fees that are provided for in General Statutes Chapter 97.

(6) To ensure that policyholders in the beach and coastal areas of the North Carolina Insurance Underwriting Association whose risks are of the same class and essentially the same hazard are charged premiums that are commensurate with the risk of loss and premiums that are actuarially correct, the North Carolina Rate Bureau shall revise, monitor, and review the existing territorial boundaries used by the Bureau when appropriate to establish geographic territories in the beach and coastal areas of the Association for rating purposes. In revising these territories, the Bureau shall use statistical data sources available to define such territories to represent relative risk factors that are actuarially sound and not unfairly discriminatory. The new territories and any subsequent amendments proposed by the North Carolina Rate Bureau or Association shall be subject to the Commissioner's approval and shall appear on the Bureau's Web site, the Association's Web site, and the Department's Web site once approved.

(7) Property insurance rates established under this Article may include a provision to reflect the cost of reinsurance to protect against catastrophic exposure within this State. Amounts to be paid to reinsurers, ceding commissions paid or to be paid to insurers by reinsurers, expected reinsurance recoveries, North Carolina exposure to catastrophic events relative to other states' exposure, and any other relevant information may be considered when determining the provision to reflect the cost of reinsurance. (1977, c. 828, s. 6; 1979, c. 824, s. 1; 1981, c. 521, s. 5; c. 790; 1987, c. 632, s. 1; 1991, c. 644, s.

39; 1999-132, s. 3.3; 2000-176, s. 1; 2004-203, s. 5(a); 2009-472, s. 2; 2012-162, s. 3.)

§ 58-36-15. Filing loss costs, rates, plans with Commissioner; public inspection of filings.

(a)   The Bureau shall file with the Commissioner copies of the rates, loss costs, classification plans, rating plans and rating systems used by its members. Each rate or loss costs filing shall become effective on the date specified in the filing, but not earlier than 210 days from the date the filing is received by the Commissioner: Provided that (1) rate or loss costs filings for workers' compensation insurance and employers' liability insurance written in connection therewith shall not become effective earlier than 210 days from the date the filing is received by the Commissioner or on the date as provided in G.S. 58-36-100, whichever is earlier; and (2) any filing may become effective on a date earlier than that specified in this subsection upon agreement between the Commissioner and the Bureau.

(b)   A filing by the Rate Bureau shall be open to public inspection immediately upon submission to the Commissioner. All property insurance rate filings shall be open to the public except as provided in this Article where necessary to maintain the confidentiality of certain testimony. At least 30 days before a notice of hearing issues, the Department shall receive comments from the public regarding a property insurance rate filing. The comments may be provided to the Department by e-mail, mail, or in person at a time and place set by the Department. All public comments shall be shared with the Rate Bureau in a timely manner.

(c)   The Bureau shall maintain reasonable records, of the type and kind reasonably adapted to its method of operation, of the experience of its members and of the data, statistics or information collected or used by it in connection with the rates, rating plans, rating systems, loss costs and other data as specified in G.S. 58-36-100, underwriting rules, policy or bond forms, surveys or inspections made or used by it.

(d)   With respect to the filing of rates for nonfleet private passenger motor vehicle insurance, the Bureau shall, on or before February 1 of each year, or later with the approval of the Commissioner, file with the Commissioner the experience, data, statistics, and information referred to in subsection (c) of this section and any proposed adjustments in the rates for all member companies of the Bureau. The filing shall include, where deemed by the Commissioner to be necessary for proper review, the data specified in subsections (c), (e), (g) and (h) of this section. Any filing that does not contain the data required by this subsection may be returned to the Bureau and not be deemed a proper filing. Provided, however, that if the Commissioner concludes that a filing does not constitute a proper filing he shall promptly notify the Bureau in writing to that effect, which notification shall state in reasonable detail the basis of the Commissioner's conclusion. The Bureau shall then have a reasonable time to remedy the defects so specified. An otherwise defective filing thus remedied shall be deemed to be a proper and timely filing, except that all periods of time specified in this Article will run from the date the Commissioner receives additional or amended documents necessary to remedy all material defects in the original filing.

(d1)   With respect to property insurance rates, the Bureau shall file no later than May 1, 2010, a schedule of credits for policyholders based on the presence of mitigation and construction features and on the condition of buildings that it insures in the beach and coastal areas of the State. The Bureau shall develop rules applicable to the operation of the schedule and the mitigation program with approval by the Commissioner. The schedule shall not be unfairly discriminatory and shall be reviewed by the Bureau annually, with the results reported annually to the Commissioner.

(e)   The Commissioner may require the filing of supporting data including:

(1)   The Bureau's interpretation of any statistical data relied upon;

(2)   Descriptions of the methods employed in setting the rates;

(3)   Analysis of the incurred losses submitted on an accident year or policy year basis into their component parts; to wit, paid losses, reserves for losses and loss expenses, and reserves for losses incurred but not reported;

(4)   The total number and dollar amount of paid claims;

(5)   The total number and dollar amount of case basis reserve claims;

(6)   Earned and written premiums at current rates by rating territory;

(7) Earned premiums and incurred losses according to classification plan categories; and

(8) Income from investment of unearned premiums and loss and loss expense reserves generated by business within this State.

Provided, however, that with respect to business written prior to January 1, 1980, the Commissioner shall not require the filing of such supporting data which has not been required to be recorded under statistical plans approved by the Commissioner.

(f) On or before September 1 of each calendar year, or later with the approval of the Commissioner, the Bureau shall submit to the Commissioner the experience, data, statistics, and information referred to in subsection (c) of this section and required under G.S. 58-36-100 and a residual market rate or prospective loss costs review based on those data for workers' compensation insurance and employers' liability insurance written in connection therewith. Any rate or loss costs increase for that insurance that is implemented under this Article shall become effective solely to insurance with an inception date on or after the effective date of the rate or loss costs increase.

(g) The following information must be included in policy form, rule, and rate or loss costs filings under this Article and under Article 37 of this Chapter:

(1) A detailed list of the rates, loss costs, rules, and policy forms filed, accompanied by a list of those superseded; and

(2) A detailed description, properly referenced, of all changes in policy forms, rules, prospective loss costs, and rates, including the effect of each change.

(h) Except to the extent the Commissioner determines that this subsection is inapplicable to filings made under G.S. 58-36-100 and except for filings made under G.S. 58-36-30, all policy form, rule, prospective loss costs, and rate filings under this Article and Article 37 of this Chapter that are based on statistical data must be accompanied by the following properly identified information:

(1) North Carolina earned premiums at the actual and current rate level; losses and loss adjustment expenses, each on paid and incurred bases without trending or other modification for the experience period, including the loss ratio anticipated at the time the rates were promulgated for the experience period;

(2) Credibility factor development and application;

(3) Loss development factor derivation and application on both paid and incurred bases and in both numbers and dollars of claims;

(4) Trending factor development and application;

(5) Changes in premium base resulting from rating exposure trends;

(6) Limiting factor development and application;

(7) Overhead expense development and application of commission and brokerage, other acquisition expenses, general expenses, taxes, licenses, and fees;

(8) Percent rate or prospective loss costs change;

(9) Final proposed rates;

(10) Investment earnings, consisting of investment income and realized plus unrealized capital gains, from loss, loss expense, and unearned premium reserves;

(11) Identification of applicable statistical plans and programs and a certification of compliance with them;

(12) Investment earnings on capital and surplus;

(13) Level of capital and surplus needed to support premium writings without endangering the solvency of member companies; and

(14) Such other information that may be required by any rule adopted by the Commissioner.

Provided, however, that no filing may be returned or disapproved on the grounds that such information has not been furnished if insurers have not been required to collect such information pursuant to statistical plans or programs or to report such information to the Bureau or to statistical agents, except where the Commissioner has given reasonable prior notice to the insurers to begin collecting and reporting such information, or except when the information is readily available to the insurers.

(i) The Bureau shall file with and at the time of any rate or prospective loss costs filing all testimony, exhibits, and other information on which the Bureau will rely at the hearing on the rate filing. The Department shall file all testimony, exhibits, and other information on which the Department will rely at the hearing on the rate filing 20 days in advance of the convening date of the hearing. Upon the issuance of a notice of hearing the Commissioner shall hold a meeting of the parties to provide for the scheduling of any additional testimony, including written testimony, exhibits or other information, in response to the notice of hearing and any potential rebuttal testimony, exhibits, or other information. This subsection also applies to rate filings made by the North Carolina Motor Vehicle Reinsurance Facility under Article 37 of this Chapter. (1977, c. 828, s. 6; 1979, c. 824, s. 2; 1981, c. 521, s. 1; 1985, c. 666, s. 3; 1985 (Reg. Sess., 1986), c. 1027, ss. 2, 3; 1993, c. 409, s. 10; 1995, c. 505, s. 2; 1999-132, ss. 3.4-3.6; 2002-187, s. 4.1; 2009-472, s. 3; 2012-162, s. 1.)

§ 58-36-16. Bureau to share information with Department of Labor and North Carolina Industrial Commission.

The Bureau shall provide to the Department of Labor and the North Carolina Industrial Commission information from the Bureau's records indicating each employer's experience rate modifier established for the purpose of setting premium rates for workers' compensation insurance and the name and business address of each employer whose workers' compensation coverage is provided through the assigned-risk pool pursuant to G.S. 58-36-1. Information provided to the Department of Labor and the North Carolina Industrial Commission with respect to experience rate modifiers shall include the name of the employer and the employer's most current intrastate or interstate experience rate modifier. The information provided to the Department and the Commission under this section shall be confidential and not open for public inspection. The Bureau shall be immune from civil liability for releasing information pursuant to this section, even if the information is erroneous, provided the Bureau acted in good faith and without malicious or wilful intent to harm in releasing the information. (1991 (Reg. Sess., 1992), c. 894, s. 4; 2012-135, s. 1(a).)

§ 58-36-17. Bureau to share information with the North Carolina Industrial Commission.

The Bureau shall provide to the North Carolina Industrial Commission information contained in the Bureau's records indicating the status of workers' compensation insurance coverage on North Carolina employers as reported to the Bureau by the Bureau's member companies. The North Carolina Industrial Commission shall take such steps, including obtaining software or software licenses, as are necessary to be able to receive and process such information from the Bureau. The records provided to the North Carolina Industrial Commission under this section shall be confidential and shall not be public records as that term is defined in G.S. 132-1. Notwithstanding the previous sentence, the North Carolina Industrial Commission may release data showing workers' compensation insurance policy information that includes only employer name and address, carrier name, address, and telephone number; policy number; policy effective dates; policy cancellation dates; and policy reinstatement dates. This data shall not be confidential data and shall be a public record as that term is defined in G.S. 132-1. The North Carolina Industrial Commission shall use the information provided pursuant to this section only to carry out its statutory duties and obligations under The North Carolina Workers' Compensation Act. The Bureau shall be immune from civil liability for releasing information pursuant to this section, even if the information is erroneous, provided the Bureau acted in good faith and without malicious or willful intent to harm in releasing the information. (2012-135, s. 1(b); 2012-194, s. 65.5; 2013-20, s. 1.)

§ 58-36-20. Disapproval; hearing, order; adjustment of premium, review of filing.

(a) At any time within 50 days after the date of any filing, the Commissioner may give written notice to the Bureau specifying in what respect and to what extent the Commissioner contends the filing fails to comply with the requirements of this Article and fixing a date for hearing not less than 30 days from the date of mailing of such notice. Once begun, hearings must proceed without undue delay. At the hearing the burden of proving that the proposed rates are not excessive, inadequate, or unfairly discriminatory is on the Bureau. At the hearing the factors specified in G.S. 58-36-10 shall be considered. If the Commissioner after hearing finds that the filing does not comply with the provisions of this Article, he may issue his order determining wherein and to what extent such filing is deemed to be improper and fixing a date thereafter, within a reasonable time, after which the filing shall no longer be effective. In the event the Commissioner finds that the proposed rates are excessive, the Commissioner shall specify the overall rates, between the existing rates and the rates proposed by the Bureau filing, that may be used by the members of the Bureau instead of the rates proposed by the Bureau filing. In any such order, the Commissioner shall make findings of fact based on the evidence presented in the filing and at the hearing. Any order issued after a hearing shall be issued within 45 days after the completion of the hearing. If no order is issued within 45 days after the completion of the hearing, the filing shall be deemed to be approved.

(b)   In the event that no notice of hearing shall be issued within 50 days from the date of any such filing, the filing shall be deemed to be approved. If the Commissioner disapproves such filing pursuant to subsection (a) as not being in compliance with G.S. 58-36-10, he may order an adjustment of the premium to be made with the policyholder either by collection of an additional premium or by refund, if the amount exceeds five dollars ($5.00). The Commissioner may thereafter review any filing in the manner provided; but if so reviewed, no adjustment of any premium on any policy then in force may be ordered.

(c)   For workers' compensation insurance and employers' liability insurance written in connection therewith, the period between the date of any filing and the date the Commissioner may give written notice as described in subsection (a) of this section and the period between the date of any filing and the deadline for giving notice of hearing as described in subsection (b) of this section shall be 60 days. (1977, c. 828, s. 6; 1979, c. 824, s. 3; 1985, c. 666, s. 2; 1993, c. 409, s. 12; 2002-187, s. 4.2; 2009-472, s. 4; 2012-162, s. 2.)

§ 58-36-25. Appeal of Commissioner's order.

(a)   Any order or decision of the Commissioner shall be subject to judicial review as provided in Article 2 of this Chapter.

(b)   Whenever a Bureau rate is held to be unfairly discriminatory or excessive and no longer effective by order of the Commissioner issued under G.S. 58-36-20, the members of the Bureau, in accordance with rules and regulations established and adopted by the governing committee, shall have the option to continue to use such rate for the interim period pending judicial review of such order, provided each such member shall place in escrow account the purportedly unfairly discriminatory or excessive portion of the premium collected during such interim period. Upon a final determination by the Court, or upon a consent agreement or consent order between the Bureau and the Commissioner, the Commissioner shall order the escrowed funds to be distributed appropriately. If refunds are to be made to policyholders, the Commissioner shall order that the members of the Bureau refund the difference between the total premium per policy using the rate levels finally determined and the total premium per policy collected during the interim period pending judicial review, except that refund amounts that are five dollars ($5.00) or less per policy shall not be required. The court may also require that purportedly excess premiums resulting from an adjustment of premiums ordered pursuant to G.S. 58-36-20(b) be placed in such escrow account pending judicial review. If refunds made to policyholders are ordered under this subsection, the amounts refunded shall bear interest at the rate determined under this subsection. That rate, to be computed by the Bureau, shall be the average of the prime rates on the effective date of the filing and each anniversary of that date occurring prior to the date of the Commissioner's order requiring refunds, with the prime rate on each of the dates being the average of the prime rates of the four largest banking institutions domiciled in this State as of that date, plus three percent (3%). (1977, c. 828, s. 6; 1979, c. 824, s. 4; 1985 (Reg. Sess., 1986), c. 1027, ss. 3.1, 4; 1995, c. 517, s. 19.)

§ 58-36-30. Deviations.

(a) Except as permitted by G.S. 58-36-100 for workers' compensation loss costs filings, no insurer and no officer, agent, or representative of an insurer shall knowingly issue or deliver or knowingly permit the issuance or delivery of any policy of insurance in this State that does not conform to the rates, rating plans, classifications, schedules, rules and standards made and filed by the Bureau. An insurer may deviate from the rates promulgated by the Bureau if the insurer has filed the proposed deviation with the Bureau and the Commissioner, if the proposed deviation is based on sound actuarial principles, and if the proposed deviation is approved by the Commissioner. Amendments to deviations are subject to the same requirements as initial filings. An insurer may terminate a deviation only if the deviation has been in effect for a period of six months before the effective date of the termination and the insurer notifies the Commissioner of the termination no later than 15 days before the effective date of the termination.

(b) A rate in excess of that promulgated by the Bureau may be charged by an insurer on any specific risk if the higher rate is charged in accordance with rules adopted by the Commissioner and with the knowledge and written consent of the insured. The insurer is not required to obtain the written consent of the insured on any renewal of or endorsement to the policy if the policy renewal or endorsement states that the rates are greater than those rates that are applicable in the State of North Carolina. The insurer shall retain the signed consent form and other policy information for each insured and make this information available to the Commissioner, upon request of the Commissioner. This subsection may be used to provide motor vehicle liability coverage limits above those required under Article 9A of Chapter 20 of the General Statutes and above those cedable to the Facility under Article 37 of this Chapter to persons whose personal excess liability insurance policies require that they maintain specific higher liability coverage limits. Any data obtained by the Commissioner under this subsection is proprietary and confidential and is not a public record under G.S. 132-1 or G.S. 58-2-100.

(c) Any approved rate under subsection (b) of this section with respect to workers' compensation and employers' liability insurance written in connection therewith shall be furnished to the Bureau.

(d) Notwithstanding any other provision of law prohibiting insurance rate differentials based on age, with respect to nonfleet private passenger motor vehicle insurance under the jurisdiction of the Bureau, any member of the Bureau may apply for and use in this State, subject to the Commissioner's approval, a downward deviation in the rates for insureds who are 55 years of age or older. A member of the Bureau may condition a deviation under this subsection or a deviation under subsection (a) of this section on the successful completion of a motor vehicle accident prevention course that has been approved by the Commissioner of Motor Vehicles, as designated in the deviation. (1977, c. 828, s. 6; 1983, c. 162, ss. 1, 2; 1985, c. 666, s. 1; 1987, c. 869, s. 1; 1993, c. 409, s. 25; 1995, c. 517, ss. 20, 21; 1995 (Reg. Sess., 1996), c. 668, s. 1; 1999-132, ss. 3.7, 3.8; 2001-423, s. 1.)

§ 58-36-35. Appeal to Commissioner from decision of Bureau.

(a) Any member of the Bureau may appeal to the Commissioner from any decision of the Bureau, except for a decision made under G.S. 58-36-1(2). After a hearing held on not fewer than 10 days' written notice to the appellant and to the Bureau, the Commissioner shall issue an order approving the decision or directing the Bureau to reconsider the decision. If the Commissioner directs the Bureau to reconsider the decision and the Bureau fails to take action satisfactory to the Commissioner, the Commissioner shall make such order as the Commissioner may see fit.

(b) No later than 20 days before the hearing, the appellant shall file with the Commissioner or the Commissioner's designated hearing officer and shall serve on the appellee a written statement of his case and any evidence the appellant intends to offer at the hearing. No later than five days before such hearing, the appellee shall file with the Commissioner or the Commissioner's designated hearing officer and shall serve on the appellant a written statement of the appellee's case and any evidence the appellee intends to offer at the hearing. Each such hearing shall be recorded and transcribed. The cost of the recording and transcribing shall be borne equally by the appellant and appellee; provided that upon any final adjudication the prevailing party shall be reimbursed for his share of such costs by the other party. Each party shall, on a date determined by the Commissioner or the Commissioner's designated hearing officer, but not sooner than 15 days after delivery of the completed transcript to the party, submit to the Commissioner or the Commissioner's designated hearing officer and serve on the other party, a proposed order. The Commissioner or the Commissioner's designated hearing officer shall then issue an order. (1977, c. 828, s. 6; 1989, c. 485, s. 28; 1989 (Reg. Sess., 1990), c. 1069, s. 16; 2001-232, s. 3.)

§ 58-36-40. Existing rates, rating systems, territories, classifications and policy forms.

Rates, rating systems, territories, classifications and policy forms lawfully in use on September 1, 1977, may continue to be used thereafter, notwithstanding any provision of this Article. (1977, c. 828, s. 6.)

§ 58-36-41. Development of policy endorsement for exclusive use of original equipment manufactured crash parts.

The Rate Bureau shall develop an optional policy endorsement to be filed with the Commissioner for approval that permits policyholders to elect nonfleet private passenger motor vehicle physical damage coverage specifying the exclusive use of original equipment manufactured crash parts. (2003-395, s. 3.)

§ 58-36-42. Development of policy form or endorsement for residential property insurance that does not include coverage for perils of windstorm or hail.

With respect to residential property insurance under its jurisdiction, the Bureau shall develop an optional policy form or endorsement to be filed with the Commissioner for approval that provides residential property insurance coverage in the coastal and beach areas defined in G.S. 58-45-5(2) and (2b) without coverage for the perils of windstorm or hail. Insurers that sell such policies shall comply with the provisions of G.S. 58-44-60 and through such compliance shall be deemed to have given notice to all insured and persons claiming benefits under such policies that such policies do not include coverage for the perils of windstorm or hail. (2012-162, s. 4; 2013-199, s. 8.)

§ 58-36-45. Notice of coverage or rate change.

Whenever an insurer changes the coverage other than at the request of the insured or changes the premium rate, it shall give the insured written notice of such coverage change or premium rate change at least 15 days in advance of the effective date of such change or changes with a copy of such notice to the agent. This section shall apply to all policies and coverages subject to the provisions of this Article except workers' compensation insurance and employers' liability insurance written in connection therewith. (1977, c. 828, s. 6; 1985, c. 666, s. 4.)

§ 58-36-50. Limitation.

Nothing in this Article shall apply to any town or county farmers mutual fire insurance association restricting its operations to not more than six adjacent counties in this State, or to domestic insurance companies, associations, orders or fraternal benefit societies now doing business in this State on the assessment plan. (1977, c. 828, s. 6; 1985 (Reg. Sess., 1986), c. 1013, s. 10.1; 1989, c. 485, s. 53.)

§ 58-36-55. Policy forms.

No policy form applying to insurance on risks or operations covered by this Article may be delivered or issued for delivery unless it has been filed with the Commissioner by the Bureau and either he has approved it, or 90 days have elapsed and he has not disapproved it. (1979, c. 824, s. 6.)

§ 58-36-60. Payment of dividends not prohibited or regulated; plan for payment into rating system.

Nothing in this Article will be construed to prohibit or regulate the payment of dividends, savings, or unabsorbed premium deposits allowed or returned by insurers to their policyholders, members, or subscribers. Individual policyholder loss experience may be considered as a factor in determining dividends for workers' compensation insurance and employers' liability insurance written in connection therewith. A plan for the payment of dividends, savings, or unabsorbed premium deposits allowed or returned by insurers to their policyholders, members, or subscribers will not be deemed a rating plan or system. (1979, c. 824, s. 6; 1983, c. 374, s. 1.)

§ 58-36-65. Classifications and Safe Driver Incentive Plan for nonfleet private passenger motor vehicle insurance.

(a) The Bureau shall file, subject to review, modification, and promulgation by the Commissioner, such rate classifications, schedules, or rules that the Commissioner deems to be desirable and equitable to classify drivers of nonfleet private passenger motor vehicles for insurance purposes. Subsequently, the Commissioner may require the Bureau to file modifications of the classifications, schedules, or rules. If the Bureau does not file the modifications within a reasonable time, the Commissioner may promulgate the modifications. In promulgating or modifying these classifications, schedules, or rules, the Commissioner may give consideration to the following:

(1) Uses of vehicles, including without limitation to farm use, pleasure use, driving to and from work, and business use;

(2) Principal and occasional operation of vehicles;

(3) Years of driving experience of insureds as licensed drivers;

(4) The characteristics of vehicles; or

(5) Any other factors, not in conflict with any law, deemed by the Commissioner to be appropriate.

(b) The Bureau shall file, subject to review, modification, and promulgation by the Commissioner, a Safe Driver Incentive Plan ("Plan") that adequately and factually distinguishes among various classes of drivers that have safe driving records and various classes of drivers that have a record of at-fault accidents; a record of convictions of major moving traffic violations; a record of convictions of minor moving traffic violations; or a combination thereof; and that provides for premium differentials among those classes of drivers. Subsequently, the Commissioner may require the Bureau to file modifications of the Plan. If the Bureau does not file the modifications within a reasonable time, the Commissioner may promulgate the modifications. The Commissioner is authorized to structure the Plan to provide for surcharges above and discounts below the rate otherwise charged.

(c) The classifications and Plan filed by the Bureau shall be subject to the filing, hearing, modification, approval, disapproval, review, and appeal procedures provided by law; provided that the 210-day disapproval period in G.S. 58-36-20(a) and the 50-day deemer period in G.S. 58-36-20(b) do not apply to filings or modifications made under this section. The classifications or Plan filed by the Bureau and promulgated by the Commissioner shall of itself not be designed to bring about any increase or decrease in the overall rate level.

(d) Whenever any policy loses any safe driver discount provided by the Plan or is surcharged due to an accumulation of points under the Plan, the insurer shall, pursuant to rules adopted by the Commissioner, prior to or simultaneously with the billing for additional premium, inform the named insured of the surcharge or loss of discount by mailing to such insured a notice that states the basis for the surcharge or loss of discount, and that advises that upon receipt of a written request from the named insured it will promptly mail to the named insured a statement of the amount of increased premium attributable to the surcharge or loss of discount. The statement of the basis of the surcharge or loss of discount is privileged, and does not constitute grounds for any cause of action for defamation or invasion of privacy against the insurer or its representatives, or against any person who furnishes to the insurer the information upon which the insurer's reasons are based, unless the statement or furnishing of information is made with malice or in bad faith.

(e) Records of convictions for moving traffic violations to be considered under this section shall be obtained at least annually from the Division of Motor Vehicles and applied by the Bureau's member companies in accordance with rules to be established by the Bureau.

(f) The Bureau is authorized to establish reasonable rules providing for the exchange of information among its member companies as to chargeable accidents and similar information involving persons to be insured under policies. Neither the Bureau, any employee of the Bureau, nor any company or individual serving on any committee of the Bureau has any liability for defamation or invasion of privacy to any person arising out of the adoption, implementation, or enforcement of any such rule. No insurer or individual requesting, furnishing, or otherwise using any information that such insurer or person reasonably believes to be for purposes authorized by this section has any liability for defamation or invasion of privacy to any person on account of any such requesting, furnishing, or use. The immunity provided by this subsection does not apply to any acts made with malice or in bad faith.

(g) If an applicant for the issuance or renewal of a nonfleet private passenger motor vehicle insurance policy knowingly makes a material misrepresentation of the years of driving experience or the driving record of any named insured or of any other operator who resides in the same household and who customarily operates a motor vehicle to be insured under the policy, the insurer may:

(1) Cancel or refuse to renew the policy;

(2) Surcharge the policy in accordance with rules to be adopted by the Bureau and approved by the Commissioner; or

(3) Recover from the applicant the appropriate amount of premium or surcharge that would have been collected by the insurer had the applicant furnished the correct information.

(h)   If an insured disputes his insurer's determination that the operator of an insured vehicle was at fault in an accident, such dispute shall be resolved pursuant to G.S. 58-36-1(2), unless there has been an adjudication or admission of negligence of such operator.

(i)   As used in this section, "conviction" means a conviction as defined in G.S. 20-279.1 and means an infraction as defined in G.S. 14-3.1.

(j)   Subclassification plan surcharges shall be applied to a policy for a period of not less nor more than three policy years.

(k)   The subclassification plan may provide for premium surcharges for insureds having less than three years' driving experience as licensed drivers.

(l)   Except as provided in G.S. 58-36-30(d), no classification or subclassification plan for nonfleet private passenger motor vehicle insurance shall be based, in whole or in part, directly or indirectly, upon the age or gender of insureds.

(m)   Notwithstanding any other provision of law, with respect to motorcycle insurance under the jurisdiction of the Bureau, any member of the Bureau may apply for and use in this State, subject to the Commissioner's approval, a downward deviation in the rates of insureds who show proof of satisfactory completion of the Motorcycle Safety Instruction Program or a comparable motorcycle safety program provided by federally certified instructors for members of the military. (1985 (Reg. Sess., 1986), c. 1027, s. 1; 1987, c. 864, ss. 28, 33; c. 869, s. 9; 1987 (Reg. Sess., 1988), c. 975, ss. 4, 5; 1989, c. 755, s. 3; 1993, c. 320, s. 5; 2002-187, s. 4.3; 2012-176, s. 1.)

§ 58-36-70. Rate filings and hearings for motor vehicle insurance.

(a)   With respect to nonfleet private passenger motor vehicle insurance, except as provided in G.S. 58-36-25, a filing made by the Bureau under G.S. 58-36-15(d) is not effective until approved by the Commissioner or unless 60 days have elapsed since the making of a proper filing under that subsection and the Commissioner has not called for a hearing on the filing. If the Commissioner calls for a hearing, he must give written notice to the Bureau, specify in the notice in what respect the filing fails to comply with this Article, and fix a date for the hearing that is not less than 30 days from the date the notice is mailed.

(b)   At least 15 days before the date set for the convening of the hearing the respective staffs and consultants of the Bureau and Commissioner shall meet at a prehearing conference to review the filing and discuss any points of disagreement that are likely to be in issue at the hearing. At the prehearing conference, the parties shall list the names of potential witnesses and, where possible, stipulate to their qualifications as expert witnesses, stipulate to the sequence of appearances of witnesses, and stipulate to the relevance of proposed exhibits to be offered by the parties. Minutes of the prehearing conference shall be made and reduced to writing and become part of the hearing record. Any agreements reached as to preliminary matters shall be set forth in writing and consented to by the Bureau and the Commissioner. The purpose of this subsection is to avoid unnecessary delay in the rate hearings.

(c) Once begun, hearings must proceed without undue delay. At the hearing the burden of proving that the proposed rates are not excessive, inadequate, or unfairly discriminatory is on the Bureau. The Commissioner may disregard at the hearing any exhibits, judgments, or conclusions offered as evidence by the Bureau that were developed by or available to or could reasonably have been obtained or developed by the Bureau at or before the time the Bureau made its proper filing and which exhibits, judgments, or conclusions were not included and supported in the filing; unless the evidence is offered in response to inquiries made at the hearing by the Department, the notice of hearing, or as rebuttal to the Department's evidence. If relevant data becomes available after the filing has been properly made, the Commissioner may consider such data as evidence in the hearing. The order of presenting evidence shall be (1) by the Bureau; (2) by the Department; (3) any rebuttal evidence by the Bureau regarding the Department's evidence; and (4) any rebuttal evidence by the Department regarding the Bureau's rebuttal evidence. Neither the Bureau nor the Department shall present repetitious testimony or evidence relating to the same issues.

(d)   If the Commissioner finds that a filing complies with the provisions of this Article, either after the hearing or at any other time after the filing has been properly made, he may issue an order approving the filing. If the Commissioner after the hearing finds that the filing does not comply with the provisions of this Article, he may issue an order disapproving the filing, determining in what respect the filing is improper, and specifying the appropriate rate level or levels that may be used by the members of the Bureau instead of the rate level or levels proposed by the Bureau filing, unless there has not been data admitted into evidence in the hearing that is sufficiently credible for arriving at the appropriate rate level or levels. Any order issued after a hearing shall be issued within 45 days after the completion of the hearing. If no order is issued within 45 days after the completion of the hearing, the filing shall be deemed to be approved. The Commissioner may thereafter review any filing in the manner provided; but if so reviewed, no adjustment of any premium on any policy then in force may be ordered. The escrow provisions of G.S. 58-36-25(b) apply to any order of the Commissioner under this subsection.

(e) No person shall willfully withhold information required by this Article from or knowingly furnish false or misleading information to the Commissioner, any statistical agency designated by the Commissioner, any rating or advisory organization, the Bureau, the North Carolina Motor Vehicle Reinsurance Facility, or any insurer, which information affects the rates, rating plans, classifications, or policy forms subject to this Article or Article 37 of this Chapter. (1985 (Reg. Sess., 1986), c. 1027, s. 5; 1987, c. 864, s. 65; 1987 (Reg. Sess., 1988), c. 975, s. 6; 1989 (Reg. Sess., 1990), c. 1069, s. 23; 1995, c. 507, s. 11A(c).)

§ 58-36-75. At-fault accidents and certain moving traffic violations under the Safe Driver Incentive Plan.

(a) The subclassification plan promulgated pursuant to G.S. 58-36-65(b) may provide for separate surcharges for major, intermediate, and minor accidents. A "major accident" is an at-fault accident that results in either (i) bodily injury or death or (ii) only property damage of three thousand dollars ($3,000) or more. An "intermediate accident" is an at-fault accident that results in only property damage of more than one thousand eight hundred dollars ($1,800) but less than three thousand dollars ($3,000). A "minor accident" is an at-fault accident that results in only property damage of one thousand eight hundred dollars ($1,800) or less. The subclassification plan may also exempt certain minor accidents from the Facility recoupment surcharge. The Bureau shall assign varying Safe Driver Incentive Plan point values and surcharges for bodily injury in at-fault accidents that are commensurate with the severity of the injury, provided that the point value and surcharge assigned for the most severe bodily injury shall not exceed the point value and surcharge assigned to a major accident involving only property damage.

(a1) The subclassification plan shall provide that there shall be no premium surcharge, increase in premium on account of cession to the Reinsurance Facility, or assessment of points against an insured where: (i) the insured is involved and is at fault in a "minor accident," as defined in subsection (a) of this section; (ii) the insured is not convicted of a moving traffic violation in connection with the accident; (iii) neither the vehicle owner, principal operator, nor any licensed operator in the owner's household has a driving record consisting of one or more convictions for a moving traffic violation or one or more at-fault accidents during the three-year period immediately preceding the date of the application for a policy or the date of the preparation of the renewal of a policy; and (iv) the insured has been covered by liability insurance with the same company or company group continuously for at least the six months immediately preceding the accident. Notwithstanding (iv) of this subsection, if the insured has been covered by liability insurance with the same company or company group for at least six continuous months, some or all of which were after the accident, the insurance company shall remove any premium surcharge or assessment of points against the insured if requirements (i), (ii), and (iii) of this subsection are met. Also notwithstanding (iv) of this subsection, an insurance company may choose not to assess a premium surcharge or points against an insured who has been covered by liability insurance with that company or with the company's group for less than six months immediately preceding the accident, if requirements (i), (ii), and (iii) are met.

(a2) The subclassification plan shall provide that there shall be no premium surcharge or assessment of points against an insured where (i) the insured's driver's license has been revoked under G.S. 20-16.5; and (ii) the insured is subsequently acquitted of the offense involving impaired driving, as defined in G.S. 20-4.01(24a), that is related to the revocation, or the charge for that offense is dismissed. In addition, no insurer shall use, for rating, underwriting, or classification purposes, including ceding any risk to the Facility or writing any kind of coverage subject to this Article, any license revocation under G.S. 20-16.5 if the insured is acquitted or the charge is dismissed as described in this subsection.

(b) Repealed by Session Laws 1999-294, s. 12(a), effective July 14, 1999.

(c) Repealed by Session Laws 1999-132, s. 8.1, effective June 4, 1999.

(d) There shall be no Safe Driver Incentive Plan surcharges under G.S. 58-36-65 for accidents occurring when only operating a firefighting, rescue squad, or law enforcement vehicle in accordance with G.S. 20-125(b) and in response to an emergency if the operator of the vehicle at the time of the accident was a paid or volunteer member of any fire department, rescue squad, or any law enforcement agency. This exception does not include an accident occurring after the vehicle ceases to be used in response to the emergency and the emergency ceases to exist.

(e)   Repealed by Session Laws 1999-294, s. 12(a), effective July 14, 1999.

(f)   The subclassification plan shall provide that with respect to a conviction for a "violation of speeding 10 miles per hour or less over the speed limit" there shall be no premium surcharge nor any assessment of points unless there is a driving record consisting of a conviction or convictions for a moving traffic violation or violations, except for a prayer for judgment continued for any moving traffic violation, during the three years immediately preceding the date of application or the preparation of the renewal. The subclassification plan shall also provide that with respect to a prayer for judgment continued for any moving traffic violation, there shall be no premium surcharge nor any assessment of points unless the vehicle owner, principal operator, or any licensed operator in the owner's household has a driving record consisting of a prayer or prayers for judgment continued for any moving traffic violation or violations during the three years immediately preceding the date of application or the preparation of the renewal. For the purpose of this subsection, a "prayer for judgment continued" means a determination of guilt by a jury or a court though no sentence has been imposed. For the purpose of this subsection, a "violation of speeding 10 miles per hour or less over the speed limit" does not include the offense of speeding in a school zone in excess of the posted school zone speed limit.

(f1)   The subclassification plan shall provide that in the event an insured is at fault in an accident and is convicted of a moving traffic violation in connection with the accident, only the higher plan premium surcharge between the accident and the conviction shall be assessed on the policy.

(g)   As used in this section "conviction" means a conviction as defined in G.S. 20-279.1 and means an infraction as defined in G.S. 14-3.1.

(h)   The North Carolina Rate Bureau shall assign one insurance point under the Safe Driver Incentive Plan for persons who fail to yield to a pedestrian under G.S. 20-158(b)(2)b.(1987, c. 869, s. 6; 1991, c. 101, s. 1; c. 713, s. 1; c. 720, s. 90; 1991 (Reg. Sess., 1992), c. 837, s. 11; c. 997, s. 1; 1993, c. 285, s. 11; 1995 (Reg. Sess., 1996), c. 730, s. 3; 1997-332, s. 1; 1997-443, s. 19.26(d); 1999-132, s. 8.1; 1999-294, s. 12(a), (b); 2003-137, s. 1; 2004-172, s. 4.)

§ 58-36-80. Coverage for damage to rental vehicles authorized.

As used in this section, "property damage" means damage or loss to a rented vehicle in excess of two hundred fifty dollars ($250.00), including loss of use and any costs or expenses incident to the damage or loss, for which the renter is legally obligated to pay; and "rented" means rented on a daily rate basis for a period of 21 consecutive days or less. The Bureau is authorized to promulgate rates and policy forms for insurance against property damage to rented private passenger motor vehicles. Such coverage may be offered at the option of the individual member companies of the Bureau. (1989, c. 631, s. 1; 1989 (Reg. Sess., 1990), c. 1021, s. 10.)

§ 58-36-85. Termination of a nonfleet private passenger motor vehicle insurance policy.

(a) Definitions. - The following definitions apply in this section:

(1) Policy. - A nonfleet private passenger motor vehicle liability insurance policy, including a policy that provides medical payments, uninsured motorist, or underinsured motorist coverage, whose named insured is one individual or two or more individuals who reside in the same household.

(2) Terminate. - To cancel or refuse to renew a policy.

(b) Termination Restrictions. - An insurer shall not terminate a policy for a reason that is not specified in G.S. 58-2-164(g), 58-36-65(g), or 58-37-50. A termination of a policy is not effective unless the insurer either has notified a named insured of the termination by sending a written termination notice by first class mail to the insured's last known address or is not required by this subsection to send a written termination notice. Proof of mailing of a written termination notice is proof that the notice was sent.

An insurer is not required to send a written termination notice if any of the following applies:

(1) The insurer has manifested its willingness to renew the policy by issuing or offering to issue a renewal policy, a certificate, or other evidence of renewal.

(2) The insurer has manifested its willingness to renew the policy by any means not described in subdivision (1) of this subsection, including mailing a premium notice or expiration notice by first class mail to the named insured and the failure of the insured to pay the required premium on or before the premium due date.

(3) A named insured has given written notification to the insurer or its agent that the named insured wants the policy to be terminated.

(c) Contents of Notice. - The form of a written termination notice used by an insurer must be approved by the Commissioner before it is used. A written termination notice must state the reason for the termination and the date the termination is effective. If the policy is terminated for nonpayment of the premium, the effective date may be 15 days from the date the notice is mailed. If the policy is terminated for any other reason, the effective date must be at least 60 days after the notice is mailed. A written termination notice must include or be accompanied by a statement that advises the insured of the penalty for driving a vehicle without complying with Article 13 of Chapter 20 of the General Statutes and that the insured has the right to request the Department to review the termination.

(d) Request for Review. - An insured who receives from an insurer a written termination notice may obtain review of the termination by filing with the Department a written request for review within 10 days after receiving a termination notice that complies with subsection (c) of this section. An insured who does not file a request within the required time waives the right to a review.

(e) Administrative Review. - When the Department receives a written request to review a termination, it must investigate and determine the reason for the termination. The Department shall issue a letter requiring one of the following upon completing its review:

(1) Approval of the termination, if it finds the termination complies with the law.

(2) Renewal or reinstatement of the policy, if it finds the termination does not comply with the law.

(3) Renewal or reinstatement of the policy and payment by the insurer of the costs of the Department's review, not to exceed one thousand dollars

($1,000), if it finds the termination does not comply with the law and the insurer willfully violated this section.

The Department shall mail the letter to the insured and the insurer. An insured or an insurer who disagrees with the determination of the Department in the letter may file a petition for a contested case under Article 3A of Chapter 150B of the General Statutes and the rules adopted by the Commissioner to implement that Article. The petition must be filed within 30 days after receiving the copy of the letter.

(f) Delegation. - The Commissioner shall designate an employee or a deputy to conduct the departmental review of a termination. The Commissioner may designate a deputy to conduct a contested case hearing concerning a termination. The Commissioner may not designate a deputy who conducted the departmental review of a termination to conduct a contested case hearing concerning the same termination.

(g) Effect of Review on Policy. - A policy shall remain in effect during administrative and judicial review of an insurer's action to terminate the policy.

(h) Liability Limit. - There is no liability on the part of and no cause of action for defamation or invasion of privacy arises against an insurer, an insurer's authorized representatives, agents, or employees, or a licensed insurance agent or broker for a communication or statement made concerning a written notice of termination.

(i) Records. - An insurer shall keep a record of a termination for three years. (1993 (Reg. Sess., 1994), c. 761, s. 30; 1995, c. 517, s. 22; 2008-124, s. 4.2.)

§ 58-36-90. Prohibitions on using credit scoring to rate noncommercial private passenger motor vehicle and residential property insurance; exceptions.

(a) Definitions. - As used in this section:

(1) "Adverse action" has the same meaning as in section 1681a(k) of the federal Fair Credit Reporting Act and includes a denial or cancellation of, an increase in any charge for, or a reduction or other adverse or unfavorable

change in the terms of coverage or amount of any insurance, existing or applied for, in connection with the underwriting of insurance.

(2) "Credit report" means any written, oral, or other communication of any information by a consumer reporting agency that bears on a consumer's credit worthiness, credit standing, or credit capacity. Credit report does not include accident or traffic violation records as maintained by the North Carolina Division of Motor Vehicles or any other law enforcement agency, a property loss report or claims history that does not include information that bears on a consumer's credit worthiness, credit standing, or credit capacity, or any report containing information solely as to transactions or experiences between the consumer and the person making the report.

(3) "Credit score" means a score that is derived by utilizing data from an individual's credit report in an algorithm, computer program, model, or other process that reduces the data to a number or rating.

(4) "Noncommercial private passenger motor vehicle" means a "private passenger motor vehicle," as defined by G.S. 58-40-10, that is neither insured under a commercial policy nor used for commercial purposes.

(5) "Private passenger motor vehicle" has the same meaning as set forth in G.S. 58-40-10.

(6) "Residential property" means real property with not more than four housing units located in this State, the contents thereof and valuable interest therein, and insurance coverage written in connection with the sale of that property. It also includes mobile homes, modular homes, townhomes, condominiums, and insurance on contents of apartments and rental property used for residential purposes.

(b) Prohibitions; Exceptions. - In the rating and underwriting of noncommercial private passenger motor vehicle and residential property insurance coverage, insurers shall not use credit scoring as the sole basis for terminating an existing policy or any coverage in an existing policy or subjecting a policy to consent to rate as specified in G.S. 58-36-30(b) without consideration of any other risk factors, but insurers may use credit scoring as the sole basis for discounting rates. For purposes of this subsection only, "existing policy" means a policy that has been in effect for more than 60 days.

(c) Notification. - If a credit report is used in conjunction with other criteria to take an adverse action, the insurer shall provide the applicant or policyholder with written notice of the action taken, in a form approved by the Commissioner. The notification shall include, in easily understandable language:

(1) The specific reason for the adverse action and, if the adverse action was based upon a credit score, a description of the factors that were the primary influence on the score.

(2) The name, address, and toll-free telephone number of the credit bureau that provided the insurer with the credit-based information.

(3) The fact that the consumer has the right to obtain a free copy of the consumer's credit report from the appropriate credit bureau.

(4) The fact that the consumer has the right to challenge information contained in the consumer's credit report.

(d) Disputed Credit Report Information. - If it is determined through the dispute resolution process set forth in the federal Fair Credit Reporting Act, 15 U.S.C. § 1681i(a)(5), that the credit information of a current insured was incorrect or incomplete and if the insurer receives notice of such determination from either the consumer reporting agency or from the insured, the insurer shall re-underwrite or re-rate the consumer within 30 days of receiving the notice. After re-underwriting or re-rating the insured, the insurer shall make any adjustments necessary, consistent with its underwriting guidelines. If an insurer determines the insured has overpaid premium, the insurer shall refund to the insured the amount of overpayment calculated back to the shorter of either the last 12 months of coverage or the actual policy period.

(e) Indemnification. - An insurer shall indemnify, defend, and hold agents harmless from and against all liability, fees, and costs arising out of or relating to the actions, errors, or omissions of an agent who obtains or uses credit information or credit scores for an insurer, provided the agent follows the instructions or procedures established by the insurer and complies with any applicable law or regulation. Nothing in this subsection shall be construed to provide a consumer or other insured with a cause of action that does not exist in the absence of this subsection.

(f) Filing. - Insurers that use credit scores to underwrite and rate risks shall file their scoring models, or other scoring processes, with the Department. A filing that includes credit scoring may include loss experience justifying the applicable surcharge or credit. A filer may request that its credit score data be considered a trade secret and may designate parts of its filings accordingly. (2003-216, s. 1; 2004-199, ss. 20(f), 20(g).)

§ 58-36-95. Use of nonoriginal crash repair parts.

(a)   As used in this section, the following definitions apply:

(1)   "Insurer" includes any person authorized to represent an insurer with respect to a claim.

(2)   "Nonoriginal crash repair part" refers to sheet metal and/or plastic parts - generally components of the exterior of a motor vehicle - that are not manufactured by or for the original equipment manufacturer of the vehicle.

(b)   An insurer shall disclose to a claimant in writing, either on the estimate or on a separate document attached to the estimate, the following in no smaller than ten point type: "THIS ESTIMATE HAS BEEN PREPARED BASED ON THE USE OF AUTOMOBILE PARTS NOT MADE BY THE ORIGINAL MANUFACTURER. PARTS USED IN THE REPAIR OF YOUR VEHICLE MADE BY OTHER THAN THE ORIGINAL MANUFACTURER ARE REQUIRED TO BE AT LEAST EQUIVALENT IN TERMS OF FIT, QUALITY, PERFORMANCE, AND WARRANTY TO THE ORIGINAL MANUFACTURER PARTS THEY ARE REPLACING."

(c)   It is a violation of G.S. 58-3-180 for an automobile repair facility or parts person to place a nonoriginal crash repair part, nonoriginal windshield, or nonoriginal auto glass on a motor vehicle and to submit an invoice for an original repair part.

(d)   Any insurer or other person who has reason to believe that fraud has occurred under this section shall report that fraud to the Commissioner for further action pursuant to G.S. 58-2-160. (2003-395, s. 2; 2006-105, s. 1.6.)

§ 58-36-100. Prospective loss costs filings and final rate filings for workers' compensation and employers' liability insurance.

(a)   Except as provided in subsections (k) and (m) of this section, the Bureau shall no longer develop or file any minimum premiums, minimum premium formulas, or expense constants. If an insurer wishes to amend minimum premium formulas or expense constants, it must file the minimum premium rules, formulas, or amounts it proposes to use. A copy of each filing submitted to the Commissioner under subsections (e) and (g) of this section shall also be sent to the Bureau.

(b)   Definitions. As used in this section, the following terms have the following meanings:

(1)   "Expenses". - That portion of a rate attributable to acquisition, field supervision, collection expenses, any tax levied by the State or by any political subdivision of the State, licensing costs, fees, and general expenses, as determined by the insurer.

(2)   "Developed losses". - Losses (including loss adjustment expenses) adjusted, using standard actuarial techniques, to eliminate the effect of differences between current payment or reserve estimates and those needed to provide actual ultimate loss (including loss adjustment expense) payments.

(3)   "Insurer". - A member insurer or group.

(4)   "Loss trending". - Any procedure for projecting developed losses to the average date of loss for the period during which the policies are to be effective.

(5)   "Multiplier". - An insurer's determination of the expenses, other than loss expense and loss adjustment expense, associated with writing workers' compensation and employers' liability insurance, which shall be expressed as a single nonintegral number to be applied equally and uniformly to the prospective loss costs approved by the Commissioner in making rates for each classification of risks utilized by that insurer.

(6)   "Prospective loss costs". - That portion of a rate that does not include provisions for expenses (other than loss adjustment expenses) or profit; and that are based on historical aggregate losses and loss adjustment expenses adjusted through development to their ultimate value and projected through trending to a future point in time.

(7) "Rate". - The cost of insurance per exposure unit, whether expressed as a single number or as a prospective loss cost with an adjustment to account for the treatment of expenses, profit, and variations in loss experience, prior to any application of individual risk variations based on loss or expense considerations, and does not include minimum premiums.

(8) "Supplementary rating information". - Includes any manual or plan of rates, classification, rating schedule, minimum premium, policy fee, rating rule, rate-related underwriting rule, experience rating plan, statistical plan and any other similar information needed to determine the applicable rate in effect or to be in effect.

(c) Except as provided in subsection (m) of this section, for workers' compensation and employers' liability insurance written in connection with workers' compensation insurance, the Bureau shall no longer develop or file advisory final rates that contain provisions for expenses (other than loss adjustment expenses) and profit. The Bureau shall instead develop and file for approval with the Commissioner, in accordance with this section, reference filings containing advisory prospective loss costs and the underlying loss data and other supporting statistical and actuarial information for any calculations or assumptions underlying these loss costs. Loss-based assessments will be included in prospective loss costs.

(d) After a reference filing has been filed with the Commissioner and approved, the Bureau shall provide its member insurers with a copy of the approved reference filing. The Bureau may print and distribute manuals of prospective loss costs as well as rules and other supplementary rating information described in subsection (k) of this section.

(e) Each insurer shall independently and individually determine the final rates it will file and the effective date of any rate changes. If an insurer decides to use the prospective loss costs in the approved reference filing in support of its own filing, the insurer shall make a filing using the reference filing adoption form. The insurer's rates shall be the combination of the prospective loss costs and the loss multiplier contained in the reference filing adoption form. Insurers may file modifications of the prospective loss costs in the approved reference filing based on their own anticipated experience. Supporting documentation is required for any upward or downward modifications of the prospective loss costs in the approved reference filing.

(f) The summary of supporting information form shall contain a reference to examples of how to apply an insurer's loss cost modification factor to the Bureau's prospective loss costs. Insurers may vary expense loads by individual classification or grouping. Insurers may use variable or fixed expense loads or a combination of these to establish their expense loadings. Each filing that varies the expense load by class shall specify the expense factor applicable to each class and shall include information supporting the justification for the variation. However, insurers shall file data in accordance with the uniform statistical plan approved by the Commissioner. Insurers may offer premium discount plans.

(g) An insurer may request to have its loss multiplier remain on file and reference all subsequent prospective loss costs reference filings. Upon receipt of subsequent approved Bureau reference filings, the insurer's rates shall be the combination of the prospective loss costs and the loss multiplier contained in the reference filing adoption form on file with the Commissioner, and will be effective on or after the effective date of the prospective loss costs. The insurer need not file anything further with the Commissioner. If an insurer that has filed to have its loss multiplier remain on file with the Department intends to delay, modify, or not adopt a particular Bureau reference filing, the insurer must make an appropriate filing with the Commissioner. The insurer's filed loss multiplier shall remain in effect until the insurer withdraws it or files a revised reference filing adoption form. The provisions of G.S. 58-40-20, 58-40-30, 58-40-35, and 58-40-45 apply to filings made by insurers under this section.

(h) An insurer may file such other information that the insurer considers relevant and shall provide such other information as may be requested by the Commissioner. When a filing is not accompanied by the information required under this section, the Commissioner shall inform the filer within 30 days after the initial filing that the filing is incomplete and describe what additional information is required. A filing is complete when the required information is furnished or when the filer certifies to the Commissioner that the additional information required by the Commissioner is not maintained or cannot be provided.

(i) To the extent that an insurer's final rates are determined solely by applying its loss multiplier, as presented in the reference filing adoption form, to the prospective loss costs contained in the Bureau's reference filing and printed in the Bureau's rating manual, the insurer need not develop or file its final rate pages with the Commissioner. If an insurer chooses to print and distribute final rate pages for its own use, based solely upon the application of its filed loss costs, the insurer need not file those pages with the Commissioner. If the

Bureau does not print the loss costs in its manual, the insurer must submit its rates to the Commissioner.

(j) For reference filings filed by the Bureau:

(1) If the insurer has filed to have its loss multiplier remain on file, applicable to subsequent reference filings, and a new reference filing is filed and approved and if:

a. The insurer decides to use the revision of the prospective loss costs and effective date as filed, then the insurer does not file anything with the Commissioner. Rates are the combination of the prospective loss costs and the on-file loss multiplier and become effective on the effective date of the loss costs.

b. The insurer decides to use the prospective loss costs as filed but with a different effective date, then the insurer must notify the Commissioner of its effective date before the effective date of the loss costs.

c. The insurer decides to use the revision of the prospective loss costs, but wishes to change its loss multiplier, then the insurer must file a revised reference filing adoption form before the effective date of the reference filing.

d. The insurer decides not to revise its rates using the prospective loss costs, then the insurer must notify the Commissioner before the effective date of the loss costs.

(2) If an insurer has not elected to have its loss multiplier remain on file, applicable to future prospective loss costs reference filings, and a new reference filing is filed and approved, and if:

a. The insurer decides to use the prospective loss costs to revise its rates, then the insurer must file a reference filing adoption form including its effective date.

b. The insurer decides not to use the revisions, then the insurer does not file anything with the Commissioner.

c. The insurer decides to change its multiplier, then the insurer must file a reference filing adoption form referencing the current approved prospective loss costs, including its effective date and, if applicable, its loss costs modification factor and supporting documentation. The insurer shall not make a change to its loss costs multiplier based on any reference filing other than the current approved reference filing.

(k) The Bureau shall file with the Commissioner, for approval, filings containing a revision of rules and supplementary rating information. This includes policy-writing rules, rating plans, classification codes and descriptions, and rules that include factors or relativities, such as increased limits factors and related minimum premiums classification relativities, or similar factors. The Bureau may print and distribute manuals of rules and supplementary rating information.

(l) If a new filing of rules, relativities, and supplementary rating information is filed by the Bureau and approved and if:

(1) The insurer decides to use the revisions and effective date as filed together with the loss multiplier on file with the Commissioner, then the insurer shall not file anything with the Commissioner.

(2) The insurer decides to use the revisions as filed but with a different effective date, then the insurer must notify the Commissioner of its effective date before the approved Bureau filing's effective date.

(3) The insurer decides not to use the revision, then the insurer must notify the Commissioner before the Bureau filing's effective date.

(4) The insurer decides to use the revision with modifications, then the insurer must file the modification with the Commissioner, specifying the basis for the modification and the insurer's proposed effective date if different than the Bureau filing's effective date.

(m) The Bureau shall file all of the following with the Commissioner:

(1) Final workers' compensation rates and rating plans for the residual market.

(2) The uniform classification plan and rules.

(3) The uniform experience rating plan and rules.

(4)　A uniform policy form to be used by member insurers for voluntary and residual market business.

(5)　Advisory manual workers' compensation rates to be used for the sole purpose of computing the premium tax liability of self-insurers under G.S. 105-228.5.

(n)　The rates filed under subdivision (m)(1) of this section shall be set at levels to self-fund the residual market, provide adequate premiums to pay losses and expenses, establish appropriate reserves, and provide a reasonable margin for underwriting profit and contingencies.

(o)　Every insurer shall adhere to the uniform classification plan, experience rating plan, and policy form filed by the Bureau. (1995, c. 505, ss. 3-8; 1999-132, ss. 3.9-3.12; 2001-232, s. 2.)

§ 58-36-105. Certain workers' compensation insurance policy cancellations prohibited.

(a)　No policy of workers' compensation insurance or employers' liability insurance written in connection with a policy of workers' compensation insurance shall be cancelled by the insurer before the expiration of the term or anniversary date stated in the policy and without the prior written consent of the insured, except for any one of the following reasons:

(1)　Nonpayment of premium in accordance with the policy terms.

(2)　An act or omission by the insured or the insured's representative that constitutes material misrepresentation or nondisclosure of a material fact in obtaining the policy, continuing the policy, or presenting a claim under the policy.

(3)　Increased hazard or material change in the risk assumed that could not have been reasonably contemplated by the parties at the time of assumption of the risk.

(4)　Substantial breach of contractual duties, conditions, or warranties that materially affects the insurability of the risk.

(5) A fraudulent act against the company by the insured or the insured's representative that materially affects the insurability of the risk.

(6) Willful failure by the insured or the insured's representative to institute reasonable loss control measures that materially affect the insurability of the risk after written notice by the insurer.

(7) Loss of facultative reinsurance or loss of or substantial changes in applicable reinsurance as provided in G.S. 58-41-30.

(8) Conviction of the insured of a crime arising out of acts that materially affect the insurability of the risk.

(9) A determination by the Commissioner that the continuation of the policy would place the insurer in violation of the laws of this State.

(10) The named insured fails to meet the requirements contained in the corporate charter, articles of incorporation, or bylaws of the insurer, when the insurer is a company organized for the sole purpose of providing members of an organization with insurance coverage in this State.

(b) Any cancellation permitted by subsection (a) of this section is not effective unless written notice of cancellation has been given to the insured not less than 15 days before the proposed effective date of cancellation. The notice may be given by registered or certified mail, return receipt requested, to the insured and any other person designated in the policy to receive notice of cancellation at their addresses shown in the policy or, if not indicated in the policy, at their last known addresses. The notice shall state the precise reason for cancellation. Whenever notice of intention to cancel is given by registered or certified mail, no cancellation by the insurer shall be effective unless and until such method is employed and completed. Notice of cancellation, termination, or nonrenewal may also be given by any method permitted for service of process pursuant to Rule 4 of the North Carolina Rules of Civil Procedure. Failure to send this notice, as provided in this section, to any other person designated in the policy to receive notice of cancellation invalidates the cancellation only as to that other person's interest.

(c) This section does not apply to any policy that has been in effect for fewer than 60 days and is not a renewal of a policy. That policy may be cancelled for any reason by giving at least 30 days' prior written notice of and reasons for cancellation to the insured by registered or certified mail, return receipt requested.

(d) Cancellation for nonpayment of premium is not effective if the amount due is paid before the effective date set forth in the notice of cancellation.

(e) Copies of the notice required by this section shall also be sent to the agent or broker of record though failure to send copies of the notice to those persons shall not invalidate the cancellation. Mailing copies of the notice by regular first-class mail to the agent or broker of record satisfies the requirements of this subsection. (2001-241, s. 2; 2013-413, s. 13(a).)

§ 58-36-110. Notice of nonrenewal, premium rate increase, or change in workers' compensation insurance coverage required.

(a) No insurer shall refuse to renew a policy of workers' compensation insurance or employers' liability insurance written in connection with a policy of workers' compensation insurance except in accordance with the provisions of this section, and any nonrenewal attempted or made that is not in compliance with this section is not effective. This section does not apply if the policyholder has obtained insurance elsewhere, has accepted replacement coverage, or has requested or agreed to nonrenewal.

(b) An insurer may refuse to renew a policy that has been written for a term of one year or less at the policy's expiration date by mailing written notice of nonrenewal to the insured not less than 45 days prior to the expiration date of the policy.

(c) An insurer may refuse to renew a policy that has been written for a term of more than one year or for an indefinite term at the policy anniversary date by mailing written notice of nonrenewal to the insured not less than 45 days prior to the anniversary date of the policy.

(d) Whenever an insurer lowers coverage limits, raises deductibles, or raises premium rates for reasons within the exclusive control of the insurer or other than at the request of the policyholder, the insurer shall mail to the policyholder written notice of the change at least 30 days in advance of the effective date of the change. As used in this subsection, the phrase, "reasons within the exclusive control of the insurer" does not mean experience modification changes, exposure changes, or loss cost rate changes.

(e) The notice required by this section shall be given by mail to the insured and any other person designated in the policy to receive this notice at their addresses shown in the policy or, if not indicated in the policy, at their last known addresses. The notice of nonrenewal shall state the precise reason for nonrenewal. Failure to send this notice, as provided in this section, to any other person designated in the policy to receive this notice invalidates the nonrenewal only as to that other person's interest.

(f) Copies of the notice required by this section shall also be sent to the agent or broker of record, though failure to send copies of the notice to such persons shall not invalidate the nonrenewal.

(g) Mailing copies of the notice by regular first-class mail satisfies the notice requirements of this section. (2001-241, s. 2.)

§ 58-36-115. Prohibitions on using inquiries to terminate a policy, refuse to issue or renew a policy, or to subject a policy to consent to rate.

An insurer writing residential real property insurance subject to this Article shall not terminate an existing policy or any coverage under an existing policy, refuse to write a policy, refuse to renew a policy, or subject a policy to consent to rate as specified in G.S. 58-36-30(b) based solely on either of the following:

(1) An inquiry about policy provisions that does not result in a claim; or

(2) A claim that was closed without payment, provided the notice of loss that was the subject of the claim was only an inquiry regarding policy provisions, and no claim for payment was requested by the insured or a third party. (2004-111, s. 1.)

§ 58-36-120. Public notice of certain filings.

Whenever the North Carolina Rate Bureau files for an increase in insurance rates for residential property insurance, the Bureau shall give public notice in at least two newspapers with statewide distribution and in the North Carolina Register, within 10 business days after the filing, which notice shall state that the Commissioner may or may not schedule and conduct a hearing with respect to the filing. The same information shall be posted on the Web site for the North Carolina Rate Bureau and the North Carolina Department of Insurance Web site within three days after the filing. The requirements of this section shall not apply to filings proposing changes as to forms, relativities, and classifications that are filed at no increase in the overall rate level. (2009-472, s. 5.)

Article 37.

North Carolina Motor Vehicle Reinsurance Facility.

§ 58-37-1. Definitions.

As used in this Article:

(1)   "Cede" or "cession" means the act of transferring the risk of loss from the individual insurer to all insurers through the operation of the facility.

(2)   Repealed by Session Laws 1991, c. 720, s. 6.

(3)   "Company" means each member of the Facility.

(4)   "Eligible risk," for the purpose of motor vehicle insurance other than nonfleet private passenger motor vehicle insurance, means:

a.   A person who is a resident of this State who owns a motor vehicle registered or principally garaged in this State;

b.   A person who has a valid driver's license in this State;

c.   A person who is required to file proof of financial responsibility under Article 9A or 13 of Chapter 20 of the General Statutes in order to register his or her motor vehicle or to obtain a driver's license in this State;

d. A nonresident of this State who owns a motor vehicle registered or principally garaged in this State; or

e. The State and its agencies and cities, counties, towns and municipal corporations in this State and their agencies.

However, no person shall be deemed an eligible risk if timely payment of premium is not tendered or if there is a valid unsatisfied judgment of record against such person for recovery of amounts due for motor vehicle insurance premiums and such person has not been discharged from paying said judgment, or if such person does not furnish the information necessary to effect insurance.

(4a) "Eligible risk," for the purpose of nonfleet private passenger motor vehicle insurance, means:

a. A resident of this State who owns a motor vehicle registered or principally garaged in this State;

b. A resident of this State and who has a valid driver's license issued by this State;

c. A person who is required to file proof of financial responsibility under Article 9A or 13 of Chapter 20 of the General Statutes in order to register his or her vehicle or to obtain a driver's license in this State;

d. A nonresident of this State who owns a motor vehicle registered and principally garaged in this State;

e. A nonresident of the State who is one of the following:

1. A member of the Armed Forces of the United States stationed in this State, or deployed outside this State from a home base in this State, who intends to return to his or her home state;

2. The spouse of a nonresident member of the Armed Forces of the United States stationed in this State, or deployed outside this State from a home base in this State, who intends to return to his or her home state;

3. An out-of-state student who intends to return to his or her home state upon completion of his or her time as a student enrolled in school in this State; or

f. The State and its agencies and cities, counties, towns, and municipal corporations in this State and their agencies.

However, no person shall be deemed an eligible risk if timely payment or premium is not tendered or if there is a valid unsatisfied judgment of record against the person for recovery of amounts due for motor vehicle insurance premiums and the person has not been discharged from paying the judgment or if the person does not furnish the information necessary to effect insurance.

(5) "Facility" means the North Carolina Motor Vehicle Reinsurance Facility established under this Article.

(6) "Motor vehicle" means every self-propelled vehicle that is designed for use upon a highway, including trailers and semitrailers designed for use with such vehicles (except traction engines, road rollers, farm tractors, tractor cranes, power shovels, and well drillers). "Motor vehicle" also means a motorcycle, as defined in G.S. 20-4.01(27)d.

(7) "Motor vehicle insurance" means direct insurance against liability arising out of the ownership, operation, maintenance or use of a motor vehicle for bodily injury including death and property damage and includes medical payments and uninsured and underinsured motorist coverages.

With respect to motor carriers who are subject to the financial responsibility requirements established under the Motor Carrier Act of 1980, the term, "motor vehicle insurance" includes coverage with respect to environmental restoration. As used in this subsection the term, "environmental restoration" means restitution for the loss, damage, or destruction of natural resources arising out of the accidental discharge, dispersal, release, or escape into or upon the land, atmosphere, watercourse, or body of water of any commodity transported by a motor carrier. Environmental restoration includes the cost of removal and the cost of necessary measures taken to minimize or mitigate damage to human health, the natural environment, fish, shellfish, and wildlife.

(8) "Person" means every natural person, firm, partnership, association, trust, limited liability company, firm, corporation, government, or governmental agency.

(9) "Plan of operation" means the plan of operation approved pursuant to the provisions of this Article.

(10) Repealed by Session Laws 1977, c. 828, s. 10.

(11) "Principally garaged" means the vehicle is garaged for six or more months of the current or preceding year on property in this State which is owned, leased, or otherwise lawfully occupied by the owner of the vehicle. (1973, c. 818, s. 1; 1977, c. 828, s. 10; 1981, c. 776, s. 1; 1985, c. 666, s. 48; 1989, c. 485, s. 48; 1991, c. 720, s. 6; 1999-132, s. 8.2; 2001-389, s. 4; 2002-187, s. 1.1; 2007-443, s. 1; 2007-481, s. 8; 2007-495, s. 8; 2011-183, s. 43.)

§ 58-37-5. North Carolina Motor Vehicle Reinsurance Facility; creation; membership.

There is created a nonprofit unincorporated legal entity to be known as the North Carolina Motor Vehicle Reinsurance Facility consisting of all insurers licensed to write and engaged in writing within this State motor vehicle insurance or any component thereof. Every such insurer, as a prerequisite to further engaging in writing such insurance in this State, shall be a member of the Facility and shall be bound by the rules of operation thereof as provided for in this Article and as promulgated by the Board of Governors. No company may withdraw from membership in the Facility unless it ceases to write motor vehicle insurance in this State or ceases to be licensed to write such insurance. (1973, c. 818, s. 1; 1983, c. 416, s. 6.)

§ 58-37-10. Obligations after termination of membership.

Any company whose membership in the Facility has been terminated by withdrawal shall, nevertheless, with respect to its business prior to midnight of the effective date of such termination continue to be governed by this Article. (1973, c. 818, s. 1.)

§ 58-37-15. Insolvency.

Any unsatisfied net liability to the Facility of any insolvent member shall be assumed by and apportioned among the remaining members in the Facility in the same manner in which assessments are apportioned by the Facility. The Facility shall have all rights allowed by law in behalf of the remaining members against the estate or funds of such insolvent for sums due the Facility in accordance with this Article. (1973, c. 818, s. 1; 1977, c. 828, s. 12.)

§ 58-37-20. Merger, consolidation or cession.

When a member has been merged or consolidated into another insurer, or has reinsured its entire motor vehicle liability insurance business in the State with another insurer, such company or its successor in interest shall remain liable for all obligations hereunder and such company and its successor in interest and the other insurers with which it has been merged or consolidated shall continue to participate in the Facility according to the rules of operation. (1973, c. 818, s. 1; 1977, c. 828, s. 13.)

§ 58-37-25. General obligations of insurers.

(a) Except as otherwise provided in this Article all insurers as a prerequisite to the further engaging in this State in the writing of motor vehicle insurance or any component thereof shall accept and insure any otherwise unacceptable applicant therefor who is an eligible risk if cession of the particular coverage and coverage limits applied for are permitted in the Facility. All such insurers shall equitably share the results of such otherwise unacceptable business through the Facility and shall be bound by the acts of their agents in accordance with the provisions of this Article. No insurer shall impose upon any of its agents, solely on account of ceded business received from such agents, any quota or matching requirement for any other insurance as a condition for further acceptance of ceded business from such agents.

(b) Each insurer will provide the same type of service to ceded business that it provides for its voluntary market. Records provided to agents and brokers will include an indication that the business is ceded. When an insurer cedes a policy or renewal thereof to the Facility and the Facility premium for such policy is higher than the premium that the insurer would normally charge for such policy if retained by the insurer, the policyholder will be informed that (i) his policy is ceded, (ii) the coverages are written at the Facility rate, which rate differential must be specified, (iii) the reason or reasons for the cession to the Facility, (iv) the specific reason or reasons for the cession to the Facility will be provided upon the written request of the policyholder to the insurer, and (v) the policyholder may seek insurance through other insurers who may elect not to cede his policy. If such policyholder obtains motor vehicle liability insurance through another insurer who elects not to cede his policy to the Facility and the policyholder cancels his ceded policy within 45 days of the effective date of such ceded policy, the earned premium for such ceded policy shall be calculated on the pro rata basis, except that the pro rata calculation shall not apply to a cancellation by any insurance premium finance company as provided in G.S. 58-35-85.

(c) Upon the written request of any eligible risk who has been notified pursuant to subsection (b) of this section that his motor vehicle insurance policy has been ceded to the Facility, the insurer ceding the insurance policy must provide in writing to that eligible risk the specific reason or reasons for the decision to cede that policy to the Facility. Proof of mailing of the written reason or reasons is sufficient proof of compliance with this obligation. With regard to any notice of cession or any written or oral communications specifying the reason or reasons for cession, there will be no liability on the part of, and no cause of action of any nature will arise against, (i) any insurer or its authorized representatives, agents, or employees, or (ii) any licensed agent, broker, or persons who furnish to the insurer information as to the reason or reasons for the cession, for any communications or statements made by them, unless the communications or statements are shown to have been made in bad faith with malice in fact. (1973, c. 818, s. 1; 1979, c. 732.)

§ 58-37-30. General obligations of agents.

(a) Except as otherwise provided in this Article, no licensed agent of an insurer authorized to solicit and accept premiums for motor vehicle insurance or any component thereof by the company he represents shall refuse on behalf of said company to accept any application from an eligible risk for such insurance and to immediately bind the coverage applied for and for a period of not less than six months if cession of the particular coverage and coverage limits applied for are permitted in the Facility, provided the application is submitted during the agent's normal business hours, at his customary place of business and in accordance with the agent's customary practices and procedures. The commission paid on the insurance coverages provided in this Article shall not be less than the commission on insurance coverage written through the North Carolina Insurance Plan on May 1, 1973. The same commission shall apply uniformly statewide.

(b)   It shall be the responsibility of the agent to write the coverage applied for at what he believes to be the appropriate rate level. If coverage is written at the Facility rate level and the company elects not to cede, the policy shall be rated at a rate under Article 36 of this Chapter. Coverage written at a rate under Article 36 of this Chapter that is not acceptable to the company must either be placed with another company or rated at the Facility rate level by the agent. (1973, c. 818, s. 1; 1977, c. 828, s. 11; 1995, c. 517, s. 23.)

§ 58-37-35. The Facility; functions; administration.

(a)   The operation of the Facility shall assure the availability of motor vehicle insurance to any eligible risk and the Facility shall accept all placements made in accordance with this Article, the plan of operation adopted pursuant thereto, and any amendments to either.

(b)   The Facility shall reinsure for each coverage available in the Facility to the standard percentage of one hundred percent (100%) or lesser equitable percentage established in the Facility's plan of operation as follows:

(1)   For the following coverages of motor vehicle insurance and in at least the following amounts of insurance:

a.   Bodily injury liability: thirty thousand dollars ($30,000) each person, sixty thousand dollars ($60,000) each accident;

b.   Property damage liability: twenty-five thousand dollars ($25,000) each accident;

c.   Medical payments: one thousand dollars ($1,000) each person; except that this coverage shall not be available for motorcycles;

d.   Uninsured motorist: thirty thousand dollars ($30,000) each person; sixty thousand dollars ($60,000) each accident for bodily injury; twenty-five thousand dollars ($25,000) each accident property damage (one hundred dollars ($100.00) deductible);

e. Any other motor vehicle insurance or financial responsibility limits in the amounts required by any federal law or federal agency regulation; by any law of this State; or by any rule duly adopted under Chapter 150B of the General Statutes or by the North Carolina Utilities Commission.

(2) Additional ceding privileges for motor vehicle insurance shall be provided by the Board of Governors up to the following:

a. Bodily injury liability: one hundred thousand dollars ($100,000) each person, three hundred thousand dollars ($300,000) each accident;

b. Property damage liability: fifty thousand dollars ($50,000) each accident;

c. Medical payments: two thousand dollars ($2,000) each person; except that this coverage shall not be available for motorcycles;

d. Underinsured motorist: one million dollars ($1,000,000) each person and each accident for bodily injury liability; and

e. Uninsured motorist: one million dollars ($1,000,000) each person and each accident for bodily injury and fifty thousand dollars ($50,000) each accident for property damage (one hundred dollars ($100.00) deductible).

(2a) For persons who must maintain liability coverage limits above those available under subdivision (2) of this subsection in order to obtain or continue coverage under personal excess liability or personal "umbrella" insurance policies, additional ceding privileges for motor vehicle insurance shall be provided by the Board of Governors up to the following:

a. Bodily injury liability: two hundred fifty thousand dollars ($250,000) each person, five hundred thousand dollars ($500,000) each accident.

b. Property damage liability: one hundred thousand dollars ($100,000) each accident.

c. Medical payments: five thousand dollars ($5,000) each person; except that this coverage shall not be available for motorcycles.

d. Uninsured motorist: one hundred thousand dollars ($100,000) each accident for property damage (one hundred dollars ($100.00) deductible).

(3) Whenever the additional ceding privileges are provided as in G.S. 58-37-35(b)(2) for any component of motor vehicle insurance, the same additional ceding privileges shall be available to "all other" types of risks subject to the rating jurisdiction of the North Carolina Rate Bureau.

(c) The Facility shall require each member to adjust losses for ceded business fairly and efficiently in the same manner as voluntary business losses are adjusted and to effect settlement where settlement is appropriate.

(d) The Facility shall be administered by a Board of Governors. The Board of Governors shall consist of 12 members having one vote each from the classifications specified in this subsection and the Commissioner, who shall serve ex officio without vote. Each Facility insurance company member serving on the Board shall be represented by a senior officer of the company. Not more than one company in a group under the same ownership or management shall be represented on the Board at the same time. Five members of the Board shall be selected by the member insurers, which members shall be fairly representative of the industry. To insure representative member insurers, one each shall be selected from the following: the American Insurance Association (or its successors), the Property Casualty Insurers Association of America (or its successors), stock insurers not affiliated with those trade associations, nonstock insurers not affiliated with those trade associations, and the industry at large regardless of trade affiliation. The at-large insurer shall be selected by the insurer company members of the Board. The Commissioner shall appoint two members of the Board who are Facility insurance company members domiciled in this State. The Commissioner shall appoint five members of the Board who shall be fire and casualty insurance agents licensed in this State and actively engaged in writing motor vehicle insurance in this State. The term of office of the Board members shall be three years. All members of the Board of Governors shall serve until their successors are selected and qualified and the Commissioner may fill any vacancy on the Board from any of the classifications specified in this subsection until the vacancies are filled in accordance with this Article. The Board of Governors of the Facility shall also have as nonvoting members two persons who are not employed by or affiliated with any insurance company or the Department and who are appointed by the Governor to serve at the Governor's pleasure.

(e) The Commissioner and member companies shall provide for a Board of Governors. The Board of Governors shall elect from its membership a chair and shall meet at the call of the chair or at the request of four members of the Board of Governors. The chair shall retain the right to vote on all issues. Seven members of the Board of Governors shall constitute a quorum. The same member may not serve as chair for more than two consecutive years; provided, however, that a member may continue to serve as chair until a successor chair is elected and qualified.

(f) The Board of Governors shall have full power and administrative responsibility for the operation of the Facility. Such administrative responsibility shall include but not be limited to:

(1) Proper establishment and implementation of the Facility.

(2) Employment of a manager who shall be responsible for the continuous operation of the Facility and such other employees, officers and committees as it deems necessary.

(3) Provision for appropriate housing and equipment to assure the efficient operation of the Facility.

(4) Promulgation of reasonable rules and regulations for the administration and operation of the Facility and delegation to the manager of such authority as it deems necessary to insure the proper administration and operation thereof.

(g) Except as may be delegated specifically to others in the plan of operation or reserved to the members, power and responsibility for the establishment and operation of the Facility is vested in the Board of Governors, which power and responsibility include but is not limited to the following:

(1) To sue and be sued in the name of the Facility. No judgment against the Facility shall create any direct liability in the individual member companies of the Facility.

(2) To receive and record cessions.

(3) To assess members on the basis of participation ratios established in the plan of operation to cover anticipated or incurred costs of operation and administration of the Facility at such intervals as are established in the plan of operation.

(4)   To contract for goods and services from others to assure the efficient operation of the Facility.

(5)   To hear and determine complaints of any company, agent or other interested party concerning the operation of the Facility.

(6)   Upon the request of any licensed fire and casualty agent meeting any two of the standards set forth below as determined by the Commissioner within 10 days of the receipt of the application, the Facility shall contract with one or more members within 20 days of receipt of the determination to appoint such licensed fire and casualty agent as designated agents in accordance with reasonable rules as are established by the plan of operation. The standards shall be:

a.   Whether the agent's evidence establishes that he has been conducting his business in a community for a period of at least one year;

b.   Whether the agent's evidence establishes that he had a gross premium volume during the 13 months next preceding the date of his application of at least twenty thousand dollars ($20,000) from motor vehicle insurance;

c.   Whether the agent's evidence establishes that the number of eligible risks served by him during the 13 months next preceding the date of application was 200 or more;

d.   Whether the agent's evidence establishes a growth in eligible risks served and premium volume during his years of service as an agent;

e.   Whether the agent's evidence establishes that he made available to eligible risks premium financing or any other plan for deferred payment of premiums.

With respect to business produced by designated agents, adequate provision shall be made by the Facility to assure that such business is rated using Facility rates. All business produced by designated agents may be ceded to the Facility, except designated agents appointed before September 1, 1987, may place liability insurance policies with a voluntary carrier, provided that all policies written by the voluntary carrier are retained by the voluntary carrier unless ceded to the Facility using Facility rates. Designated agents must provide the Facility with a list of such policies written by the voluntary carrier at least annually, or as requested by the Facility, on a form approved by the Facility. If no insurer is willing to contract with any such agent on terms acceptable to the Board, the Facility shall license such agent to write directly on behalf of the Facility. However, for this purpose the Facility does not act as an insurer, but acts only as the statutory agent of all of the members of the Facility, which shall be bound on risks written by the Facility's appointed agent. The Facility may contract with one or more servicing carriers and shall promulgate fair and reasonable underwriting procedures to require that business produced by Facility agents and written through those servicing carriers shall be rated using Facility rates. All business produced by Facility agents may be ceded to the Facility. Any designated agent who is disabled or retiring or the estate of any deceased designated agent may transfer the designation and the book of business to some other licensed fire and casualty agent meeting the requirements of this section and under rules established by the Facility, and a transfer from a designated agent appointed before September 1, 1987, shall entitle the transferee designated agent to place liability insurance policies with a voluntary carrier.

The Commissioner shall require, as a condition precedent to the issuance, renewal, or continuation of a resident agent's license to any designated agent to act for the company appointing such designated agent under contract with the Facility, that the designated agent file and thereafter maintain in force while so licensed a bond in favor of the State of North Carolina executed by an authorized corporate surety approved by the Commissioner, cash, mortgage on real property, or other securities approved by the Commissioner, in the amount of ten thousand dollars ($10,000) for the use of aggrieved persons. Such bond, cash, mortgage, or other securities shall be conditioned on the accounting by the designated agent (i) to any person requesting the designated agent to obtain motor vehicle insurance for moneys or premiums collected in connection therewith, and (ii) to the company providing coverage with respect to any such moneys or premiums under contract with the Facility. Any such bond shall remain in force until the surety is released from liability by the Commissioner, or until the bond is cancelled by the surety. Without prejudice to any liability accrued prior to such cancellation, the surety may cancel the bond upon 30 days' advance notice in writing filed with the Commissioner.

No agent may be designated under this subdivision to any insurer that does not actively write voluntary market business.

(7) To maintain all loss, expense, and premium data relative to all risks reinsured in the Facility, and to require each member to furnish such statistics

relative to insurance reinsured by the Facility at such times and in such form and detail as may be required.

(8)   To establish fair and reasonable procedures for the sharing among members of any loss on Facility business that cannot be recouped under G.S. 58-37-40(e) and other costs, charges, expenses, liabilities, income, property and other assets of the Facility and for assessing or distributing to members their appropriate shares. The shares may be based on the member's premiums for voluntary business for the appropriate category of motor vehicle insurance or by any other fair and reasonable method.

(9)   To receive or distribute all sums required by the operation of the Facility.

(10)   To accept all risks submitted in accordance with this Article.

(11)   To establish procedures for reviewing claims practices of member companies to the end that claims to the account of the Facility will be handled fairly and efficiently.

(12)   To adopt and enforce all rules and to do anything else where the Board is not elsewhere herein specifically empowered which is otherwise necessary to accomplish the purpose of the Facility and is not in conflict with the other provisions of this Article.

(h)   Each member company shall authorize the Facility to audit that part of the company's business which is written subject to the Facility in a manner and time prescribed by the Board of Governors.

(i)   The Board of Governors shall fix a date for an annual meeting and shall annually meet on that date. Twenty days' notice of such meeting shall be given in writing to all members of the Board of Governors.

(j)   There shall be furnished to each member an annual report of the operation of the Facility in such form and detail as may be determined by the Board of Governors.

(k)   Each member shall furnish statistics in connection with insurance subject to the Facility as may be required by the Facility. Such statistics shall be furnished at such time and in such form and detail as may be required but at least will include premiums charged, expenses and losses.

(l) The classifications, rules, rates, rating plans and policy forms used on motor vehicle insurance policies reinsured by the Facility may be made by the Facility or by any licensed or statutory statistical organization or bureau on its behalf and shall be filed with the Commissioner. The Board of Governors shall establish a separate subclassification within the Facility for "clean risks". For the purpose of this Article, a "clean risk" is any owner of a nonfleet private passenger motor vehicle as defined in G.S. 58-40-10, if the owner, principal operator, and each licensed operator in the owner's household have two years' driving experience as licensed drivers and if none of the persons has been assigned any Safe Driver Incentive Plan points under Article 36 of this Chapter during the three-year period immediately preceding either (i) the date of application for a motor vehicle insurance policy or (ii) the date of preparation of a renewal of a motor vehicle insurance policy. The filings may incorporate by reference any other material on file with the Commissioner. Rates shall be neither excessive, inadequate nor unfairly discriminatory. If the Commissioner finds, after a hearing, that a rate is either excessive, inadequate or unfairly discriminatory, the Commissioner shall issue an order specifying in what respect it is deficient and stating when, within a reasonable period thereafter, the rate is no longer effective. The order is subject to judicial review as set out in Article 2 of this Chapter. Pending judicial review of said order, the filed classification plan and the filed rates may be used, charged and collected in the same manner as set out in G.S. 58-40-45 of this Chapter. The order shall not affect any contract or policy made or issued before the expiration of the period set forth in the order. All rates shall be on an actuarially sound basis and shall be calculated, insofar as is possible, to produce neither a profit nor a loss. However, the rates made by or on behalf of the Facility with respect to "clean risks" shall not exceed the rates charged "clean risks" who are not reinsured in the Facility. The difference between the actual rate charged and the actuarially sound and self-supporting rates for "clean risks" reinsured in the Facility may be recouped in similar manner as assessments under G.S. 58-37-40(f). Rates shall not include any factor for underwriting profit on Facility business, but shall provide an allowance for contingencies. There shall be a strong presumption that the rates and premiums for the business of the Facility are neither unreasonable nor excessive.

(m) In addition to annual premiums, the rules of the Facility shall allow semiannual and quarterly premium terms. (1973, c. 818, s. 1; 1977, c. 710; c. 828, ss. 14-19; 1977, 2nd Sess., c. 1135; 1979, c. 676, ss. 1, 2; 1981, c. 776, ss. 2, 3; c. 776, ss. 2, 3; 1983, c. 416, ss. 3, 4; c. 690; 1985, c. 666, s. 49; 1985 (Reg. Sess., 1986), c. 1027, ss. 7, 19, 33, 43; 1987, c. 869, ss. 3, 4(1), (2), 15; 1989, c. 67; 1991, c. 469, s. 7; c. 562, s. 2; c. 709, s. 1; c. 720, s. 4; 1999-132, ss. 6.2, 8.3, 8.4, 8.7, 8.8; 1999-228, s. 8; 2001-236, s. 1; 2001-423, s. 3; 2002-185, s. 6; 2002-187, ss. 1.2, 1.3; 2005-210, s. 19; 2005-242, s. 1; 2006-105, s. 1.7; 2006-264, s. 83.)

§ 58-37-40. Plan of operation.

(a) Within 60 days after the initial organizational meeting, the Facility shall submit to the Commissioner, for his approval, a proposed plan of operation, consistent with the provisions of this Article, which shall provide for economical, fair and nondiscriminating administration and for the prompt and efficient provision of motor vehicle insurance to eligible risks. Should no plan be submitted within the aforesaid 60-day period, then the Commissioner of Insurance shall formulate and place into effect a plan consistent with the provisions of this Article.

(b) The plan of operation, unless sooner approved in writing, shall be deemed to meet the requirements of the Article if it is not disapproved by order of the Commissioner within 30 days from the date of filing. Prior to the disapproval of all or any part of the proposed plan of operation the Commissioner shall notify the Facility in what respect the plan of operation fails to meet the specific requirements of this Article. The Facility shall, within 30 days thereafter, submit for his approval a revised plan of operation which meets the specific requirements of this Article. In the event the Facility fails to submit a revised plan of operation which meets the specific requirements of this Article within the aforesaid 30-day period, the Commissioner shall enter an order accordingly and shall immediately thereafter formulate and place into effect a plan consistent with the provisions of this Article.

(c) Any revision of the proposed plan of operation or any subsequent amendments to an approved plan of operation shall be subject to approval or disapproval by the Commissioner in the manner herein provided in subsection (b) with respect to the initial plan of operation.

(d) Any order of the Commissioner with respect to the plan of operation or any revision or amendment thereof shall be subject to court review as provided in G.S. 58-2-75.

(e) Upon approval of the Commissioner of the plan so submitted or promulgation of a plan deemed approved by the Commissioner, all insurance companies licensed to write motor vehicle insurance in this State or any component thereof as a prerequisite to further engaging in writing the insurance shall formally subscribe to and participate in the plan so approved.

The plan of operation shall provide for, among other matters, (i) the establishment of necessary facilities; (ii) the management of the Facility; (iii) the preliminary assessment of all members for initial expenses necessary to commence operations; (iv) the assessment of members if necessary to defray losses and expenses; (v) the distribution of gains to defray losses incurred since September 1, 1977; (vi) the distribution of gains by credit or reduction of recoupment surcharges to policies subject to recoupment surcharges pursuant to this Article (the Facility may apportion the distribution of gains among the coverages eligible for cession pursuant to this Article); (vii) the recoupment of losses sustained by the Facility since September 1, 1977, pursuant to this Article, which losses may be recouped by equitable pro rata assessment of companies or by way of a surcharge on motor vehicle policies issued by member companies or through the Facility; (viii) the standard amount (one hundred percent (100%) or any equitable lesser amount) of coverage afforded on eligible risks which a member company may cede to the Facility; and (ix) the procedure by which reinsurance shall be accepted by the Facility. The plan shall further provide that:

(1)   Members of the Board of Governors shall receive reimbursement from the Facility for their actual and necessary expenses incurred on Facility business, en route to perform Facility business, and while returning from Facility business plus a per diem allowance of twenty-five dollars ($25.00) a day which may be waived.

(2)   In order to obtain a transfer of business to the Facility effective when the binder or policy or renewal thereof first becomes effective, the company must within 30 days of the binding or policy effective date notify the Facility of the identification of the insured, the coverage and limits afforded, classification data, and premium. The Facility shall accept risks at other times on receipt of necessary information, but acceptance shall not be retroactive. The Facility shall accept renewal business after the member on underwriting review elects to again cede the business.

(f)   The plan of operation shall provide that every member shall, following payment of any pro rata assessment, begin recoupment of that assessment by way of a surcharge on motor vehicle insurance policies issued by the member or through the Facility until the assessment has been recouped. Any surcharge under this subsection or under subsection (e) of this section shall be a percentage of premium adopted by the Board of Governors of the Facility; and the charges determined on the basis of the surcharge shall be combined with and displayed as a part of the applicable premium charges. Recoupment of losses sustained by the Facility since September 1, 1977, with respect to nonfleet private passenger motor vehicles may be made only by surcharging nonfleet private passenger motor vehicle insurance policies. If the amount collected during the period of surcharge exceeds assessments paid by the member to the Facility, the member shall pay over the excess to the Facility on a date specified by the Board of Governors. If the amount collected during the period of surcharge is less than the assessments paid by the member to the Facility, the Facility shall pay the difference to the member. Except as otherwise provided in this Article, the amount of recoupment shall not be considered or treated as a rate or premium for any purpose. The Board of Governors shall adopt and implement a plan for compensation of agents of Facility members when recoupment surcharges are imposed; that compensation shall not exceed the compensation or commission rate normally paid to the agent for the issuance or renewal of the automobile liability policy issued through the North Carolina Reinsurance Facility affected by the surcharge. However, the surcharge shall include an amount necessary to recover the amount of the assessment to member companies and the compensation paid by each member, under this section, to agents.

(g)   The plan of operation shall provide that all investment income from the premium on business reinsured by the Facility shall be retained by or paid over to the Facility. In determining the cost of operation of the Facility, all investment income shall be taken into consideration.

(h)   The plan of operation shall provide for audit of the annual statement of the Facility by independent auditor approved by the Legislative Services Commission.

(i)   The Facility shall file with the Commissioner revisions in the Facility plan of operation for his approval or modification. Such revisions shall be made for the purpose of revising the classification and rating plans for other than nonfleet private passenger motor vehicle insurance ceded to the Facility. (1973, c. 818, s. 1; 1975, c. 19, s. 18; 1977, c. 828, ss. 20, 21; 1981, c. 590; c. 916, ss. 2, 3; 1985 (Reg. Sess., 1986), c. 1027, s. 34; 1987, c. 869, s. 5(1)-5(3); 1989, c. 424, s. 1; 1991, c. 720, s. 4; 1995, c. 517, s. 24; 1999-132, ss. 8.5, 8.6.)

§ 58-37-45. Procedure for cession provided in plan of operation.

Upon receipt by the company of a risk which it does not elect to retain, the company shall follow such procedures for ceding the risk as are established by the plan of operation. (1973, c. 818, s. 1; 1977, c. 828, s. 22.)

§ 58-37-50. Termination of insurance.

No member may terminate insurance to the extent that cession of a particular type of coverage and limits is available under the provisions of this Article except for the following reasons:

(1)   Nonpayment of premium when due to the insurer or producing agent.

(2)   The named insured has become a nonresident of this State and would not otherwise be entitled to insurance on submission of new application under this Article.

(3)   A member company has terminated an agency contract for reasons other than the quality of the agent's insureds or the agent has terminated the contract and such agent represented the company in taking the original application for insurance.

(4)   When the insurance contract has been cancelled pursuant to a power of attorney given a company licensed pursuant to the provisions of G.S. 58-35-5.

(5)   The named insured, at the time of renewal, fails to meet the requirements contained in the corporate charter, articles of incorporation, and/or bylaws of the insurer, when the insurer is a company organized for the sole purpose of providing members of an organization with insurance policies in North Carolina.

(6)   The named insured is no longer an eligible risk under G.S. 58-37-1. (1973, c. 818, s. 1; 1979, c. 497; 2007-443, s. 2.)

§ 58-37-55. Exemption from requirements of this Article of companies and their agents.

The Board of Governors may exempt a company and its agents from the requirements of this Article, insofar as new business is concerned. The Board may further exempt a company and its agents from the requirements of this Article regarding the selling and servicing a particular category of business, if the company is not qualified to service the business. (1973, c. 818, s. 1; 1977, c. 828, s. 23.)

§ 58-37-60. Physical damage insurance availability.

No physical damage insurer shall refuse to make physical damage coverage available to any applicant for the reason that such applicant has, or may acquire, auto liability insurance through the Facility plan as provided herein; further that no such insurer may levy a surcharge or increased rate for such physical damage coverage on the basis that such applicant has, or may acquire, auto liability insurance through the Facility plan as provided herein.

Any insurer or representative thereof who fails to comply with or violates this section shall be subject to suspension or revocation of his certificate or license and shall be subject to the provisions of G.S. 58-2-70. (1973, c. 818, s. 1; 1985, c. 666, s. 37.)

§ 58-37-65. Hearings; review.

(a)   Any applicant for a policy from any carrier, any person insured under such a policy, any member of the Facility and any agent duly licensed to write motor vehicle insurance, may request a formal hearing and ruling by the Board of Governors of the Facility on any alleged violation of or failure to comply with the plan of operation or the provisions of this Article or any alleged improper act or ruling of the Facility directly affecting him as to coverage or premium or in the case of a member directly affecting its assessment, and in the case of an agent, any matter affecting his appointment to a carrier or his account therewith. The request for hearing must be made within 15 days after the date of the alleged violation or improper act or ruling. The hearing shall be held within 15 days after the receipt of the request. The hearing may be held by any panel of the Board of Governors consisting of not less than three members thereof, and the ruling of a majority of the panel shall be deemed to be the formal ruling of the Board, unless the full Board on its own motion shall modify or rescind the action of the panel.

(b)   Any formal ruling by the Board of Governors may be appealed to the Commissioner by filing notice of appeal with the Facility and Commissioner within 30 days after issuance of the ruling.

(c)   The Commissioner shall, after a hearing held on not less than 30 days written notice to the appellant and to the Board, (i) issue an order approving the decision of the Board or (ii) after setting out the findings and conclusions as to how the action of the Board is not in accordance with the plan of operation, the Standard Practice Manual, or other provisions of this Article, direct the Board to reconsider its decision. In the event the Commissioner directs the Board to reconsider its decision and the Board fails to take action in accordance with the plan of operation, the Standard Practice Manual, or other provisions of this Article, the Commissioner may issue an order modifying the action of the Board to the extent necessary to comply with the plan of operation, the Standard Practice Manual, or other provisions of this Article.

No later than 20 days before each hearing, the appellant shall file with the Commissioner or his designated hearing officer and shall serve on the appellee a written statement of his case and any evidence he intends to offer at the hearing. No later than five days before such hearing, the appellee shall file with the Commissioner or his designated hearing officer and shall serve on the appellant a written statement of his case and any evidence he intends to offer at the hearing. Each such hearing shall be recorded and transcribed. The cost of such recording and transcribing shall be borne equally by the appellant and appellee; provided that upon any final adjudication the prevailing party shall be reimbursed for his share of such costs by the other party. Each party shall, on a date determined by the Commissioner or his designated hearing officer, but not sooner than 15 days after delivery of the completed transcript to the party, submit to the Commissioner or his designated hearing officer and serve on the other party, a proposed order. The Commissioner or his designated hearing officer shall then issue an order.

(d)   Any aggrieved person or organization, any member of the Facility or the Facility may request a public hearing and ruling by the Commissioner on the provisions of the plan of operation, rules, regulations or policy forms approved by the Commissioner. The request for hearing shall specify the matter or matters to be considered. The hearing shall be held within 30 days after receipt of the request. The Commissioner shall give public notice of the hearing and the matter or matters to be considered not less than 15 days in advance of the hearing date.

(e)   In any hearing held pursuant to this section by the Board of Governors or the Commissioner, the Board or the Commissioner as the case may be, shall issue a ruling or order within 30 days after the close of the hearing.

(f)   All rulings or orders of the Commissioner under this section shall be subject to judicial review as approved in G.S. 58-2-75. (1973, c. 818, s. 1; 1989, c. 424, s. 3; 1989 (Reg. Sess., 1990), c. 1069, s. 17.)

§ 58-37-70: Repealed by Session Laws 1991, c. 720, s. 6.

§ 58-37-75. Repealed by Session Laws 1999-132, s. 8.9.

Article 38.

Readable Insurance Policies.

§ 58-38-1. Title.

This Article is known and may be cited as the "Readable Insurance Policies Act." (1979, c. 755, s. 1.)

§ 58-38-5. Purpose.

The purpose of this Article is to provide that insurance policies and contracts be readable by a person of average intelligence, experience, and education. All insurers are required by this Article to use policy and contract forms and, where applicable, benefit booklets that are written in simple and commonly used language, that are logically and clearly arranged, and that are printed in a legible format. (1979, c. 755, s. 1.)

§ 58-38-10. Scope of application.

(a) Except as provided in subsection (b) of this section, the provisions of this Article apply to the policies and contracts of direct insurance that are described in G.S. 58-38-35(a).

(b) Nothing in this Article applies to:

(1) Any policy that is a security subject to federal jurisdiction;

(2) Any group policy covering a group of 1,000 or more lives at date of issue, other than a group credit life insurance policy, nor any group policy delivered or issued for delivery outside of this State; however, this does not exempt any certificate issued pursuant to a group policy delivered or issued for delivery in this State;

(3) Any group annuity contract that serves as a funding vehicle for pension, profit-sharing, or deferred compensation plans;

(4) Any form used in connection with, as a conversion from, as an addition to, or in exchange pursuant to a contractual provision for, a policy delivered or issued for delivery on a form approved or permitted to be issued prior to the dates such forms must be approved under this Article;

(5) The renewal of a policy delivered or issued for delivery prior to the date such policy must be approved under this Article; nor

(6) Insurers who issue benefit booklets on group and nongroup bases for the policies described in G.S. 58-38-35(a)(2). In such cases, the provisions of this Article apply to the benefit booklets furnished to the persons insured.

(7) Insurance on farm buildings (other than farm dwellings and their appurtenant structures); farm personal property; travel or camper trailers designed to be pulled by private passenger motor vehicles unless insured under policies covering nonfleet private passenger motor vehicles; nonfleet private

passenger motor vehicles insured under a commercial motor vehicle insurance policy when combined with a commercial risk; residential real and personal property insured in multiple line insurance policies covering business activities as the primary insurable interest; and marine, general liability, burglary and theft, glass, and animal collision insurance except when such coverages are written as an integral part of a multiple line insurance policy for which there is an indivisible premium.

(c) No other provision of the General Statutes setting language simplification standards shall apply to any policy forms covered by this Article.

(d) Any non-English language policy delivered or issued for delivery in this State shall be deemed to be in compliance with this Article if the insurer certifies that such policy is translated from an English language policy which does comply with this Article. (1979, c. 755, s. 1; 1981, c. 888, s. 6; 1983, c. 393, s. 1.)

§ 58-38-15. Definitions.

As used in this Article, unless the context clearly indicates otherwise:

(1) "Benefit booklet" means any written explanation of insurance coverages or benefits issued by an insurer and which is supplemental to and not a part of an insurance policy or contract.

(2) Repealed by Session Laws 1991, c. 720, s. 6.

(3) "Flesch scale analysis readability score" means a measurement of the ease of readability of an insurance policy or contract made pursuant to the procedures described in G.S. 58-38-35.

(4) "Insurance policy or contract" or "policy" means an agreement as defined by G.S. 58-1-10.

(5) "Insurer" means every person entering insurance policies or contracts as a principal, as described in G.S. 58-1-5(3).

(6) "Person" means any individual, corporation, partnership, association, business trust, or voluntary organization. (1979, c. 755, s. 1; 1987, c. 864, s. 10; 1991, c. 720, s. 6.)

§ 58-38-20. Format requirements.

(a) All insurance policies and contracts covered by G.S. 58-38-35 must be printed in a typeface at least as large as 10 point modern type, one point leaded, be written in a logical and clear order and form, and contain the following items:

(1) On the cover, first, or insert page of the policy a statement that the policy is a legal contract between the policy owner and the insurer and the statement, printed in larger or other contrasting type or color, "Read your policy carefully";

(2) An index of the major provisions of the policy, which may include the following items:

a. The person or persons insured by the policy;

b. The applicable events, occurrences, conditions, losses, or damages covered by the policy;

c. The limitations or conditions on the coverage of the policy;

d. Definitional sections of the policy;

e. Provisions governing the procedure for filing a claim under the policy;

f. Provisions governing cancellation, renewal, or amendment of the policy by either the insurer or the policyholder;

g. Any options under the policy; and

h. Provisions governing the insurer's duties and powers in the event that suit is filed against the insured.

(b) In determining whether or not a policy is written in a logical and clear order and form the Commissioner must consider the following factors:

(1) The extent to which sections or provisions are set off and clearly identified by titles, headings, or margin notations;

(2) The use of a more readable format, such as narrative or outline forms;

(3) Margin size and the amount and use of space to separate sections of the policy; and

(4) Contrast and legibility of the colors of the ink and paper and the use of contrasting titles or headings for sections. (1979, c. 755, s. 1.)

§ 58-38-25. Flesch scale analysis readability score; procedures.

(a) A Flesch scale analysis readability score will be measured as provided in this section.

(b) For policies containing 10,000 words or less of text, the entire policy must be analyzed. For policies containing more than 10,000 words, the readability of two 200-word samples per page may be analyzed in lieu of the entire policy. The samples must be separated by at least 20 printed lines. For the purposes of this subsection a word will be counted as five printed characters or spaces between characters.

(c) The number of words and sentences in the text must be counted and the total number of words divided by the total number of sentences. The figure obtained must be multiplied by a factor of 1.015. The total number of syllables must be counted and divided by the total number of words. The figure obtained must be multiplied by a factor of 84.6. The sum of the figures computed under this subsection subtracted from 206.835 equals the Flesch scale analysis readability score for the policy.

(d) For the purposes of subsection (c) of this section the following procedures must be used:

(1) A contraction, hyphenated word, or numbers and letters, when separated by spaces, will be counted as one word;

(2) A unit of words ending with a period, semicolon, or colon, but excluding headings and captions, will be counted as a sentence; and

(3) A syllable means a unit of spoken language consisting of one or more letters of a word as divided by an accepted dictionary. Where the dictionary shows two or more equally acceptable pronunciations of a word, the pronunciation containing fewer syllables may be used.

(e) The term "text" as used in this section includes all printed matter except the following:

(1) The name and address of the insurer; the name, number or title of the policy; the table of contents or index; captions and subcaptions; specification pages, schedules or tables; and

(2) Any policy language that is drafted to conform to the requirements of any law, regulation, or agency interpretation of any state or the federal government; any policy language required by any collectively bargained agreement; any medical terminology; and any words that are defined in the policy: Provided, however, that the insurer submits with his filing under G.S. 58-38-30 a certified document identifying the language or terminology that is entitled to be excepted by this subdivision. (1979, c. 755, s. 1.)

§ 58-38-30. Filing requirements; duties of the Commissioner.

(a) No insurer may make, issue, amend, or renew any insurance policy or contract after the dates specified in G.S. 58-38-35 for the applicable type of insurance unless the policy is in compliance with the provisions of G.S. 58-38-20 and G.S. 58-38-25 and unless the policy is filed with the Commissioner for his approval. The policy will be deemed approved 90 days after filing unless disapproved within the 90-day period. The Commissioner may not unreasonably withhold his approval. Any disapproval must be delivered to the insurer in writing and must state the grounds for disapproval. Any policy filed with the Commissioner must be accompanied by a certified Flesch scale readability analysis and test score and by the insurer's certification that the policy is, in the insurer's judgment, readable based on the factors specified in G.S. 58-38-20 and G.S. 58-38-25.

(b)   The Commissioner must disapprove any policy covered by subsection (a) of this section if he finds that:

(1)   It is not accompanied by a certified Flesch scale analysis readability score of 50 or more.

(2)   It is not accompanied by the insurer's certification that the policy is, in the judgment of the insurer, readable under the standards of this Article; or

(3)   It does not comply with the format requirements of G.S. 58-38-20. (1979, c. 755, s. 1; 1979, 2nd Sess., c. 1161, s. 2.)

§ 58-38-35. Application to policies; dates; duties of the Commissioner.

(a)   The filing requirements of G.S. 58-38-30 apply as follows:

(1)   As described in Article 36 of this Chapter, to all policies of private passenger nonfleet motor vehicle insurance except as excluded by G.S. 58-38-10(b)(7), to all policies of insurance against loss to residential real property with not more than four housing units located in this State and any contents thereof and valuable interest therein, and other insurance coverages written in connection with the sale of such property insurance except as excluded in G.S. 58-38-10(b)(7), that are made, issued, amended, or renewed after March 1, 1981; and

(2)   To all policies of life insurance as described in Article 58 of this Chapter, to all benefit certificates issued by fraternal orders and societies as described in Articles 24 and 25 of this Chapter, to all policies of accident and health insurance as described in Articles 50 through 55 of this Chapter, to all subscribers' contracts of hospital, medical, and dental service corporations as described in Articles 65 and 66 of this Chapter, and to all health maintenance organization evidences of coverage as described in Article 67 of this Chapter, that are made, issued, amended, or renewed after July 1, 1983.

(b)   Repealed by Session Laws 1991, c. 720, s. 6. (1979, c. 755, s. 1; 1979, 2nd Sess., c. 1161, s. 3; 1981, c. 888, s. 7; 1983, c. 393, s. 2; 1987, c. 864, s. 11; 1991, c. 720, ss. 6, 42.)

§ 58-38-40. Construction.

(a) The provisions of this Article will not operate to relieve any insurer from any provision of law regulating the contents or provisions of insurance policies or contracts nor operate to reduce an insured's or beneficiary's rights or protection granted under any statute or provision of law.

(b) The provisions of this Article shall not be construed to mandate, require, or allow alteration of the legal effect of any provision of any insurance policy or contract.

(c) In any action brought by a policyholder or claimant arising out of a policy approved pursuant to this Article, the policyholder or claimant may base such an action on either or both (i) the substantive language prescribed by such other statute or provision of law or (ii) the wording of the approved policy. (1979, c. 755, s. 1.)

Article 39.

Consumer and Customer Information Privacy.

Part 1. Insurance Information and Privacy Protection.

§ 58-39-1. Short titles.

This Article may be cited as the Consumer and Customer Information Privacy Act. Part 1 of this Article may be cited as the Insurance Information and Privacy Protection Act. Part 3 of this Article may be cited as the Customer Information Safeguards Act. (1981, c. 846, s. 1; 2003-262, s. 3.)

§ 58-39-5. Purpose.

The purpose of this Article is to establish standards for the collection, use, and disclosure of information gathered in connection with insurance transactions by insurance institutions, agents, or insurance-support organizations; to maintain a balance between the need for information by those conducting the business of insurance and the public's need for fairness in insurance information practices, including the need to minimize intrusiveness; to establish a regulatory mechanism to enable natural persons to ascertain what information is being or has been collected about them in connection with insurance transactions and to have access to such information for the purpose of verifying or disputing its accuracy; to limit the disclosure of information collected in connection with insurance transactions; and to enable insurance applicants and policyholders to obtain the reasons for any adverse underwriting decision. (1981, c. 846, s. 1; 2003-262, s. 2(1).)

§ 58-39-10. Scope.

(a) The obligations imposed by this Article shall apply to those insurance institutions, agents, or insurance-support organizations that:

(1) In the case of life, health, or disability insurance:

a. Collect, receive, or maintain information in connection with insurance transactions that pertains to natural persons who are residents of this State; or

b. Engage in insurance transactions with applicants, individuals, or policyholders who are residents of this State; and

(2) In the case of property or casualty insurance:

a. Collect, receive, or maintain information in connection with insurance transactions involving policies, contracts, or certificates of insurance delivered, issued for delivery, or renewed in this State;

b. Engage in insurance transactions involving policies, contracts, or certificates of insurance delivered, issued for delivery, or renewed in this State; or

c. Engage in transactions involving mortgage guaranty insurance where the mortgage guaranty policies, contracts, or certificates of insurance are delivered, issued for delivery, or renewed in this State.

(b) The rights granted by this Article shall extend to:

(1) In the case of life, health, or disability insurance, the following persons who are residents of this State:

a. Natural persons who are the subject of information collected, received, or maintained in connection with insurance transactions; and

b. Applicants, individuals, or policyholders who engage in or seek to engage in insurance transactions;

(2) In the case of property or casualty insurance, the following persons:

a. Natural persons who are the subject of information collected, received, or maintained in connection with insurance transactions involving policies, contracts, or certificates of insurance delivered, issued for delivery, or renewed in this State; and

b. Applicants, individuals, or policyholders who engage in or seek to engage in (i) insurance transactions involving policies, contracts, or certificates of insurance delivered, issued for delivery, or renewed in this State; or (ii) mortgage guaranty insurance transactions involving policies, contracts, or certificates of insurance delivered, issued for delivery, or renewed in this State.

(c) For purposes of this section, a person shall be considered a resident of this State if the person's last known mailing address, as shown in the records of the insurance institution, agent, or insurance-support organization, is located in this State.

(d) Notwithstanding subsections (a) and (b) of this section, this Article shall not apply to information collected from the public records of a governmental authority and maintained by an insurance institution or its representatives for the purpose of insuring the title to real property located in this State.

(e) This Article applies to credit insurance that is subject to Article 57 of this Chapter. (1981, c. 846, s. 1; 2001-351, s. 1; 2003-262, s. 2(1).)

§ 58-39-15. Definitions.

As used in this Article:

(1)   "Adverse underwriting decision" means:

a.   Any of the following actions with respect to insurance transactions involving insurance coverage that is individually underwritten:

1.   A declination of insurance coverage;

2.   A termination of insurance coverage;

3.   Failure of an agent to apply for insurance coverage with a specific insurance institution that an agent represents and that is requested by an applicant;

4.   In the case of a property or casualty insurance coverage:

I.   Placement by an insurance institution or agent of a risk with a residual market mechanism, an unauthorized insurer, or an insurance institution that specializes in substandard risks; or

II.   The charging of a higher rate on the basis of information that differs from that which the applicant or policyholder furnished; or

5.   In the case of a life, health, or disability insurance coverage, an offer to insure at higher than standard rates.

b.   Notwithstanding subdivision (1)a. of this section, the following actions shall not be considered adverse underwriting decisions, but the insurance institution or agent responsible for their occurrence shall nevertheless provide the applicant or policyholder with the specific reason or reasons for their occurrence:

1.   The termination of an individual policy form on a class or statewide basis;

2.   A declination of insurance coverage solely because such coverage is not available on a class or statewide basis; or

3.   The rescission of a policy.

(2) "Affiliate" or "affiliated" means a person that directly, or indirectly through one or more intermediaries, controls, is controlled by, or is under common control with another person.

(3) "Agent" has the meaning as set forth in G.S. 58-33-10, and includes limited representatives, limited line credit insurance producers, limited lines producers, insurance producers, and surplus lines licensees.

(4) "Applicant" means any person who seeks to contract for insurance coverage other than a person seeking group insurance that is not individually underwritten.

(5) "Consumer report" means any written, oral, or other communication of information bearing on a natural person's credit worthiness, credit standing, credit capacity, character, general reputation, personal characteristics, or mode of living that is used or expected to be used in connection with an insurance transaction.

(6) "Consumer reporting agency" means any person who:

a. Regularly engages, in whole or in part, in the practice of assembling or preparing consumer reports for a monetary fee;

b. Obtains information primarily from sources other than insurance institutions; and

c. Furnishes consumer reports to other persons.

(7) "Control," including the terms "controlled by" or "under common control with," means the possession, direct or indirect, of the power to direct or cause the direction of the management and policies of a person, whether through the ownership of voting securities, by contract other than a commercial contract for goods or nonmanagement services, or otherwise, unless the power is the result of an official position with or corporate office held by the person.

(8) "Declination of insurance coverage" means a denial, in whole or in part, by an insurance institution or agent of requested insurance coverage.

(9) "Individual" means any natural person who:

a. In the case of property or casualty insurance, is a past, present, or proposed named insured or certificate holder;

b. In the case of life, health, or disability insurance, is a past, present, or proposed principal insured or certificate holder;

c. Is a past, present or proposed policy owner;

d. Is a past or present applicant;

e. Is a past or present claimant;

f. Derived, derives, or is proposed to derive insurance coverage under an insurance policy or certificate subject to this Article; or

g. Is the subject of personal information collected or maintained by an insurance institution, agent, or insurance-support organization in connection with mortgage guaranty insurance.

(10) "Institutional source" means any person or governmental entity that provides information about an individual to an agent, insurance institution, or insurance-support organization, other than:

a. An agent;

b. The individual who is the subject of the information; or

c. A natural person acting in a personal capacity rather than in a business or professional capacity.

(11) "Insurance institution" means any corporation, association, partnership, reciprocal exchange, inter-insurer, Lloyd's insurer, fraternal benefit society, or other person engaged in the business of insurance, including health maintenance organizations and medical, surgical, hospital, dental, and optometric service plans, governed by Articles 65 through 67 of this Chapter. "Insurance institution" shall not include agents or insurance-support organizations.

(12) "Insurance-support organization" means any person who regularly engages, in whole or in part, in the practice of assembling or collecting information about natural persons for the primary purpose of providing the

information to an insurance institution or agent for insurance transactions, including: (i) the furnishing of consumer reports or investigative consumer reports to an insurance institution or agent for use in connection with an insurance transaction; or (ii) the collection of personal information from insurance institutions, agents, or other insurance-support organizations for the purpose of detecting or preventing fraud, material misrepresentation, or material nondisclosure in connection with insurance underwriting or insurance claim activity; provided, however, the following persons shall not be considered "insurance-support organizations" for purposes of this Article: agents, governmental institutions, insurance institutions, medical-care institutions, and medical professionals.

(13)   "Insurance transaction" means any transaction involving insurance primarily for personal, family, or household needs rather than business or professional needs that entails:

a.   The determination of an individual's eligibility for an insurance coverage, benefit, or payment; or

b.   The servicing of an insurance application, policy, contract, or certificate.

(14)   "Investigative consumer report" means a consumer report or portion thereof in which information about a natural person's character, general reputation, personal characteristics, or mode of living is obtained through personal interviews with the person's neighbors, friends, associates, acquaintances, or others who may have knowledge concerning such items of information.

(15)   "Life insurance" includes annuities.

(16)   "Medical-care institution" means any facility or institution that is licensed to provide health care services to natural persons, including but not limited to, hospitals, skilled nursing facilities, home-health agencies, medical clinics, rehabilitation agencies, public health agencies, or health-maintenance organizations.

(17)   "Medical professional" means any person licensed or certified to provide health care services to natural persons, including but not limited to, a physician, dentist, nurse, chiropractor, optometrist, physical or occupational therapist, licensed clinical social worker, clinical dietitian, clinical psychologist, pharmacist, or speech therapist.

(18) "Medical-record information" means personal information that:

a. Relates to an individual's physical or mental condition, medical history, or medical treatment; and

b. Is obtained from a medical professional or medical-care institution, from the individual, or from the individual's spouse, parent, or legal guardian.

(19) "Personal information" means any individually identifiable information gathered in connection with an insurance transaction from which judgments can be made about an individual's character, habits, avocations, finances, occupation, general reputation, credit, health, or any other personal characteristics. "Personal information" includes an individual's name and address and medical-record information, but does not include privileged information.

(20) "Policyholder" means any person who:

a. In the case of individual property or casualty insurance, is a present named insured;

b. In the case of individual life or accident and health insurance, is a present policy owner; or

c. In the case of group insurance that is individually underwritten, is a present group certificate holder.

(21) "Pretext interview" means an interview whereby a person, in an attempt to obtain information about a natural person, performs one or more of the following acts:

a. Pretends to be someone he is not;

b. Pretends to represent a person he is not in fact representing;

c. Misrepresents the true purpose of the interview; or

d. Refuses to identify himself upon request.

(22) "Privileged information" means any individually identifiable information that (i) relates to a claim for insurance benefits or a civil or criminal proceeding involving an individual, and (ii) is collected in connection with or in reasonable anticipation of a claim for insurance benefits or civil or criminal proceeding involving an individual: Provided, however, information otherwise meeting the requirements of this subsection shall nevertheless be considered personal information under this Article if it is disclosed in violation of G.S. 58-39-75.

(23) "Residual market mechanism" means any reinsurance facility, joint underwriting association, assigned risk plan, or other similar plan established under the laws of this State.

(24) "Termination of insurance coverage" or "termination of an insurance policy" means either a cancellation or nonrenewal of an insurance policy, in whole or in part, for any reason other than the failure to pay a premium as required by the policy.

(25) "Unauthorized insurer" means an insurance institution that has not been granted a license by the Commissioner to transact the business of insurance in this State. (1981, c. 846, s. 1; 1987, c. 629, s. 13; 1993, c. 464, s. 1; 2001-203, s. 30; 2001-351, ss. 2, 3; 2001-487, s. 40(f); 2003-262, s. 2(1).)

§ 58-39-20. Pretext interviews.

No insurance institution, agent, or insurance-support organization shall use or authorize the use of pretext interviews to obtain information in connection with an insurance transaction: Provided, however, a pretext interview may be undertaken to obtain information from a person or institution that does not have a generally or statutorily recognized privileged relationship with the person about whom the information relates for the purpose of investigating a claim where, based upon specific information available for review by the Commissioner, there is a reasonable basis for suspecting criminal activity, fraud, material misrepresentation, or material nondisclosure in connection with the claim. (1981, c. 846, s. 1; 2003-262, s. 2(1).)

§ 58-39-25. Notice of insurance information practices.

(a) An insurance institution or agent shall provide a notice of information practices to all applicants or policyholders in connection with insurance transactions as provided in this section:

(1) In the case of an application for insurance a notice shall be provided no later than:

a. At the time of the delivery of the insurance policy or certificate when personal information is collected only from the applicant or from public records; or

b. At the time the collection of personal information is initiated when personal information is collected from a source other than the applicant or public records;

(2) In the case of a policy renewal, a notice shall be provided no later than the policy renewal date, except that no notice shall be required in connection with a policy renewal if:

a. Personal information is collected only from the policyholder or from public records; or

b. A notice meeting the requirements of this section has been given within the previous 24 months; or

(3) In the case of a policy reinstatement or change in insurance benefits, a notice shall be provided no later than the time a request for a policy reinstatement or change in insurance benefits is received by the insurance institution, except that no notice shall be required if personal information is collected only from the policyholder or from public records.

(b) The notice required by subsection (a) of this section shall be in writing and shall state:

(1) Whether personal information may be collected from persons other than the individual or individuals proposed for coverage;

(2) The types of personal information that may be collected and the types of sources and investigative techniques that may be used to collect such information;

(3) The types of disclosures identified in subsections (2), (3), (4), (5), (6), (9), (11), (12), and (14) of G.S. 58-39-75 and the circumstances under which such disclosures may be made without prior authorization: Provided, however, only those circumstances need be described that occur with such frequency as to indicate a general business practice;

(4) A description of the rights established under G.S. 58-39-45 and 58-39-50 and the manner in which such rights may be exercised; and

(5) That information obtained from a report prepared by an insurance-support organization may be retained by the insurance-support organization and disclosed to other persons.

(c) In lieu of the notice prescribed in subsection (b) of this section, the insurance institution or agent may provide an abbreviated notice informing the applicant or policyholder that:

(1) Personal information may be collected from persons other than the individual or individuals proposed for coverage;

(2) Such information, as well as other personal or privileged information subsequently collected by the insurance institution or agent, in certain circumstances, may be disclosed to third parties without authorization;

(3) A right of access and correction exists with respect to all personal information collected; and

(4) The notice prescribed in subsection (b) of this section will be furnished to the applicant or policyholder upon request.

(d) The obligations imposed by this section upon an insurance institution or agent may be satisfied by another insurance institution or agent authorized to act on its behalf. (1981, c. 846, s. 1; 2003-262, s. 2(1).)

§ 58-39-26. Federal privacy disclosure notice requirements.

(a) Disclosure Required. - In addition to the notice requirements of G.S. 58-39-25, an insurance institution or agent shall provide, to all applicants and policyholders no later than (i) before the initial disclosure of personal information under G.S. 58-39-75(11) or (ii) the time of the delivery of the insurance policy or certificate, a clear and conspicuous notice, in written or electronic form, of the insurance institution or agent's policies and practices with respect to:

(1) Disclosing nonpublic personal information to affiliates and nonaffiliated third parties, consistent with section 502 of Public Law 106-102, including the categories of information that may be disclosed.

(2) Disclosing nonpublic personal information of persons who have ceased to be customers of the financial institution.

(3) Protecting the nonpublic personal information of consumers.

These disclosures shall be made in accordance with the regulations prescribed under section 505 of Public Law 106-102.

(b) Information to Be Included. - The disclosure required by subsection (a) of this section shall include:

(1) The policies and practices of the insurance institution or agent with respect to disclosing nonpublic personal information to nonaffiliated third parties, other than agents of the insurance institution or agent, consistent with section 502 of Public Law 106-102, and including:

a. The categories of persons to whom the information is or may be disclosed, other than the persons to whom the information may be provided under section 502(e) of Public Law 106-102.

b. The policies and practices of the insurance institution or agent with respect to disclosing of nonpublic personal information of persons who have ceased to be customers of the insurance institution or agent.

(2) The categories of nonpublic personal information that are collected by the insurance institution or agent.

(3) The policies that the insurance institution or agent maintains to protect the confidentiality and security of nonpublic personal information in accordance with section 501 of Public Law 106-102.

(4) The disclosures required, if any, under section 603(d)(2)(A)(iii) of the Fair Credit Reporting Act.

(c) In the case of a policyholder, the notice required by this section shall be provided not less than annually during the continuation of the policy. As used in this subsection, "annually" means at least once in any period of 12 consecutive months during which the policy is in effect. (2001-351, s. 4; 2003-262, s. 2(1).)

§ 58-39-27. Privacy notice and disclosure requirement exceptions.

(a) Under G.S. 58-39-25 and G.S. 58-39-26, an insurance institution or agent may provide a joint notice from the insurance institution or agent and one or more of its affiliates or other financial institutions, as defined in the notice, as long as the notice is accurate with respect to the insurance institution or agent and the other institutions.

(b) An insurance institution or agent may satisfy the notice requirements of G.S. 58-39-25 and G.S. 58-39-26 by providing a single notice if two or more applicants or policyholders jointly obtain or apply for an insurance product.

(c) An insurance institution or agent may satisfy the notice requirements of G.S. 58-39-25 and G.S. 58-39-26 through the use of separate or combined notices.

(d) An insurance institution or agent is not required to provide the notices required by G.S. 58-39-25 and G.S. 58-39-26 to:

(1) Any applicant or policyholder whose last known address, according to the insurance institution's or agent's records is deemed invalid. The applicant's or policyholder's last known address shall be deemed invalid if mail sent to that address has been returned by the postal authorities as undeliverable and if subsequent reasonable attempts to obtain a current valid address for the applicant or policyholder have been unsuccessful; or

(2) Any policyholder whose policy is lapsed, expired, or otherwise inactive or dormant under the insurance institution's business practices, and the insurance institution has not communicated with the policyholder about the relationship for a period of 12 consecutive months, other than annual privacy notices, material required by law or regulation, or promotional materials.

(e) If an agent does not share information with any person other than the agent's principal or an affiliate of the principal, and if the principal provides all notices required by G.S. 58-39-25 and G.S. 58-39-26, the agent is not required to provide the notices required by G.S. 58-39-25 and G.S. 58-39-26. G.S. 58-39-75 applies to the sharing of information with an affiliate under this subsection.

(f) When an agent discloses a policyholder's personal information, other than medical information, to an insurance institution solely for the purposes of renewal, transfer, replacement, reinstatement, or modification of an existing policy, the agent is not required to provide the notices required by G.S. 58-39-25 and G.S. 58-39-26.

(g) For the purposes of G.S. 58-39-26 only, the terms "applicant" or "policyholder" include respectively a person who applies for, or a certificate holder who obtains, insurance coverage under a group or blanket insurance contract, employee benefit plan, or group annuity contract, regardless of whether the coverage is individually underwritten. An insurance institution or agent that does not disclose personal information about an applicant or policyholder under a group or blanket insurance contract, employee benefit plan, or group annuity contract, except as permitted under G.S. 58-39-75(1) through (10) and G.S. 58-39-75(12) through (21), may satisfy any notice requirement that otherwise exists under G.S. 58-39-26 with respect to that applicant or policyholder by providing a notice of information practices to the holder of the group or blanket insurance or annuity contract or the employee benefit plan sponsor. If an insurance institution or agent discloses personal information about an applicant or policyholder as permitted by G.S. 58-39-75(11), it shall provide the notice required by G.S. 58-39-26 to the applicant or policyholder not less than 30 days before the information is disclosed, and it may satisfy any other notice requirement that otherwise exists under this section with respect to that applicant or policyholder by providing a notice of information practices to the holder of the group or blanket insurance or annuity contract or employee benefit plan sponsor. (2001-351, s. 5; 2003-262, s. 2(1).)

§ 58-39-28. Exception for title and mortgage guaranty insurance.

(a) A title insurance company shall give notice of its insurance information practices under G.S. 58-39-25 and G.S. 58-39-26 only at the time the final policy of title insurance is issued and is not subject to any annual notice requirement thereafter.

(b) In the case of mortgage guaranty insurance, the notice required by G.S. 58-39-25 and G.S. 58-39-26 shall be provided at the time a master policy is issued and thereafter only if there is a material change in the insurer's policies and practices regarding the use or disclosure of personal information. (2001-351, s. 6; 2003-262, s. 2(1).)

§ 58-39-30. Marketing and research surveys.

An insurance institution or agent shall clearly specify those questions designed to obtain information solely for marketing or research purposes from an individual in connection with an insurance transaction. (1981, c. 846, s. 1; 2003-262, s. 2(1).)

§ 58-39-35. Content of disclosure authorization forms.

Notwithstanding any other provision of law of this State, no insurance institution, agent, or insurance-support organization shall utilize as its disclosure authorization form in connection with insurance transactions involving insurance policies or contracts issued after July 1, 1982, a form or statement that authorizes the disclosure of personal or privileged information about an individual to the insurance institution, agent, or insurance-support organization unless the form or statement:

(1) Complies with the provisions of Article 38 of this Chapter;

(2) Is dated;

(3) Specifies the types of persons authorized to disclose information about the individual;

(4) Specifies the nature of the information authorized to be disclosed;

(5) Names the insurance institution or agent and identifies by generic reference representatives of the insurance institution to whom the individual is authorizing information to be disclosed;

(6) Specifies the purposes for which the information is collected;

(7) Specifies the length of time such authorization shall remain valid, which shall be no longer than:

a. In the case of authorizations signed for the purpose of collecting information in connection with an application for an insurance policy, a policy reinstatement, or a request for change in policy benefits:

1. Thirty months from the date the authorization is signed if the application or request involves life, health, or disability insurance; or

2. One year from the date the authorization is signed if the application or request involves property or casualty insurance;

b. In the case of authorizations signed for the purpose of collecting information in connection with a claim for benefits under an insurance policy:

1. The term of coverage of the policy if the claim is for a health insurance benefit; or

2. The duration of the claim if the claim is not for a health insurance benefit; and

(8) Advises the individual or a person authorized to act on behalf of the individual that the individual or the individual's authorized representative is entitled to receive a copy of the authorization form. (1981, c. 846, s. 1; c. 1127, s. 56; 2003-262, s. 2(1).)

§ 58-39-40. Investigative consumer reports.

(a) No insurance institution, agent, or insurance-support organization may prepare or request an investigative consumer report about an individual in connection with an insurance transaction involving an application for insurance, a policy renewal, a policy reinstatement, or a change in insurance benefits unless the insurance institution or agent informs the individual:

(1) That he may request to be interviewed in connection with the preparation of the investigative consumer report; and

(2) That upon a request pursuant to G.S. 58-39-45 he is entitled to receive a copy of the investigative consumer report.

(b) If an investigative consumer report is to be prepared by an insurance institution or agent, the insurance institution or agent shall institute reasonable procedures to conduct a personal interview requested by an individual.

(c) If an investigative consumer report is to be prepared by an insurance-support organization, the insurance institution or agent desiring such report shall inform the insurance-support organization whether a personal interview has been requested by the individual. The insurance-support organization shall institute reasonable procedures to conduct such interviews, if requested. (1981, c. 846, s. 1; 2003-262, s. 2(1).)

§ 58-39-45. Access to recorded personal information.

(a) If any individual, after proper identification, submits a written request to an insurance institution, agent, or insurance-support organization for access to recorded personal information about the individual that is reasonably described by the individual and reasonably locatable and retrievable by the insurance institution, agent, or insurance-support organization, the insurance institution, agent, or insurance-support organization shall within 30 business days from the date such request is received:

(1) Inform the individual of the nature and substance of such recorded personal information in writing, by telephone, or by other oral communication, whichever the insurance institution, agent, or insurance-support organization prefers;

(2) Permit the individual to see and copy, in person, such recorded personal information pertaining to him or to obtain a copy of such recorded personal information by mail, whichever the individual prefers, unless such recorded

personal information is in coded form, in which case an accurate translation in plain language shall be provided in writing;

(3) Disclose to the individual the identity, if recorded, of those persons to whom the insurance institution, agent, or insurance-support organization has disclosed such personal information within two years prior to such request, and if the identity is not recorded, the names of those insurance institutions, agents, insurance-support organizations or other persons to whom such information is normally disclosed; and

(4) Provide the individual with a summary of the procedures by which he may request correction, amendment, or deletion of recorded personal information.

(b) Any personal information provided pursuant to subsection (a) of this section shall identify the source of the information if such source is an institutional source.

(c) Medical-record information supplied by a medical-care institution or medical professional and requested under subsection (a) of this section together with the identity of the medical professional or medical-care institution that provided such information, shall be supplied either directly to the individual or to a medical professional designated by the individual and licensed to provide medical care with respect to the condition to which the information relates, whichever the insurance institution, agent, or insurance-support organization prefers. If it elects to disclose the information to a medical professional designated by the individual, the insurance institution, agent, or insurance-support organization shall notify the individual, at the time of the disclosure, that it has provided the information to the medical professional.

(d) Except for personal information provided under G.S. 58-39-55, an insurance institution, agent, or insurance-support organization may charge a reasonable fee to cover the costs incurred in providing a copy of recorded personal information to individuals.

(e) The obligations imposed by this section upon an insurance institution or agent may be satisfied by another insurance institution or agent authorized to act on its behalf. With respect to the copying and disclosure of recorded personal information pursuant to a request under subsection (a) of this section, an insurance institution, agent, or insurance-support organization may make arrangements with an insurance-support organization or a consumer reporting agency to copy and disclose recorded personal information on its behalf.

(f) The rights granted to individuals in this section shall extend to all natural persons to the extent information about them is collected and maintained by an insurance institution, agent, or insurance-support organization in connection with an insurance transaction. The rights granted to all natural persons by this subsection shall not extend to information about them that relates to and is collected in connection with or in reasonable anticipation of a claim or civil or criminal proceeding involving them.

(g) For purposes of this section, the term, "insurance-support organization" does not include the term, "consumer reporting agency." (1981, c. 846, s. 1; 2003-262, s. 2(1).)

§ 58-39-50. Correction, amendment, or deletion of recorded personal information.

(a) Within 30 business days from the date of receipt of a written request from an individual to correct, amend, or delete any recorded personal information about the individual within its possession, an insurance institution, agent, or insurance-support organization shall either:

(1) Correct, amend, or delete the portion of the recorded personal information in dispute; or

(2) Notify the individual of:

a. Its refusal to make such correction, amendment, or deletion;

b. The reasons for the refusal; and

c. The individual's right to file a statement as provided in subsection (c) of this section.

(b) If the insurance institution, agent, or insurance-support organization corrects, amends, or deletes recorded personal information in accordance with subdivision (a)(1) of this section, the insurance institution, agent, or insurance-support organization shall so notify the individual in writing and furnish the correction, amendment, or fact of deletion to:

(1)   Any person specifically designated by the individual who, within the preceding two years, may have received such recorded personal information;

(2)   Any insurance-support organization whose primary source of personal information is insurance institutions if the insurance-support organization has systematically received such recorded personal information from the insurance institution within the preceding seven years. The correction, amendment, or fact of deletion need not be furnished if the insurance-support organization no longer maintains recorded personal information about the individual; and

(3)   Any insurance-support organization that furnished the personal information that has been corrected, amended, or deleted.

(c)   Whenever an individual disagrees with an insurance institution's, agent's, or insurance-support organization's refusal to correct, amend, or delete recorded personal information, the individual shall be permitted to file with the insurance institution, agent, or insurance-support organization:

(1)   A concise statement setting forth what the individual thinks is the correct, relevant, or fair information; and

(2)   A concise statement of the reasons why the individual disagrees with the insurance institution's, agent's, or insurance-support organization's refusal to correct, amend, or delete recorded personal information.

(d)   In the event an individual files either statement as described in subsection (c) of this section, the insurance institution, agent, or support organization shall:

(1)   File the statement with the disputed personal information and provide a means by which anyone reviewing the disputed personal information will be made aware of the individual's statement and have access to it; and

(2)   In any subsequent disclosure by the insurance institution, agent, or support organization of the recorded personal information that is the subject of disagreement, clearly identify the matter or matters in dispute and provide the individual's statement along with the recorded personal information being disclosed; and

(3) Furnish the statement to the persons and in the manner specified in subsection (b) of this section.

(e) The rights granted to individuals in this section shall extend to all natural persons to the extent information about them is collected and maintained by an insurance institution, agent, or insurance-support organization in connection with an insurance transaction. The rights granted to all natural persons by this subsection shall not extend to information about them that relates to and is collected in connection with or in reasonable anticipation of a claim or civil or criminal proceeding involving them.

(f) For purposes of this section, the term, "insurance-support organization" does not include the term, "consumer reporting agency." (1981, c. 846, s. 1; 1991, c. 720, s. 74; 2003-262, s. 2(1).)

§ 58-39-55. Reasons for adverse underwriting decisions.

(a) In the event of an adverse underwriting decision, the insurance institution or agent responsible for the decision shall give a written notice in a form approved by the Commissioner that:

(1) Either provides the applicant, policyholder, or individual proposed for coverage with the specific reason or reasons for the adverse underwriting decision in writing or advises such person that upon written request he may receive the specific reason or reasons in writing; and

(2) Provides the applicant, policyholder, or individual proposed for coverage with a summary of the rights established under subsection (b) of this section and G.S. 58-39-45 and 58-39-50.

(b) Upon receipt of a written request within 90 business days from the date of the mailing of notice or other communication of an adverse underwriting decision to an applicant, policyholder or individual proposed for coverage, the insurance institution or agent shall furnish to such person within 21 business days from the date of receipt of such written request:

(1) The specific reason or reasons for the adverse underwriting decision, in writing, if such information was not initially furnished in writing pursuant to subdivision (a)(1) of this section;

(2) The specific items of personal and privileged information that support those reasons: Provided, however:

a. The insurance institution or agent shall not be required to furnish specific items of privileged information if it has a reasonable suspicion, based upon specific information available for review by the Commissioner, that the applicant, policyholder, or individual proposed for coverage has engaged in criminal activity, fraud, material misrepresentation, or material nondisclosure, and

b. Specific items of medical-record information supplied by a medical-care institution or medical professional shall be disclosed either directly to the individual about whom the information relates or to the medical professional designated by the individual and licensed to provide medical care with respect to the condition to which the information relates, whichever the insurance institution or agent prefers; and

(3) The names and addresses of the institutional sources that supplied the specific items of information given pursuant to subdivision (b)(2) of this section: Provided, however, the identity of any medical professional or medical-care institution shall be disclosed either directly to the individual or to the designated medical professional, whichever the insurance institution or agent prefers.

(c) The obligations imposed by this section upon an insurance institution or agent may be satisfied by another insurance institution or agent authorized to act on its behalf.

(d) When an adverse underwriting decision results solely from an oral request or inquiry, the explanation of reasons and summary of rights required by this section may be given orally. (1981, c. 846, s. 1; 2003-262, s. 2(1).)

§ 58-39-60. Information concerning previous adverse underwriting decisions.

No insurance institution, agent, or insurance-support organization may seek information in connection with an insurance transaction concerning: (i) any previous adverse underwriting decision experienced by an individual; or (ii) any previous insurance coverage obtained by an individual through a residual market mechanism, unless such inquiry also requests the reasons for any previous adverse underwriting decision or the reasons why insurance coverage was previously obtained through a residual market mechanism. (1981, c. 846, s. 1; 2003-262, s. 2(1).)

§ 58-39-65. Previous adverse underwriting decisions.

No insurance institution or agent may base an adverse underwriting decision in whole or in part:

(1)   On the fact of a previous adverse underwriting decision or on the fact that an individual previously obtained insurance coverage through a residual market mechanism: Provided, however, an insurance institution or agent may base an adverse underwriting decision on further information obtained from an insurance institution or agent responsible for a previous adverse underwriting decision;

(2)   On personal information received from an insurance-support organization whose primary source of information is insurance institutions: Provided, however, an insurance institution or agent may base an adverse underwriting decision on further personal information obtained as the result of information received from such insurance-support organization. (1981, c. 846, s. 1; 2003-262, s. 2(1).)

§ 58-39-70: Recodified as G.S. 58-39-125 by Session Laws 2003-262, s. 2(3), effective June 26, 2003.

§ 58-39-75. Disclosure limitations and conditions.

An insurance institution, agent, or insurance-support organization shall not disclose any personal or privileged information about an individual collected or received in connection with an insurance transaction unless the disclosure is:

(1)   With the written authorization of the individual, provided:

a. If such authorization is submitted by another insurance institution, agent, or insurance-support organization, the authorization meets the requirements of G.S. 58-39-35; or

b. If such authorization is submitted by a person other than an insurance institution, agent, or insurance-support organization, the authorization meets the requirements of G.S. 58-39-35 and is:

1. Dated;

2. Signed by the individual; and

3. Obtained one year or less before the date a disclosure is sought pursuant to this paragraph; or

(2) To a person other than an insurance institution, agent, or insurance-support organization, provided such disclosure is reasonably necessary:

a. To enable that person to perform a business, professional, or insurance function for the disclosing insurance institution, agent, or insurance-support organization, including, but not limited to, performing marketing functions and other functions regarding the provision of information concerning the disclosing institution's own products, services, and programs, and that person agrees not to disclose the information further without the individual's written authorization unless the further disclosure:

1. Would otherwise be permitted by this section if made by an insurance institution, agent, or insurance-support organization; or

2. Is reasonably necessary for that person to perform its function for the disclosing insurance institution, agent, or insurance-support organization; or

b. To enable that person to provide information to the disclosing insurance institution, agent, or insurance-support organization for the purpose of:

1. Determining an individual's eligibility for an insurance benefit or payment; or

2. Detecting or preventing criminal activity, fraud, material misrepresentation, or material nondisclosure in connection with an insurance transaction; or

(3) To an insurance institution, agent, insurance-support organization, or self-insurer, provided the information disclosed is limited to that which is reasonably necessary:

a. To detect or prevent criminal activity, fraud, material misrepresentation, or material nondisclosure in connection with insurance transactions; or

b. For either the disclosing or receiving insurance institution, agent, or insurance-support organization to perform its function in connection with an insurance transaction involving the individual; or

(4) To a medical-care institution or medical professional for the purpose of (i) verifying insurance coverage or benefits, (ii) informing an individual of a medical problem of which the individual may not be aware, or (iii) conducting an operations or services audit, provided only such information is disclosed as is reasonably necessary to accomplish the foregoing purposes; or

(4a) To a person making an inquiry under G.S. 58-58-97 when providing funeral service to a deceased insured; or

(5) To an insurance regulatory authority; or

(6) To a law-enforcement or other government authority:

a. To protect the interests of the insurance institution, agent, or insurance-support organization in preventing or prosecuting the perpetration of fraud upon it; or

b. If the insurance institution, agent, or insurance-support organization reasonably believes that illegal activities have been conducted by the individual; or

(7) Otherwise permitted or required by law; or

(8) In response to a facially valid administrative or judicial order, including a search warrant or subpoena; or

(9) Made for the purpose of conducting actuarial or research studies, provided:

a. No individual may be identified in any actuarial or research report;

b. Materials allowing the individual to be identified are returned or destroyed as soon as they are no longer needed; and

c. The actuarial or research organization agrees not to disclose the information unless the disclosure would otherwise be permitted by this section if made by an insurance institution, agent, or insurance-support organization; or

(10) To a party or a representative of a party to a proposed or consummated sale, transfer, merger, or consolidation of all or part of the business of the insurance institution, agent, or insurance-support organization, provided:

a. Prior to the consummation of the sale, transfer, merger, or consolidation only such information is disclosed as is reasonably necessary to enable the recipient to make business decisions about the purchase, transfer, merger, or consolidation, and

b. The recipient agrees not to disclose the information unless the disclosure would otherwise be permitted by this section if made by an insurance institution, agent or insurance-support organization; or

(11) To a person whose only use of such information will be in connection with the marketing of a product or service, provided:

a. No medical-record information, privileged information, or personal information relating to an individual's character, personal habits, mode of living, or general reputation is disclosed, and no classification derived from such information is disclosed;

b. The individual has been given an opportunity to indicate that he does not want personal information disclosed for marketing purposes and has given no indication that such individual does not want the information disclosed; and

c. The person receiving such information agrees not to use it except in connection with the marketing of a product or service; or

(12) To an affiliate whose only use of the information will be in connection with an audit of the insurance institution or agent or the marketing of an insurance product or service, provided the affiliate agrees not to disclose the information for any other purpose or to unaffiliated persons; and further provided that no medical record information may be disclosed to the affiliate for the marketing of an insurance product or service; or

(13) By a consumer reporting agency, provided the disclosure is to a person other than an insurance institution or agent; or

(14) To a group policyholder for the purpose of reporting claims experience or conducting an audit of the insurance institution's or agent's operations or services, provided the information disclosed is reasonably necessary for the group policyholder to conduct the review or audit; or

(15) To a professional peer review organization for the purpose of reviewing the service or conduct of a medical-care institution or medical professional; or

(16) To a governmental authority for the purpose of determining the individual's eligibility for health benefits for which the governmental authority may be liable; or

(17) To a certificate holder or policyholder for the purpose of providing information regarding the status of an insurance transaction; or

(18) To a lienholder, mortgagee, assignee, lessor, or other person shown on the records of an insurance institution or agent as having a legal or beneficial interest in a policy of insurance only if:

a. No medical record information is disclosed unless the disclosure would otherwise be permitted by this section; and

b. The information disclosed is limited to that which is reasonably necessary to permit such person to protect its interest in such policy; or

(19) To authorized personnel of the Division of Motor Vehicles upon requests pursuant to G.S. 20-309(c) or G.S. 20-309(f).

(20) To the Department of Health and Human Services and the information disclosed is immunization information described in G.S. 130A-153.

(21) To a person whose only use of an applicant's or policyholder's personal information, but not including medical record information, will be in connection with the marketing of a financial product or service intended to be provided by participants in a marketing program where the program participants and the types of information to be shared are identified to the applicant or policyholder when the applicant or policyholder is first offered the financial product or service. As used in this subdivision:

a. "Financial institution" means any institution the business of which is engaging in activities that are financial in nature or incidental to such financial activities as described in section 4(k) of the Bank Holding Company Act of 1956 (12 U.S.C. § 1843(k)).

b. "Financial product or service" means any product or service that a financial holding company could offer by engaging in an activity that is financial in nature or incidental to such financial activity under section 4(k) of the Bank Holding Company Act of 1956 (12 U.S.C. § 1843(k)).

c. "Marketing program" includes only those programs established by written agreement by the insurance institution and one or more financial institutions under which they jointly offer, endorse, or sponsor a financial product or service. (1981, c. 846, s. 1; 1985, c. 666, s. 68; 1993, c. 134, s. 2; 1997-443, s. 11A.20A; 2001-351, ss. 7, 8, 10, 11, 12; 2003-262, s. 2(1); 2009-566, s. 24.)

§ 58-39-76. Limits on sharing account number information for marketing purposes.

(a) General Prohibition on Disclosure of Account Numbers. - An insurance institution, insurance agent, or insurance-support organization shall not disclose, other than to a consumer reporting agency, an account number or similar form of access number or access code for a credit card account, deposit account, or transaction account of a consumer to any nonaffiliated third party for use in telemarketing, direct mail marketing, or other marketing through electronic mail to the consumer.

(b) Definitions. - As used in this section:

(1) "Account number" means an account number, or similar form of access number or access code, but does not include a number or code in an encrypted

form, as long as the insurance institution, insurance agent, or insurance-support organization does not provide the recipient with a means to decode the number or code.

(2) "Transaction account" means an account other than a deposit account or credit card account. A transaction account does not include an account to which third parties cannot initiate charges.

(c) Exceptions. - Subsection (a) of this section does not apply if an insurance institution, insurance agent, or insurance-support organization discloses an account number or similar form of access number or access code:

(1) To the insurance institution's, insurance agent's, or insurance-support organization's agent or service provider solely in order to perform marketing for the insurance institution's, insurance agent's, or insurance-support organization's own products or services, as long as the agent or service provider is not authorized to directly initiate charges to the account; or

(2) To a participant in a private label credit card program or an affinity or similar program where the participants in the program are identified to the customer when the customer enters into the program. (2001-351, s. 9; 2003-262, s. 2(1).)

Part 2. Enforcement, Sanctions, Remedies, and Rights.

§ 58-39-80. Hearings and procedures.

(a) Whenever the Commissioner has reason to believe that an insurance institution, agent, or insurance-support organization has been or is engaged in conduct in this State that violates this Article, or whenever the Commissioner has reason to believe that an insurance-support organization has been or is engaged in conduct outside this State that has an effect on a person residing in this State and that violates this Article, the Commissioner may issue and serve upon such insurance institution, agent, or insurance-support organization a statement of charges and notice of hearing to be held at a time and place fixed in the notice. The date for such hearing shall be not less than 10 days after the date of service.

(b) At the time and place fixed for such hearing the insurance institution, agent, or insurance-support organization charged shall have an opportunity to answer the charges against it and present evidence on its behalf. Upon good cause shown, the Commissioner shall permit any adversely affected person to intervene, appear, and be heard at such hearing by counsel or in person. (1981, c. 846, s. 1; 2003-262, s. 2(2).)

§ 58-39-85. Service of process; insurance-support organizations.

For the purpose of this Article, an insurance-support organization transacting business outside this State that has an effect on a person residing in this State shall be deemed to have appointed the Commissioner to accept service of process on its behalf. The provisions of G.S. 58-16-30 and 58-16-45 shall apply to service of process under this section, except that such service shall be mailed to the insurance-support organization at its last known principal place of business. (1981, c. 846, s. 1; 1985, c. 666, s. 9; 2003-262, s. 2(2).)

§ 58-39-90. Cease and desist orders.

If, after a hearing pursuant to G.S. 58-39-80, the Commissioner determines that the insurance institution, agent, or insurance-support organization charged has engaged in conduct or practices in violation of this Article, he may issue an order requiring such insurance institution, agent, or insurance-support organization to cease and desist from the conduct or practices constituting a violation of this Article. (1981, c. 846, s. 1; 2003-262, s. 2(2).)

§ 58-39-95. Penalties.

(a) In any case where a hearing pursuant to G.S. 58-39-80 results in the findings of a violation of this Article, the Commissioner, in addition to the issuance of a cease and desist order as prescribed in G.S. 58-39-90, may levy a civil penalty under G.S. 58-2-70.

(b) Any person who violates a cease and desist order of the Commissioner under G.S. 58-39-90, after notice and hearing and upon order of the court, may be subject to one or more of the following penalties, at the discretion of the court:

(1) A monetary fine of not more than ten thousand dollars ($10,000) for each violation; or

(2) A monetary fine of not more than fifty thousand dollars ($50,000) if the court finds that violations have occurred with such frequency as to constitute a general business practice; or

(3) Suspension or revocation of an insurance institution's or agent's license.

(c) The clear proceeds of any civil penalties levied pursuant to this section shall be remitted to the Civil Penalty and Forfeiture Fund in accordance with G.S. 115C-457.2. (1981, c. 846, s. 1; 1991, c. 720, s. 73; 1998-215, s. 89(b); 2003-262, s. 2(2).)

§ 58-39-100. Appeal of right.

From any final order of the Commissioner issued pursuant to the provisions of this Article there shall be an appeal as provided in G.S. 58-2-75. (1981, c. 846, s. 1; 2003-262, s. 2(2).)

§ 58-39-105. Individual remedies.

(a) If any insurance institution, agent, or insurance-support organization fails to comply with G.S. 58-39-45, 58-39-50, or 58-39-55 with respect to the rights granted under those sections, any person whose rights are violated may apply to the superior court in the county in which such person resides for appropriate equitable relief.

(b) An insurance institution, agent, or insurance-support organization that discloses information in violation of G.S. 58-39-75 shall be liable for damages sustained by the individual to whom the information relates. No individual, however, shall be entitled to a monetary award that exceeds the actual damages sustained by the individual as a result of a violation of G.S. 58-39-75.

(c) In any action brought pursuant to this section, the court may award the cost of the action and reasonable attorney's fees to the prevailing party.

(d) An action under this section must be brought within two years from the date the alleged violation is or should have been discovered.

(e) Except as specifically provided in this section, there shall be no remedy or recovery available to individuals for any occurrence that constitutes a violation of any provision of this Article. (1981, c. 846, s. 1; 2003-262, s. 2(2).)

§ 58-39-110. Immunity.

No cause of action in the nature of defamation, invasion of privacy, or negligence shall arise against any person for disclosing personal or privileged information in accordance with this Article, nor shall such a cause of action arise against any person for furnishing personal or privileged information to an insurance institution, agent, or insurance-support organization: Provided, however, this section shall provide no immunity for disclosing or furnishing false information with malice or willful intent to injure any person. (1981, c. 846, s. 1; 2003-262, s. 2(2).)

§ 58-39-115. Obtaining information under false pretenses.

Any person who knowingly and willfully obtains information about an individual from an insurance institution, agent, or insurance-support organization under false pretenses shall, upon conviction, be guilty of a Class 1 misdemeanor. (1981, c. 846, s. 1; 1985, c. 666, s. 33; 1993, c. 539, s. 465; 1994, Ex. Sess., c. 24, s. 14(c); 2003-262, s. 2(2).)

§ 58-39-120. Rights.

The rights granted under G.S. 58-39-45, 58-39-50, and 58-39-75 shall take effect on July 1, 1982, regardless of the date of the collection or receipt of the information that is the subject of such sections. (1981, c. 846, s. 1; c. 1127, s. 56; 2003-262, s. 2(2).)

§ 58-39-125. Powers of the Commissioner.

(a) The Commissioner shall have the power to examine and investigate into the affairs of every insurance institution or agent doing business in this State to determine whether the insurance institution or agent has been or is engaged in any conduct in violation of this Article.

(b) The Commissioner shall have the power to examine and investigate the affairs of every insurance-support organization that acts on behalf of an insurance institution or agent and that either (i) transacts business in this State, or (ii) transacts business outside this State and has an effect on a person residing in this State in order to determine whether such insurance-support organization has been or is engaged in any conduct in violation of this Article. (1981, c. 846, s. 1; 2003-262, ss. 2(1), 2(3).)

Part 3. Customer Information Safeguards.

§ 58-39-130. Purpose.

The purpose of this Part is to establish standards for developing and implementing administrative, technical, and physical safeguards to protect the security, confidentiality, and integrity of customer information, as required by sections 501, 505(b), and 507 of the federal Gramm-Leach-Bliley Act (Public Law 106-102), codified as 15 U.S.C. §§ 6801, 6805(b), and 6807. The purpose of this Part is also to provide privacy and security protection consistent with federal regulations governing the privacy and security of medical records when this Part is consistent with those federal regulations. In those instances in which this Part and the federal regulations are inconsistent and this Part provides privacy and security protection beyond that offered by the federal regulations, the purpose of this Part is to provide that additional privacy and security protection. (2003-262, s. 4.)

§ 58-39-135. Scope.

The safeguards established under this Part apply to all customer information as defined in G.S. 58-39-140. (2003-262, s. 4.)

§ 58-39-140. Definitions.

As used in this Part, in addition to the definitions in G.S. 58-39-15:

(1)   "Customer" means an applicant with or policyholder of a licensee.

(2)   "Customer information" means nonpublic personal information about a customer, whether in paper, electronic, or other form that is maintained by or on behalf of the licensee.

(3)   "Customer information systems" means the electronic or physical methods used to access, collect, store, use, transmit, protect, or dispose of customer information.

(4)   "Licensee" means any producer, as defined in G.S. 58-33-10(7), insurer, MEWA, HMO, or service corporation governed by this Chapter. "Licensee" does not mean:

a.   An insurance-support organization.

b.   A licensee who is a natural person operating within the scope of the licensee's employment by or affiliation with an insurer or producer.

c.   A surplus lines insurer or licensee under Article 21 of this Chapter.

(5)   "Service provider" means a person that maintains, processes, or otherwise is permitted access to customer information through its provision of services directly to the licensee and includes an insurance support organization. (2003-262, s. 4.)

§ 58-39-145. Information security program.

Each licensee shall implement a comprehensive written information security program that includes administrative, technical, and physical safeguards for the protection of customer information. The administrative, technical, and physical safeguards included in the information security program shall be appropriate to the size and complexity of the licensee and the nature and scope of its activities. (2003-262, s. 4.)

§ 58-39-150. Objectives of information security program.

A licensee's information security program shall be designed to:

(1) Ensure the security and confidentiality of customer information;

(2) Protect against any anticipated threats or hazards to the security or integrity of the information; and

(3) Protect against unauthorized access to or use of the information that could result in substantial harm or inconvenience to any customer. (2003-262, s. 4.)

§ 58-39-155. Rules.

The Commissioner may adopt rules that the Commissioner deems necessary to carry out the purposes of this Part, including rules that govern licensee oversight of service providers with which it contracts or has a relationship. (2003-262, s. 4.)

§ 58-39-160. Violation.

A violation of G.S. 58-39-145 or G.S. 58-39-150 subjects the violator to Part 2 of this Article. (2003-262, s. 4.)

§ 58-39-165. Effective date.

Each licensee shall establish an information security program, including appropriate policies and systems under this Part by April 1, 2005. (2003-262, s. 4.)

Article 40.

Regulation of Insurance Rates.

§ 58-40-1. Purposes.

The purposes of this Article are

(1) To promote the public welfare by regulating rates to the end that they shall not be excessive, inadequate, or unfairly discriminatory;

(2) To authorize the existence and operation of qualified statistical organizations and require that specified services of the organizations be generally available to all admitted insurers;

(3) To encourage, as the most effective way to produce rates that conform to the standards of subsection (1) of this section, independent action by and reasonable price competition among insurers;

(4) To authorize cooperative action among insurers in the rate-making process, and to regulate such cooperation in order to prevent practices that tend to bring about monopoly or to lessen or destroy competition; and

(5) To encourage the most efficient and economic marketing practices. (1977, c. 828, s. 2; 2005-210, s. 2.)

§ 58-40-5. Definitions.

As used in this Article:

(1)   Repealed by Session Laws 2005-210, s. 3, effective October 1, 2005.

(2)   Repealed by Session Laws 1991, c. 720, s. 6.

(3) "Inland marine insurance" shall be deemed to include insurance now or hereafter defined by statute, or by interpretation thereof, or if not so defined or interpreted, by ruling of the Commissioner or as established by general custom of the business, as inland marine insurance.

(4) "Member," unless otherwise apparent from the context, means an insurer who participates in or is entitled to participate in the management of a statistical organization.

(5) Repealed by Session Laws 2005-210, s. 3, effective October 1, 2005.

(5a) "Statistical organization" means every person, other than an admitted insurer, whether located within or outside this State, who performs one or more of the following functions:

a. Prepares policy forms or makes underwriting rules incident to, but not including, the making of rates, or rating plans or rating systems.

b. Collects and furnishes to admitted insurers or statistical organizations loss or expense statistics or other statistical information and data and acts in an advisory rather than a rate-making capacity. No duly authorized attorney-at-law acting in the usual course of his profession shall be deemed to be a statistical organization.

c. Makes rates, rating plans or rating systems, or develops loss costs. Two or more insurers that act in concert for the purpose of making rates, rating plans or rating systems, or developing loss costs and that do not operate within the specific authorizations contained in G.S. 58-40-60, 58-40-65, 58-40-70, and 58-40-75 shall be deemed to be a statistical organization.

d. Collects data and statistics from insurers and provides reports from these statistics to the Commissioner for the purpose of fulfilling the statistical reporting obligations of those insurers.

(5b) "Statistical plan" means the document used by a statistical organization to set forth which data elements are to be reported to the statistical organization and to describe the format in which the data must be reported.

(6) "Subscriber," unless otherwise apparent from the context, means an insurer which is furnished at its request (i) with rates and rating manuals by a

statistical organization of which it is not a member, or (ii) with advisory services by a statistical organization of which it is not a member.

(7)   "Willful" means in relation to an act or omission which constitutes a violation of this Article with actual knowledge or belief that such act or omission constitutes such violation and with specific intent to commit such violation.

(8),(9) Repealed by Session Laws 1987, c. 864, s. 66. (1977, c. 828, s. 2; 1987, c. 864, s. 66; 1991, c. 720, s. 6; 2005-210, s. 3.)

§ 58-40-10. Other definitions.

As used in this Article and in Articles 36 and 37 of this Chapter:

(1)   "Private passenger motor vehicle" means:

a.   A motor vehicle of the private passenger or station wagon type that is owned or hired under a long-term contract by the policy named insured and that is neither used as a public or livery conveyance for passengers nor rented to others without a driver; or

b.   A motor vehicle that is a pickup truck or van that is owned by an individual or by husband and wife or individuals who are residents of the same household if it:

1.   Has a gross vehicle weight as specified by the manufacturer of less than 14,000 pounds; and

2.   Is not used for the delivery or transportation of goods or materials unless such use is (i) incidental to the insured's business of installing, maintaining, or repairing furnishings or equipment, or (ii) for farming or ranching. Such vehicles owned by a family farm copartnership or a family farm corporation shall be considered owned by an individual for the purposes of this section; or

c.   A motorcycle, motorized scooter or other similar motorized vehicle not used for commercial purposes.

(2)   "Nonfleet" motor vehicle means a motor vehicle not eligible for classification as a fleet vehicle for the reason that the motor vehicle is one of

four or fewer motor vehicles hired under a long-term contract or owned by the insured named in the policy. (1987, c. 864, s. 67; 1989, c. 789, s. 1; 1995, c. 517, s. 25; 1995 (Reg. Sess., 1996), c. 730, s. 1; 2013-199, s. 20; 2013-410, s. 44.)

§ 58-40-15. Scope of application.

The provisions of this Article shall apply to all insurance on risks or on operations in this State, except:

(1) Reinsurance, other than joint reinsurance to the extent stated in G.S. 58-40-60;

(2) Any policy of insurance against loss or damage to or legal liability in connection with property located outside this State, or any motor vehicle or aircraft principally garaged and used outside of this State, or any activity wholly carried on outside this State;

(3) Insurance of vessels or craft, their cargoes, marine builders' risks, marine protection and indemnity, or other risks commonly insured under marine, as distinguished from inland marine, insurance policies;

(4) Accident, health, or life insurance;

(5) Annuities;

(6) Repealed by Session Laws 1985, c. 666, s. 43.

(7) Mortgage guaranty insurance;

(8) Workers' compensation and employers' liability insurance written in connection therewith;

(9) For private passenger (nonfleet) motor vehicle liability insurance, automobile medical payments insurance, uninsured motorists' coverage and other insurance coverages written in connection with the sale of such liability insurance;

(10) Theft of or physical damage to nonfleet private passenger motor vehicles; except this Article applies to insurance against theft of or physical damage to motorcycles, as defined in G.S. 20-4.01(27)d.; and

(11) Insurance against loss to residential real property with not more than four housing units located in this State or any contents thereof or valuable interest therein and other insurance coverages written in connection with the sale of such property insurance. Provided, however, that this Article shall apply to insurance against loss to farm dwellings, farm buildings and their appurtenant structures, farm personal property and other coverages written in connection with farm real or personal property; travel or camper trailers designed to be pulled by private passenger motor vehicles unless insured under policies covering nonfleet private passenger motor vehicles; residential real and personal property insured in multiple line insurance policies covering business activities as the primary insurable interest; and marine, general liability, burglary and theft, glass, and animal collision insurance except when such coverages are written as an integral part of a multiple line insurance policy for which there is an indivisible premium.

The provisions of this Article shall not apply to hospital service or medical service corporations, investment companies, mutual benefit associations, or fraternal beneficiary associations. (1977, c. 828, s. 2; 1979, c. 714, s. 2; 1981, c. 888, s. 5; 1985, c. 666, s. 43; 1991, c. 339, s. 2; 2001-389, s. 5.)

§ 58-40-20. Rate standards.

(a) In order to serve the public interest, rates shall not be excessive, inadequate, or unfairly discriminatory.

(b), (c) Repealed by Session Laws 1985 (Reg. Sess., 1986), c. 1027, s. 10.

(d) No rate is inadequate unless the rate is unreasonably low for the insurance provided and the use or continued use of the rate by the insurer has had or will have the effect of:

(1) Endangering the solvency of the insurer; or

(2) Destroying competition; or

(3)   Creating a monopoly; or

(4)   Violating actuarial principles, practices, or soundness.

(e)   A rate is not unfairly discriminatory in relation to another in the same class if it reflects equitably the differences in expected losses and expenses. Rates are not unfairly discriminatory because different premiums result for policyholders with like loss exposures but different expense factors, or like expense factors but different loss exposures, as long as the rates reflect the differences with reasonable accuracy. Rates are not unfairly discriminatory if they are averaged broadly among persons insured under a group, franchise, or blanket policy. (1977, c. 828, s. 2; 1985 (Reg. Sess., 1986), c. 1027, ss. 9.1, 10, 11.)

§ 58-40-25. Rating methods.

In determining whether rates comply with the standards under G.S. 58-40-20, the following criteria shall be applied:

(1)   Due consideration shall be given to past and prospective loss and expense experience within this State, to catastrophe hazards, to a reasonable margin for underwriting profit and contingencies, to trends within this State, to dividends or savings to be allowed or returned by insurers to their policyholders, members, or subscribers, and to all other relevant factors, including judgment factors; however, regional or countrywide expense or loss experience and other regional or countrywide data may be considered only when credible North Carolina expense or loss experience or other data is not available.

(2)   Risks may be grouped by classifications for the establishment of rates and minimum premiums. Classification rates may be modified to produce rates for individual risks in accordance with rating plans which establish standards for measuring variations in hazards or expense provisions, or both. Those standards may measure any differences among risks that have probable effect upon losses or expenses. Classifications or modifications of classifications of risks may be established based upon size, expense, management, individual experience, location or dispersion of hazard, or any other reasonable considerations. Those classifications and modifications shall apply to all risks under the same or substantially the same circumstances or conditions.

(3)   The expense provisions included in the rates to be used by an insurer may reflect the operating methods of the insurer and, as far as it is credible, its own expense experience.

(4)   In the case of property insurance rates under this Article, consideration shall be given to the insurance public protection classifications of fire districts established by the Commissioner. The Commissioner shall establish and modify from time to time insurance public protection districts for all rural areas of the State and for cities with populations of 100,000 or fewer, according to the most recent annual population estimates certified by the State Budget Officer. In establishing and modifying these districts, the Commissioner shall use standards at least equivalent to those used by the Insurance Services Office, Inc., or any successor organization. The standards developed by the Commissioner are subject to Article 2A of Chapter 150B of the General Statutes. The insurance public protection classifications established by the Commissioner issued pursuant to the provisions of this Article shall be subject to appeal as provided in G.S. 58-2-75, et seq. The exceptions stated in G.S. 58-2-75(a) do not apply. (1977, c. 828, s. 2; 1985 (Reg. Sess., 1986), c. 1027, s. 16; 1991, c. 644, s. 40; 2000-176, s. 2; 2004-203, s. 5(b).)

§ 58-40-30. Filing of rates and supporting data.

(a)   With the exception of inland marine insurance that is not written according to manual rates and rating plans, every admitted insurer and every licensed statistical organization, which has been designated by any insurer for the filing of rates under G.S. 58-40-40, shall file with the Commissioner all rates and all changes and amendments thereto made by it for use in this State prior to the time they become effective.

(b)   The Commissioner may require the filing of supporting data including:

(1)   The experience and judgment of the filer, and to the extent the filer wishes or the Commissioner requires, of other insurers or rating organizations;

(2)   The filer's interpretation of any statistical data relied upon; and

(3)   Descriptions of the methods employed in setting the rates.

(c) Upon written consent of the insured stating the insured's reasons, a rate or deductible or both in excess of that provided by an otherwise applicable filing may be used on a specific risk, in accordance with rules adopted by the Commissioner. The insurer is not required to obtain the written consent of the insured on any renewal of or endorsement to the policy if the policy renewal or endorsement states that the rates or deductible, or both, are greater than those rates or deductibles, or both, that are applicable in the State of North Carolina. The insurer shall retain the signed consent form and other policy information for each insured and make this information available to the Commissioner, upon request of the Commissioner.

(d) This section and G.S. 58-41-50 shall be construed in pari materia. (1977, c. 828, s. 2; 1985 (Reg. Sess., 1986), c. 1027, s. 17; 1987, c. 441, s. 8; 1995 (Reg. Sess., 1996), c. 668, s. 2; 2005-210, s. 4.)

§ 58-40-35. Filing open to inspection.

Each filing and supporting data filed under this Article shall, as soon as filed, be open to public inspection at any reasonable time. Copies may be obtained by any person on request and upon payment of a reasonable charge therefor. (1977, c. 828, s. 2.)

§ 58-40-40. Delegation of rate making and rate filing obligation.

(a) An insurer may itself establish rates based on the factors in G.S. 58-40-25 or it may use rates prepared by a statistical organization, with average expense factors determined by the statistical organization or with such modification for its own expense and loss experience as the credibility of that experience allows.

(b) An insurer may discharge its obligation under G.S. 58-40-30 by giving notice to the Commissioner that it uses rates prepared by a designated statistical organization, with such information about modifications thereof as are necessary to fully inform the Commissioner. The insurer's rates shall be those filed from time to time by the statistical organization, including any amendments thereto as filed, subject, however, to the modifications filed by the insurer. (1977, c. 828, s. 2; 2005-210, s. 5.)

§ 58-40-45. Disapproval of rates; interim use of rates.

(a)   If, after a hearing, the Commissioner disapproves a rate, he must issue an order specifying in what respects the rate fails to meet the requirements of G.S. 58-40-20. If the Commissioner finds a rate to be excessive, he shall order the excess premium, plus interest at a rate determined in the same manner as in G.S. 58-36-25(b) as of the dates such rates were effective for policyholders, to be refunded to those policyholders who have paid the excess premium. If the Commissioner finds a rate to be unfairly discriminatory, he shall order an appropriate adjustment for policyholders who have paid the unfairly discriminatory premium. The order must be issued within 30 business days after the close of the hearing.

(b)   Whenever a rate of an insurer is held to be unfairly discriminatory or excessive and the rate is deemed no longer effective by order of the Commissioner issued under subsection (a) of this section, the insurer shall have the option to continue to use the rate for the interim period pending judicial review of the order, provided that the insurer shall place in an escrow account approved by the Commissioner the purported unfairly discriminatory or excessive portion of the premium collected during the interim period. The court, upon a final determination, shall order the escrowed funds or any overcharge in the interim rates to be distributed appropriately, except that refunds to policyholders that are de minimis shall not be required.

(c)   No person shall willfully withhold information required by this Article from or knowingly furnish false or misleading information to the Commissioner, any statistical organization designated by the Commissioner, or any insurer, which information will affect the rates, rating plans, loss costs, classifications, or policy forms subject to this Article. (1977, c. 828, s. 2; 1985 (Reg. Sess., 1986), c. 1027, ss. 12, 12.1; 2005-210, s. 6.)

§ 58-40-50. Statistical organizations.

(a)   No statistical organization shall conduct its operations in this State, and no insurer shall utilize the service of such organization for any purpose enumerated in G.S. 58-40-5 unless the organization has obtained a license from the Commissioner.

(b) No statistical organization shall refuse to supply any services for which it is licensed in this State to any insurer admitted to do business in this State and offering to pay the fair and usual compensation for the services.

(c) A statistical organization applying for a license shall include with its application:

(1) A copy of its constitution, charter, articles of organization, agreement, association, or incorporation, and a copy of its bylaws, plan of operation, and any other rules or regulations governing the conduct of its business, all duly certified by the custodian of the originals thereof;

(2) A list of its members and subscribers;

(3) The name and address of one or more residents of this State upon whom notices, process affecting it, or orders of the Commissioner may be served;

(4) A statement showing its technical qualifications for acting in the capacity for which it seeks a license; and

(5) Any other relevant information and documents that the Commissioner may require.

(d) If the Commissioner determines that the applicant and the natural persons through whom it acts are qualified to provide the services proposed, and that all requirements of law are met, he shall issue a license specifying the authorized activity of the applicant. He shall not issue a license if the proposed activity would tend to create a monopoly or to lessen or to destroy price competition. Licenses issued pursuant to this section shall remain in effect until the licensee withdraws from the State or until the license is suspended or revoked.

(e) Any change in or amendment to any document required to be filed under this section shall be promptly filed with the Commissioner.

(f) Repealed by Session Laws 2005-210, s. 7, effective October 1, 2005.

(g) Every statistical organization shall file a statistical plan with the Commissioner for approval for each line of insurance for which the organization requests to be licensed. The Commissioner may, in the Commissioner's discretion, modify the plan to collect additional types of data.

(h) No statistical organization shall engage in any unfair or unreasonable practice with respect to its activities.

(i) A statistical organization is considered an insurance company for purposes of the applicability of G.S. 58-6-7. (1977, c. 828, s. 2; 2005-210, s. 7; 2006-264, s. 45(a).)

§ 58-40-55: Repealed by Session Laws 2005-210, s. 8, effective October 1, 2005.

§ 58-40-60. Joint underwriting and joint reinsurance organizations.

(a) Every group, association, or other organization of insurers which engages in joint underwriting or joint reinsurance through such group, association, or organization, or by standing agreement among the members thereof, shall obtain a license from and file with the Commissioner:

(1) A copy of its constitution, articles of incorporation, agreement, or association, and bylaws;

(2) A list of its members; and

(3) The name and address of a resident of this State upon whom notices, process affecting it, or orders of the Commissioner may be served.

(b) Any change in or amendment to any document required to be filed under this section shall be promptly filed with the Commissioner.

(c) If after a hearing, the Commissioner finds that any activity or practice of any such group, association, or other organization is unfair, unreasonable, or otherwise inconsistent with the provisions of this Article, he may issue a written order specifying in what respects the activity or practice is unfair, unreasonable, or otherwise inconsistent with the provisions of this Article, and requiring the discontinuance of the activity or practice. (1977, c. 828, s. 2; 1985 (Reg. Sess., 1986), c. 1027, s. 48; 1987, c. 441, s. 12; c. 864, s. 71.)

§ 58-40-65. Insurers authorized to act in concert.

Subject to and in compliance with the provisions of Articles 1 through 64 of this Chapter authorizing insurers to be members or subscribers of statistical organizations or to engage in joint underwriting or joint reinsurance, two or more insurers may act in concert with each other and with others with respect to any matters pertaining to the making of rates or rating systems, the preparation or making of insurance policy or bond forms, underwriting rules, surveys, inspections and investigations, the furnishing of loss or expense statistics or other information and data, the creation, administration, or termination of a market assistance program, or carrying on of research. (1977, c. 828, s. 2; 1986, Ex. Sess., c. 7, s. 9; 1987, c. 731, s. 1; 2005-210, s. 9.)

§ 58-40-70. Insurers authorized to act in concert; admitted insurers with common ownership or management; matters relating to co-surety bonds.

With respect to any matters pertaining to the making of rates or rating systems, the preparation or making of insurance policy or bond forms, underwriting rules, surveys, inspections and investigations, the furnishing of loss or expense statistics or other information and data, or carrying on of research, two or more admitted insurers having a common ownership or operating in this State under common management or control, are hereby authorized to act in concert between or among themselves the same as if they constituted a single insurer. To the extent that such matters relate to co-surety bonds, two or more admitted insurers executing co-surety bonds are authorized to act in concert between or among themselves the same as if they constituted a single insurer. (1977, c. 828, s. 2.)

§ 58-40-75. Agreements to adhere.

No insurer shall assume any obligation to any person, other than a policyholder or other insurers with which it is under common control or management or is a member of a market assistance program or of a joint underwriting or joint reinsurance organization, to use or adhere to certain rates or rules; and no other person shall impose any penalty or other adverse consequence for failure of an insurer to adhere to certain rates or rules. This section does not apply to mandatory or voluntary risk sharing plans established under Article 42 of this Chapter or apportionment agreements among insurers approved by the Commissioner pursuant to G.S. 58-40-95. Provided, however, that members and subscribers of statistical organizations may use the rates, rating systems, underwriting rules, or policy or bond forms of such organizations either consistently or intermittently. The fact that two or more admitted insurers, whether or not members or subscribers of a statistical organization, consistently or intermittently use the rates or rating systems made or adopted by a statistical organization, or the underwriting rules or policy or bond forms prepared by a statistical organization, shall not be sufficient in itself to support a finding that an agreement to so adhere exists, and it may be used only for the purpose of supplementing or explaining direct evidence of the existence of any such agreement. (1977, c. 828, s. 2; 1986, Ex. Sess., c. 7, ss. 10, 11; 1987, c. 731, s. 1; 2005-210, s. 10.)

§ 58-40-80. Exchange of information or experience data; consultation with statistical organizations and insurers.

Statistical organizations licensed pursuant to G.S. 58-40-50 and admitted insurers are authorized to exchange information and experience data between and among themselves in this State and with statistical organizations and insurers in other states and may consult with them with respect to rate making and the application of rating systems. (1977, c. 828, s. 2; 2005-210, s. 11.)

§ 58-40-85. Recording and reporting of experience.

The Commissioner shall promulgate or approve reasonable rules, including rules providing statistical plans, for use thereafter by all insurers in the recording and reporting of loss and expense experience, in order that the experience of such insurers may be made available to him. The Commissioner may designate one or more statistical organizations to assist him in gathering and making compilations of such experience. All insurers, for lines of insurance that require data to be reported, shall report their data to one of these designated statistical organizations. (1977, c. 828, s. 2; 2005-210, s. 12.)

§ 58-40-90. Examination of rating, joint underwriting, and joint reinsurance organizations.

The Commissioner shall, at least once every three years, make or cause to be made an examination of each statistical organization licensed pursuant to G.S. 58-40-50. The Commissioner may, as often as deemed expedient, make or cause to be made, an examination of each group, association, or other organization referred to in G.S. 58-40-60. This examination shall relate only to the activities conducted pursuant to this Article and to the organizations licensed under this Article. The officers, manager, agents and employees of any such organization may be examined at any time under oath and shall exhibit all books, records, accounts, documents or agreements governing its method of operation. In lieu of any such examination, the Commissioner may accept the report of an examination made by the insurance advisory official of another state, pursuant to the laws of that state. (1977, c. 828, s. 2; 1995, c. 360, s. 2(b); 1995 (Reg. Sess., 1996), c. 742, s. 26; 2005-210, s. 13.)

§ 58-40-95. Apportionment agreements among insurers.

Agreements may be made between or among insurers with respect to equitable apportionment among them of insurance which may be afforded applicants who are in good faith entitled to but who are unable to procure such insurance through ordinary methods. The insurers may agree between or among themselves on the use of reasonable rate modifications for such insurance, agreements, and rate modifications to be subject to the approval of the Commissioner. (1977, c. 828, s. 2.)

§ 58-40-100. Request for review of rate, rating plan, rating system or underwriting rule.

(a) Any person aggrieved by any rate charged, rating plan, rating system, or underwriting rule followed or adopted by an insurer or statistical organization may request the insurer or rating organization to review the manner in which the rate, plan, system, or rule has been applied with respect to insurance afforded him. Such request may be made by his authorized representative, and shall be in writing. If the request is not granted within 30 days after it is made, the requestor may treat it as rejected. Any person aggrieved by the action of an insurer or statistical organization in refusing the review requested or in failing or refusing to grant all or part of the relief requested, may file a written complaint and request for hearing with the Commissioner, and shall specify the grounds relied upon. If the Commissioner has information concerning a similar complaint he may deny the hearing. If the Commissioner believes that probable cause for the complaint does not exist or that the complaint is not made in good faith, he shall deny the hearing. If the Commissioner finds that the complaint charges a violation of this Article and that the complainant would be aggrieved if the violation is proven, he shall proceed as provided in G.S. 58-2-50 or 58-2-70.

(b) Repealed by Session Laws 1985 (Regular Session, 1986), c. 1027, s. 15. (1977, c. 828, s. 2; 1985, c. 733, s. 3; 1985 (Reg. Sess., 1986), c. 1027, s. 15; 1987, c. 441, s. 13; 2005-210, s. 14.)

§ 58-40-105. Hearing and judicial review.

(a) Any insurer, person, or organization to which the Commissioner has directed an order or decision made without a hearing may, within 30 days after notice to it of the order or decision, make written request to the Commissioner for a hearing thereon. The Commissioner shall hear the party or parties within 20 days after receipt of the request and shall give not less than 10 days' written notice of the time and place of hearing. Within 15 days after the hearing, the Commissioner shall affirm, reverse, or modify his previous action, and specify his reasons therefor. Pending such hearing and decision thereon, the Commissioner may suspend or postpone the effective date of his previous action.

(b) Any order or decision of the Commissioner shall be subject to judicial review as provided in Article 2 of this Chapter. (1977, c. 828, s. 2.)

§ 58-40-110. Suspension of license.

(a) Repealed by Session Laws 1985, c. 666, s. 36.

(b) Subject to the requirements of this Article and of G.S. 58-2-70, the Commissioner may suspend or revoke the license of any statistical organization or insurer or impose a monetary penalty against any statistical organization or insurer where (i) the Commissioner has reason to believe that any statistical organization or insurer has violated any provision of this Chapter, or (ii) the statistical agent fails to comply with an order of the Commissioner within the time limited by such order, or within any extension thereof that the Commissioner may grant. The Commissioner shall not suspend the license of any statistical organization or insurer for failure to comply with an order until the time prescribed for an appeal therefrom has expired or, if an appeal has been taken, until the order has been affirmed. The Commissioner may determine when a suspension of a license shall become effective, and the suspension shall remain in effect for the period fixed by him unless he modifies or rescinds the suspension, or until the order upon which the suspension is based is modified, rescinded, or reversed.

(c) No license shall be suspended or revoked, and no monetary penalty shall be imposed except upon a written order of the Commissioner stating his findings, made after a hearing held upon not less than 10 days' written notice to the person or organization, and specifying the alleged violation. (1977, c. 828, s. 2; 1985, c. 666, s. 36; 2005-210, s. 15.)

§ 58-40-115. Existing rates, rating systems, territories, classifications and policy forms.

Rates, rating systems, territories, classifications, and policy forms lawfully in use on September 1, 1977, may continue to be used thereafter, notwithstanding any provision of this Article. (1977, c. 828, s. 2.)

§ 58-40-120. Payment of dividends not prohibited or regulated; plan for payment into rating system.

Nothing in this Article shall be construed to prohibit or regulate the payment of dividends, savings, or unabsorbed premium deposits allowed or returned by insurers to their policyholders, members, or subscribers. A plan for the payment of dividends, savings, or unabsorbed premium deposits allowed or returned by insurers to their policyholders, members, or subscribers shall not be deemed a rating plan or system. (1977, c. 828, s. 2.)

§ 58-40-125. Limitation.

Nothing in this Article shall apply to any town or county farmers mutual fire insurance association restricting its operations to not more than six adjacent counties in this State, or to domestic insurance companies, associations, orders or fraternal benefit societies now doing business in this State on the assessment plan. (1977, c. 828, s. 2; 1985 (Reg. Sess., 1986), c. 1013, s. 10.1; 1989, c. 485, s. 53.)

§ 58-40-130. Financial disclosure; rate modifications; reporting requirements.

(a) The Commissioner may require each insurer subject to this Article to report, on a form prescribed by the Commissioner, its loss and expense experience, investment income, administrative expenses, and other data that he may require, for kinds of insurance or classes of risks that he designates. These reports are in addition to financial or other statements required by Articles 1 through 64 of this Chapter.

(b) The Commissioner may designate one or more statistical organizations to gather and compile the experience and data referred to in subsection (a) of this section for their member companies.

(c) Whereas the provisions enacted by the General Assembly in 1986 regarding modifications in North Carolina civil law may have a prospective effect upon the loss experience of insurers subject to this Article, the Commissioner is authorized to review each company's rates by type of insurance that are in effect on and after January 1, 1987, and, when and where appropriate, require modification of those rates.

(d) Each insurer subject to this Article shall record the experience and data referred to in subsection (a) of this section. Such experience and data shall be reported to the Commissioner on a form prescribed by the Commissioner by March 31 of each year for each one-year period ending on December 31 of the previous year.

(e) On or before July 1, 1988, and annually thereafter, the Commissioner shall report to the General Assembly the effects, if any, of changes in North Carolina civil law statutes on the experience of insurers subject to this section. (1985 (Reg. Sess., 1986), c. 1027, c. 13; 2005-210, s. 16.)

§ 58-40-135. Good faith immunity for operation of market assistance programs.

There is no liability on the part of and no cause of action of any nature arises against any director, administrator, or employee of a market assistance program, or the Commissioner or his representatives, for any acts or omissions taken by them in creation or operation of a market assistance program. The immunity established by this section does not extend to willful neglect, malfeasance, bad faith, fraud, or malice that would otherwise make an act or omission actionable. (1985 (Reg. Sess., 1986), c. 1027, s. 28.)

§ 58-40-140. Extended reporting.

(a) Any policy for commercial general liability coverage or professional liability insurance wherein the insurer offers, and the insured elects to purchase, an extended reporting period for claims arising during the expiring policy period must provide:

(1) That in the event of a cancellation permitted by G.S. 58-41-15 or nonrenewal effective under G.S. 58-41-20, there shall be a 30-day period after the effective date of the cancellation or nonrenewal during which the insured may elect to purchase coverage for the extended reporting period.

(2) That the limit of liability in the policy aggregate for the extended reporting period shall be one hundred percent (100%) of the expiring policy aggregate that was in effect at the inception of the policy.

(3) Within 45 days after the mailing or delivery of the written request of the insured, the insurer shall mail or deliver the following loss information covering a three-year period:

a. Aggregate information on total closed claims, including date and description of occurrence, and any paid losses;

b. Aggregate information on total open claims, including date and description of occurrence, and amounts of any payments;

c. Information on notice of any occurrence, including date and description of occurrence.

(b) In the event of a cancellation or nonrenewal of a health care provider's professional liability insurance policy by the insured or by the insurer, as permitted by G.S. 58-41-15 or G.S. 58-41-20, except for nonpayment of premium, there shall be a 30-day period after the effective date of the cancellation or nonrenewal during which the insured may elect to obtain an endorsement providing an extended reporting period of unlimited duration covering claims first reported during the extended reporting period and arising from the acts, errors, or omissions committed during the policy period and otherwise covered by the policy.

(c) An unlimited extended reporting period for health care provider professional liability claims must be provided if the insured: (i) dies; (ii) becomes permanently disabled and is unable to carry out his or her profession or practice; or (iii) retires permanently from his or her profession or practice after attaining the age of 65 and accumulating five or more consecutive years of claims-made coverage. (1985 (Reg. Sess., 1986), c. 1013, s. 17; c. 1027, s. 29; 1993, c. 409, s. 9; 1993 (Reg. Sess., 1994), c. 678, s. 21; 1999-294, s. 2.)

Article 41.

Insurance Regulatory Reform Act.

§ 58-41-1. Short title.

This Article is known and may be cited as the Insurance Regulatory Reform Act. (1985 (Reg. Sess., 1986), c. 1027, s. 14.)

§ 58-41-5. Legislative findings and intent.

(a)   Due to conditions in national and international property and liability insurance markets, insureds in the United States have experienced unprecedented in-term cancellations of existing policies for entire books of business, have been afforded little or no notice that existing policies would not be renewed at their expiration dates, or would be renewed only at substantially higher rates or on less favorable terms. The General Assembly finds that such conditions pose an imminent peril to the public welfare for the following reasons:

(1)   In-term cancellations of insurance coverages erode insureds' confidence and breach insureds' trust; unfairly and prematurely terminate the promised coverage; force persons to go without needed insurance protection or force the procurement of substitute insurance at greater cost; and create marketplace confusion resulting in product unavailability.

(2)   Failures to provide timely notices of nonrenewals or of renewals with altered terms deprive persons of adequate opportunities to secure affordable replacement coverages or require persons to go without needed insurance protection.

(b)   The General Assembly finds that there is no uniform requirement for the notice of cancellation, renewal, or nonrenewal for commercial property and liability insurance and that it should adopt reasonable requirements for such notices and should regulate in-term cancellations of entire books of business by companies. (1985 (Reg. Sess., 1986), c. 1027, s. 14.)

§ 58-41-10. Scope.

(a)   Except as otherwise provided, this Article applies to all kinds of insurance authorized by G.S. 58-7-15(4) through (14) and G.S. 58-7-15(18) through (22), and to all insurance companies licensed by the Commissioner to write those kinds of insurance. This Article does not apply to insurance written under Articles 21, 26, 36, 37, 45 or 46 of this Chapter; insurance written for residential risks in conjunction with insurance written under Article 36 of this Chapter; to marine insurance as defined in G.S. 58-40-15(3); to personal inland marine insurance; to commercial aircraft insurance; to policies issued in this State covering risks with multistate locations, except with respect to coverages applicable to locations within this State; to any town or county farmers mutual fire insurance association restricting its operations to not more than six adjacent counties in this State; nor to domestic insurance companies, associations, orders, or fraternal benefit societies doing business in this State on the assessment plan.

(b)   This Article is not exclusive, and the Commissioner may also consider other provisions of Articles 1 through 64 of this Chapter to be applicable to the circumstances or situations addressed in this Article. Policies may provide terms more favorable to insureds than are required by this Article. The rights provided by this Article are in addition to and do not prejudice any other rights the insured may have at common law, under statutes, or under administrative rules. (1985 (Reg. Sess., 1986), c. 1027, s. 14; 1987, c. 441, ss. 1, 2; 1989 c. 485, s. 53; 1993, c. 409, s. 21; 1993 (Reg. Sess., 1994), c. 678, s. 22; 1999-219, s. 5.2; 1999-294, s. 1.)

§ 58-41-15. Certain policy cancellations prohibited.

(a)   No insurance policy or renewal thereof may be cancelled by the insurer prior to the expiration of the term or anniversary date stated in the policy and without the prior written consent of the insured, except for any one of the following reasons:

(1)   Nonpayment of premium in accordance with the policy terms;

(2)   An act or omission by the insured or his representative that constitutes material misrepresentation or nondisclosure of a material fact in obtaining the policy, continuing the policy, or presenting a claim under the policy;

(3)   Increased hazard or material change in the risk assumed that could not have been reasonably contemplated by the parties at the time of assumption of the risk;

(4)   Substantial breach of contractual duties, conditions, or warranties that materially affects the insurability of the risk;

(5) A fraudulent act against the company by the insured or his representative that materially affects the insurability of the risk;

(6) Willful failure by the insured or his representative to institute reasonable loss control measures that materially affect the insurability of the risk after written notice by the insurer;

(7) Loss of facultative reinsurance, or loss of or substantial changes in applicable reinsurance as provided in G.S. 58-41-30;

(8) Conviction of the insured of a crime arising out of acts that materially affect the insurability of the risk; or

(9) A determination by the Commissioner that the continuation of the policy would place the insurer in violation of the laws of this State;

(10) The named insured fails to meet the requirements contained in the corporate charter, articles of incorporation, or bylaws of the insurer, when the insurer is a company organized for the sole purpose of providing members of an organization with insurance coverage in this State.

(b) Any cancellation permitted by subsection (a) of this section is not effective unless written notice of cancellation has been delivered or mailed to the insured, not less than 15 days before the proposed effective date of cancellation. The notice must be given or mailed to the insured, and any designated mortgagee or loss payee at their addresses shown in the policy or, if not indicated in the policy, at their last known addresses. The notice must state the precise reason for cancellation. Proof of mailing is sufficient proof of notice. Failure to send this notice to any designated mortgagee or loss payee invalidates the cancellation only as to the mortgagee's or loss payee's interest.

(c) This section does not apply to any insurance policy that has been in effect for less than 60 days and is not a renewal of a policy. That policy may be cancelled for any reason by furnishing to the insured at least 15 days prior written notice of and reasons for cancellation.

(d) Cancellation for nonpayment of premium is not effective if the amount due is paid before the effective date set forth in the notice of cancellation.

(e) Copies of the notice required by this section shall also be sent to the agent or broker of record; however, failure to send copies of the notice to such persons shall not invalidate the cancellation. (1985 (Reg. Sess., 1986), c. 1027, s. 14.)

§ 58-41-20. Notice of nonrenewal, premium rate increase, or change in coverage required.

(a) No insurer may refuse to renew an insurance policy except in accordance with the provisions of this section, and any nonrenewal attempted or made that is not in compliance with this section is not effective. This section does not apply if the policyholder has insured elsewhere, has accepted replacement coverage, or has requested or agreed to nonrenewal.

(b) An insurer may refuse to renew a policy that has been written for a term of one year or less at the policy's expiration date by giving or mailing written notice of nonrenewal to the insured not less than 45 days prior to the expiration date of the policy.

(c) An insurer may refuse to renew a policy that has been written for a term of more than one year or for an indefinite term at the policy anniversary date by giving or mailing written notice of nonrenewal to the insured not less than 45 days prior to the anniversary date of the policy.

(d) Except as provided in G.S. 58-41-25, whenever an insurer lowers coverage limits or raises deductibles or premium rates other than at the request of the policyholder, the insurer shall give the policyholder written notice of such change at least 30 days in advance of the effective date of the change.

(e) The notice required by this section must be given or mailed to the insured and any designated mortgagee or loss payee at their addresses shown in the policy or, if not indicated in the policy, at their last known addresses. Proof of mailing is sufficient proof of notice. The notice of nonrenewal must state the precise reason for nonrenewal. Failure to send this notice to any designated mortgagee or loss payee invalidates the nonrenewal only as to the mortgagee's or loss payee's interest.

(f) Copies of the notice required by this section shall also be sent the agent or broker of record; however, failure to send copies of the notice to such persons shall not invalidate the nonrenewal. (1985 (Reg. Sess., 1986), c. 1027, s. 14; 1987, c. 441, ss. 3, 4.)

§ 58-41-25. Notice of renewal of policies with premium rate or coverage changes.

(a) If an insurer intends to renew a policy, the insurer must furnish to the insured the renewal terms and a statement of the amount of premium due for the renewal policy period. This section applies only if the insurer intends to decrease coverage, increase deductibles, impose any kind of surcharge, or increase the premium rate in the renewal policy.

(b) If the policy being renewed was written for a term of one year or less, the renewal terms and statement of premium due must be given or mailed not less than 45 days before the expiration date of that policy. If the policy being renewed was written for a term of more than one year or for an indefinite term, the renewal terms and statement of premium due must be given or mailed not less than 45 days before the anniversary date of that policy. The renewal terms and statement of premium due must be given or mailed to the insured and any designated mortgagee or loss payee at their addresses shown in the policy, or, if not indicated in the policy, at their last known addresses.

(c) If the insurer fails to furnish the renewal terms and statement of premium due in the manner required by this section, the insured may cancel the renewal policy within the 30-day period following receipt of the renewal terms and statement of premium due. For refund purposes, earned premium for any period of coverage shall be calculated pro rata upon the premium applicable to the policy being renewed instead of the renewal policy. If an insurer fails to comply with the 45-day notice requirement of this section, the insured is entitled to the option of coverage under the policy being renewed and at the same cost of that policy until 45 days have elapsed after the insurer has provided the insured with the notice.

(d) If a policy has been issued for a term longer than one year, and for additional consideration a premium has been guaranteed for the entire term, it is unlawful for the insurer to increase that premium or require policy deductibles or other policy or coverage provisions less favorable to the insured during the term of the policy.

(e)   Copies of the notice required by this section shall also be given or mailed to any designated mortgagee or loss payee and may also be given or mailed to the agent or broker of record. (1985 (Reg. Sess., 1986), c. 1027, s. 14; 1987, c. 441, ss. 5, 6; 1989, c. 485, ss. 5, 6.)

§ 58-41-30. Loss of reinsurance.

An insurer may cancel or refuse to renew a kind of insurance when the cancellation or nonrenewal is necessary because of a loss of or substantial reduction in applicable reinsurance, by filing a plan with the Commissioner pursuant to the requirements of this section. The insurer's plan must be filed with the Commissioner at least 15 business days prior to the issuance of any notice of cancellation or nonrenewal. The insurer may implement its plan upon the approval of the Commissioner, which shall be granted or denied in writing, with the reasons for his actions, within 15 business days of the Commissioner's receipt of the plan. Any plan submitted for approval shall contain a certification by an elected officer of the company:

(1)   That the loss or substantial change in applicable reinsurance necessitates the cancellation or nonrenewal action;

(2)   That the insurer has made a good faith effort to obtain replacement reinsurance but was unable to do so because of the unavailability or unaffordability of replacement reinsurance;

(3)   Identifying the category of risks, the total number of risks written by the company in that category, and the number of risks intended to be cancelled or not renewed;

(4)   Identifying the total amount of the insurer's net retention for the risks intended to be cancelled or not renewed;

(5)   Identifying the total amount of risk ceded to each reinsurer and the portion of that total that is no longer available;

(6)   Explaining how the loss of or reduction in reinsurance affects the insurer's risks throughout the kind of insurance proposed for cancellation or nonrenewal;

(7) Explaining why cancellation or nonrenewal is necessary to cure the loss of or reduction in reinsurance; and

(8) Explaining how the cancellations or nonrenewals, if approved, will be implemented and the steps that will be taken to ensure that the cancellation or nonrenewal decisions will not be applied in an arbitrary, capricious, or unfairly discriminatory manner. (1985 (Reg. Sess., 1986), c. 1027, s. 14.)

§ 58-41-35. Repealed by Session Laws 1999-219, s. 9.

§ 58-41-40. No liability for statements or communications made in good faith; prior notice to agents or brokers.

(a) There is no liability on the part of and no cause of action for defamation or invasion of privacy arises against any insurer or its authorized representatives, agents, or employees, or any licensed insurance agent or broker, for any communication or statement made, unless shown to have been made in bad faith with malice, in any of the following:

(1) A written notice of cancellation under G.S. 58-41-15 or of nonrenewal under G.S. 58-41-20, specifying the reasons for cancellation.

(2) Communications providing information pertaining to the cancellation or nonrenewal.

(3) Evidence submitted at any court proceeding, administrative hearing, or informal inquiry in which the cancellation or nonrenewal is an issue.

(b) With respect to the notices that must be given or mailed to agents or brokers under G.S. 58-41-15, 58-41-20, and 58-41-25, the insurer may give or mail that notice at the same time or prior to giving or mailing the notice to the insured. (1985 (Reg. Sess., 1986), c. 1027, s. 14; 1987 (Reg. Sess., 1988), c. 975, s. 31; 1999-219, s. 9.1.)

§ 58-41-45. Termination of writing kind of insurance.

(a) Except as provided in G.S. 58-41-30, no insurer may terminate, by nonrenewals, an entire book of business of any kind of insurance without 60 days prior written notice to the Commissioner; unless the Commissioner determines that continuation of the line of business would impair the solvency of the insurer or unless the Commissioner determines that such termination is effected under a plan that minimizes disruption in the marketplace or that makes provisions for alternative coverage at comparable rates and terms.

(b) Except as provided in G.S. 58-41-30, in-term cancellation by an insurer of an entire book of business of any kind of insurance is presumed to be unfair, inequitable, and contrary to the public interest, unless the Commissioner determines that continuation of the line of business would impair the solvency of the insurer or unless the Commissioner determines that such termination is effected under a plan that minimizes disruption in the marketplace or that makes provisions for alternative coverage at comparable rates and terms. (1985 (Reg. Sess., 1986), c. 1027, s. 14.)

§ 58-41-50. Policy form and rate filings; punitive damages; data required to support filings.

(a) With the exception of inland marine insurance that is not written according to manual rates and rating plans, all policy forms must be filed with and either approved by the Commissioner or 90 days have elapsed and he has not disapproved the form before they may be used in this State. With respect to liability insurance policy forms, an insurer may exclude or limit coverage for punitive damages awarded against its insured.

(b) With the exception of inland marine insurance that is not written according to manual rates and rating plans, all rates or prospective loss cost multipliers by licensed fire and casualty companies or their designated statistical organizations must be filed with the Commissioner at least 60 days before they may be used in this State. Any filing may become effective on a date earlier than that specified in this subsection upon agreement between the Commissioner and the filer.

(c) A filing that does not include the statistical and rating information required by subsections (d) and (e) of this section is not a proper filing, and will be returned to the filing insurer or organization. The filer may then remedy the defects in the filing. An otherwise defective filing thus remedied shall be deemed to be a proper filing, except that all periods of time specified in this Article will run from the date the Commissioner receives additional or amended documents necessary to remedy all material defects in the filing.

(d) The following information must be included in each policy form, rule, and rate filing:

(1) A detailed list of the rates, rules, and policy forms filed, accompanied by a list of those superseded; and

(2) A detailed description, properly referenced, of all changes in policy forms, rules, and rates, including the effect of each change.

(e) Each policy form, rule, and rate filing that is based on statistical data must be accompanied by the following properly identified information:

(1) North Carolina earned premiums at the actual and current rate level; losses and loss adjustment expenses, each on paid and incurred bases without trending or other modification for the experience period, including the loss ratio anticipated at the time the rates were promulgated for the experience period;

(2) Credibility factor development and application;

(3) Loss development factor derivation and application on both paid and incurred bases and in both numbers and dollars of claims;

(4) Trending factor development and application;

(5) Changes in premium base resulting from rating exposure trends;

(6) Limiting factor development and application;

(7) Overhead expense development and application of commission and brokerage, other acquisition expenses, general expenses, taxes, licenses, and fees;

(8) Percent rate change;

(9) Final proposed rates;

(10) Investment earnings, consisting of investment income and realized plus unrealized capital gains, from loss, loss expense, and unearned premium reserves;

(11) Identification of applicable statistical plans and programs and a certification of compliance with them;

(12) Investment earnings on capital and surplus;

(13) Level of capital and surplus needed to support premium writings without endangering the solvency of the company or companies involved; and

(14) Such other information that may be required by any rule adopted by the Commissioner.

Provided, however, that no filing may be returned or disapproved on the grounds that such information has not been furnished if the filer has not been required to collect such information pursuant to statistical plans or programs or to report such information to statistical agents, except where the Commissioner has given reasonable prior notice to the filer to begin collecting and reporting such information or except when the information is readily available to the filer.

(f) It is unlawful for an insurer to charge or collect, or attempt to charge or collect, any premium for insurance except in accordance with filings made with the Commissioner under this section and Article 40 of this Chapter.

(g) An insurer subject to this Article may develop and use an individual form or rate as a result of the uniqueness of a particular risk. The form or rate shall be developed, filed, and used in accordance with rules adopted by the Commissioner. (1985 (Reg. Sess., 1986), c. 1027, s. 14; 1987, c. 441, ss. 7, 9, 10; 1991, c. 644, s. 4; 1995, c. 193, s. 37; 2005-210, s. 20.)

§ 58-41-55. Penalties; restitution.

In addition to criminal penalties for acts declared unlawful by this Article, any violation of this Article subjects an insurer to revocation or suspension of its license, or monetary penalties or payment of restitution as provided in G.S. 58-2-70. (1985 (Reg. Sess., 1986), c. 1027, s. 14; 1999-132, s. 9.1.)

Article 42.

Mandatory or Voluntary Risk Sharing Plans.

§ 58-42-1. Establishment of plans.

(a) If the Commissioner finds, after a hearing held in accordance with Article 3A of Chapter 150B of the General Statutes, that in all or any part of this State, any amount or kind of insurance authorized by G.S. 58-7-15(4) through G.S. 58-7-15(22) is not readily available in the voluntary market and that the public interest requires the availability of that insurance, he may either:

(1) Promulgate plans to provide insurance coverage for any risks in this State that are, based on reasonable underwriting standards, entitled to obtain but are otherwise unable to obtain coverage; or

(2) Call upon insurers to prepare plans for his approval.

(b) Consistent with G.S. 58-42-5(a)(2), the Commissioner shall at least annually reevaluate a plan promulgated pursuant to this section and shall terminate the plan upon determining that the insurance coverage is readily available in the voluntary market or that the public interest no longer requires the operation of the plan. (1986, Ex. Sess., c. 7, s. 1; 1999-114, ss. 1, 2.)

§ 58-42-5. Purposes, contents, and operation of risk sharing plans.

(a) Each plan promulgated or prepared pursuant to G.S. 58-42-1 shall:

(1) Give consideration to:

a. The need for adequate and readily accessible coverage;

b. Optional methods of improving the market affected;

c. The inherent limitations of the insurance mechanism;

d. The need for reasonable underwriting standards; and

e. The requirement of reasonable loss prevention measures;

(2) Establish procedures that will create minimum interference with the voluntary market;

(3) Distribute the obligations imposed by the plan, and any profits or losses experienced by the plan, equitably and efficiently among the participating insurers; and

(4) Establish procedures for applicants and participants to have their grievances reviewed by an impartial body. The filing and processing of a grievance pursuant to this subdivision does not stay the requirement for participation in a plan mandated by G.S. 58-42-10.

(b) Each plan may, on behalf of its participants:

(1) Issue policies of insurance to eligible applicants;

(2) Underwrite, adjust, and pay losses on insurance issued by the plan;

(3) Appoint a service company or companies to perform the functions enumerated in this subsection; and

(4) Obtain reinsurance for any part or all of its risks. (1986, Ex. Sess., c. 7, s. 1; 1999-114, s. 1.)

§ 58-42-10. Persons required to participate.

(a) Each plan shall require participation:

(1) By all insurers licensed in this State to write the kinds of insurance covered by the specific plan;

(2) By all agents licensed to represent those insurers for that kind of insurance; and

(3) By every statistical organization that makes rates for that kind of insurance.

(b) The Commissioner shall exclude from each plan any person if participation would impair the solvency of that person. (1986, Ex. Sess., c. 7, s. 1; 1999-114, s. 1; 2005-210, s. 21.)

§ 58-42-15. Voluntary participation.

Each plan may provide for participation by:

(1) Insurers that are not required to participate by G.S. 58-42-10;

(2) Eligible surplus lines insurers as defined in G.S. 58-21-10(3); or

(3) Reinsurers approved by the Commissioner. (1986, Ex. Sess., c. 7, s. 1; 1999-114, s. 1.)

§ 58-42-20. Classification and rates.

Each plan shall provide for:

(1) The method of classifying risks;

(2) The making and filing of rates that are not excessive, inadequate, or unfairly discriminatory and that are calculated on an actuarially sound basis and policy forms applicable to the various risks insured by the plan;

(3) The adjusting and processing of claims;

(4) The commission rates to be paid to agents or brokers for coverages written by the plan; and

(5) Any other insurance or investment functions that are necessary for the purpose of providing adequate and readily accessible coverage. (1986, Ex. Sess., c. 7, s. 1; 1999-114, s. 1.)

§ 58-42-25. Basis for participation.

Each plan shall specify the basis for participation by insurers, agents, statistical organizations, and other participants and shall specify the conditions under which risks shall be accepted and underwritten by the plan. (1986, Ex. Sess., c. 7, s. 1; 1999-114, s. 1; 2005-210, s. 22.)

§ 58-42-30. Duty to provide information.

Every participating insurer and agent shall provide to any person seeking the insurance available in each plan, information about the services prescribed in the plan, including full information on the requirements and procedures for obtaining insurance under the plan, whenever the insurance is not readily available in the voluntary market. (1986, Ex. Sess., c. 7, s. 1; 1999-114, s. 1.)

§ 58-42-35. Provision of marketing facilities.

If the Commissioner finds that the lack of participating insurers or agents in a geographic area makes the functioning of a plan difficult, he may order that the plan appoint agents on such terms as he designates or that the plan take other appropriate steps to guarantee that service is available. (1986, Ex. Sess., c. 7, s. 1; 1999-114, s. 1.)

§ 58-42-40. Voluntary risk sharing plans.

Insurers doing business within this State or reinsurers approved by the Commissioner may prepare voluntary plans that will provide any specific amount or kind of insurance or component thereof for all or any part of this State in which that insurance is not readily available in the voluntary market and in which the public interest requires the availability of the coverage. These plans shall be submitted to the Commissioner and, if approved by him, may be put into operation. (1986, Ex. Sess., c. 7, s. 1; 1999-114, s. 1.)

§ 58-42-45. Article subject to Administrative Procedure Act; legislative oversight of plans.

(a) The provisions of Chapter 150B of the General Statutes shall apply to this Article.

(b) At the same time the Commissioner issues a notice of hearing under G.S. 150B-38, the Commissioner shall provide copies of the notice to the Joint Regulatory Reform Committee and to the Joint Legislative Commission on Governmental Operations. The Commissioner shall provide the Committee and Commission with copies of any plan promulgated by or approved by the Commissioner under G.S. 58-42-1(1) or (2). (1986, Ex. Sess., c. 7, s. 1; 1999-114, s. 1; 2000-140, s. 15; 2011-291, s. 2.5.)

§ 58-42-50. Immunity of Commissioner and plan participants.

There shall be no liability on the part of, and no cause of action shall arise against the Commissioner, his representatives, or any plan, its participants, or its employee for any good faith action taken by them in the performance of their powers and duties in creating any plan pursuant to this Article. (1986, Ex. Sess., c. 7, s. 1; 1999-114, s. 1.)

§ 58-42-55: Repealed by Session Laws 2001-122, s. 1.

Article 43

General Regulations of Business-Fire Insurance.

§ 58-43-1. Performance of contracts as to devices not prohibited.

Nothing contained in Articles 1 through 64 of this Chapter shall be construed as prohibiting the performance of any contract hereafter made for the introduction or installation of automatic sprinklers or other betterments or improvements for reducing the risk by fire or water on any property located in this State, and containing provisions for obtaining insurance against loss or damage by fire or water, for a specified time at a fixed rate; provided, every policy issued under such contract shall be as provided by law. (1929, c. 145, s. 1.)

§ 58-43-5. Limitation as to amount and term; indemnity contracts for difference in actual value and cost of replacement; functional replacement.

No insurance company or agent shall knowingly issue any fire insurance policy upon property within this State for an amount which, together with any existing insurance thereon, exceeds the fair value of the property, nor for a longer term than seven years: Provided, any fire insurance company authorized to transact business in this State may, by appropriate riders or endorsements or otherwise, provide insurance indemnifying the insured for the difference between the actual value of the insured property at the time any loss or damage occurs, and the amount actually expended to repair, rebuild or replace on the premises described in the policy, or some other location within the State of North Carolina with new materials of like size, kind and quality, property that has been damaged or destroyed by fire or other perils insured against: Provided further, that the Commissioner may approve forms that permit functional replacement by the insurance company, at the insured's option. Functional replacement means to replace the property with property that performs the same function when replacement with materials of like size, kind, and quality is not possible, necessary, or less costly than obsolete, antique, or custom construction materials and methods. Forms and rating plans may also provide for credits when functional replacement cost coverage is provided. Policies issued in violation of this section are binding upon the company issuing them, but the company is liable for the forfeitures by law prescribed for such violation. (1899, c. 54, ss. 39, 99; 1903, c. 438, s. 10; Rev., s. 4755; C.S., s. 6418; 1949, c. 295, s. 1; 1991, c. 644, s. 5.)

§ 58-43-10. Limit of liability on total loss.

Subject to the provisions of G.S. 58-43-5, when buildings insured against loss by fire and situated within the State are totally destroyed by fire, the company is not liable beyond the actual cash value of the insured property at the time of the loss or damage; and if it appears that the insured has paid a premium on a sum in excess of the actual value, he shall be reimbursed the proportionate excess of premium paid on the difference between the amount named in the policy and the ascertained values, with interest at six per centum (6%) per annum from the date of issue. (1899, c. 54, s. 40; Rev., s. 4756; C.S., s. 6419; 1949, c. 295, s. 2.)

§ 58-43-15. Policies for the benefit of mortgagees.

Where by an agreement with the insured, or by the terms of a fire insurance policy taken out by a mortgagor, the whole or any part of the loss thereon is payable to a mortgagee of the property for his benefit, the company shall, upon satisfactory proof of the rights and title of the parties, in accordance with such terms or agreement, pay all mortgagees protected by such policy in the order of their priority of claim, as their claims appear, not beyond the amount for which the company is liable, and such payments are, to the extent thereof, payment and satisfaction of the liabilities of the company under the policy. Any payment due by the insuring company to mortgagees or loss payees under the terms of the policy shall be made within 90 days of the loss or within 60 days of the filing of proof of loss, whichever is the longer period; provided, the payment of or settlement of the claim of the mortgagee or loss payee under the policy shall in no way constitute an admission of liability as to the insured and the fact of such payment or settlement shall be inadmissible in any action at law. (1899, c. 54, s. 41; Rev., s. 4757; C.S., s. 6420; 1969, c. 1077, s. 1.)

§ 58-43-20: Repealed by Session Laws 1995 (Regular Session, 1996), c. 752, s. 1.

§ 58-43-25. Limitation of fire insurance risks.

No insurer authorized to do in this State the business of fire insurance shall expose itself to any loss on any one fire risk, whether located in this State or elsewhere, in an amount exceeding ten percent (10%) of its surplus to policyholders, except that in the case of risks adequately protected by automatic sprinklers or risks principally of noncombustible construction and occupancy such insurer may expose itself to any loss on any one risk in an amount not exceeding twenty-five percent (25%) of the sum of (i) its unearned premium reserve and (ii) its surplus to policyholders. Any risk or portion of any risk which shall have been reinsured shall be deducted in determining the limitation of risk prescribed in this section. (1945, c. 378.)

§ 58-43-30. Agreements restricting agent's commission; penalty.

It is unlawful for any insurance company doing the business of insurance as defined in subdivisions (3) to (22), inclusive, of G.S. 58-7-15 and employing an agent representing another such company, either directly or through any organization or association, to enter into, make or maintain any stipulation or agreement in anywise limiting the compensation such agent may receive from any such other company or forbidding or prohibiting reinsurance of the risks of any such domestic company in whole or in part by any other company holding membership in or cooperating with such organization or association. The penalty for any violation of this section shall be a fine of not less than one thousand dollars ($1,000) nor more than five thousand dollars ($5,000), and the forfeiture of license to do business in this State for a period of 12 months following conviction. (1905, c. 424; Rev., ss. 3491, 4768; 1915, c. 166, ss. 2, 3; C.S., s. 6432; 1945, c. 458; 1985, c. 666, s. 26.)

§ 58-43-35. Punishment for issuing fire policies contrary to law.

Any insurance company or agent who makes, issues, or delivers a policy of fire insurance in willful violation of the provisions of Articles 1 through 64 of this Chapter that prohibit a domestic insurance company from issuing policies before obtaining a license from the Commissioner; or that prohibit the issuing of a fire insurance policy for more than the fair value of the property or for a longer term than seven years; or that prohibit stipulations in insurance contracts restricting the jurisdiction of courts, or limiting the time within which an action may be brought to less than one year after the cause of action accrues or to less than six months after a nonsuit by the plaintiff, shall be guilty of a Class 3 misdemeanor and shall, upon conviction, be punished only by a fine of not less than one thousand dollars ($1,000) nor more than five thousand dollars ($5,000); but the policy shall be binding upon the company issuing it. (1899, c.

54, s. 99; 1903, c. 438, s. 10; Rev., s. 4832; C.S., s. 6433; 1985, c. 666, s. 27; 1993, c. 539, s. 466; 1994, Ex. Sess., c. 24, s. 14(c); 1999-132, s. 9.2.)

§ 58-43-40: Expired.

Article 44.

Property Insurance Policies.

Part 1. Policy Provisions.

§ 58-44-1. Terms and conditions must be set out in policy.

In all insurance against loss by fire the conditions of insurance must be stated in full, and the rules and bylaws of the company are not a warranty or a part of the contract, except as incorporated in full into the policy. (1899, c. 54, s. 42; Rev., s. 4758; C.S., s. 6434; 2006-145, s. 1.)

§ 58-44-5. Items to be expressed in policies.

Upon request there shall be printed, stamped, or written on each fire policy issued in this State the basis rate, deficiency charge, the credit for improvements, and the rate at which written, and whenever a rate is made or changed on any property situated in this State upon request a full statement thereof showing in detail the basis rate, deficiency charges and credits, as well as rate proposed to be made, shall be delivered to the owner or his representative having the insurance on the property in charge, by the company, association, their agent or representative. (1915, c. 109, s. 3; C.S., s. 6435; 1925, c. 70, s. 3; 1945, c. 378.)

§ 58-44-10: Repealed by Session Laws 1995, c. 517, s. 27.

§ 58-44-15: Repealed by Session Laws 2009-171, s. 6, effective January 1, 2010, and applicable to fire insurance policies issued or renewed on and after that date.

§ 58-44-16. Fire insurance policies; standard fire insurance policy provisions.

(a) The provisions of a fire insurance policy, as set forth in subsection (f) of this section, shall be known and designated as the "standard fire insurance policy."

(b) With the exception of policies covering (i) automobile fire, theft, comprehensive, and collision or (ii) marine and inland marine insurance, no fire insurance policy shall be made, issued, or delivered by any insurer or by any agent or representative of the insurer on any property in this State, unless it conforms in substance with all of the provisions, stipulations, agreements, and conditions in subsection (f) of this section.

(c) There shall be printed at the head of the policy the name of the insurer or insurers issuing the policy; the location of the home office of the insurer or insurers; a statement whether the insurer or insurers are stock or mutual corporations or are reciprocal insurers. This section does not limit an insurer to the use of any particular size or manner of folding the paper upon which the policy is printed; provided, however, that any insurer organized under special charter provisions may so indicate upon its policy and add a statement of the plan under which it operates in this State.

(d) The standard fire insurance policy need not be used for effecting reinsurance between insurers.

(e) The provisions of the standard fire policy are stated in this section and shall be incorporated in fire insurance policies subject to this section. If any conditions of this section are construed to be more liberal than any other policy conditions relating to the perils of fire, lightning, or removal, the provisions of this section shall apply.

(f) The following subdivisions comprise all of the provisions, stipulations, agreements, and conditions of the standard fire insurance policy:

(1) General provisions. - In consideration of the provisions, stipulations, agreements, and conditions in this policy or added to this policy, and of the premium specified in the declarations or in endorsements made a part of this policy, this insurer, for the term of years specified in the declarations from inception date shown in the declarations at 12:01 A.M. to expiration date shown in the declarations at 12:01 A.M. at the location of the property covered, to an amount not exceeding the limit of liability specified in the declarations, does insure the insured named in the declarations and legal representatives to the extent of the actual cash value of the property at the time of loss but not exceeding the amount that it would cost to repair or replace the property with material of like kind and quality within a reasonable time after the loss, without allowance for any increased cost of repair or reconstruction by reason of any ordinance or law regulating construction or repair and without compensation for loss resulting from interruption of business or manufacture, nor in any event for more than the interest of the insured against all direct loss by fire, lightning, and other perils insured against in this policy, including removal from premises endangered by the perils insured against in this policy, except as hereinafter provided, to the property described in the declarations while located or contained as described in this policy, or pro rata for five days at each proper place to which any of the property shall necessarily be removed for preservation from the perils insured against in this policy but not elsewhere. Assignment of this policy shall not be valid except with the written consent of this insurer. This policy is made and accepted subject to the provisions, stipulations, agreements, and conditions in this section, which are hereby made a part of this policy, together with such other provisions, stipulations, agreements, and conditions that may be added to this policy as provided in this policy.

(2) Concealment or fraud. - This entire policy shall be void if, whether before or after a loss, the insured has willfully concealed or misrepresented any material fact or circumstance concerning this insurance or the subject of this insurance, or the interest of the insured in the subject of this insurance, or in the case of any fraud or false swearing by the insured relating the subject of this insurance.

(3) Uninsurable and excepted property. - This policy shall not cover accounts, bills, currency, deeds, evidences of debt, money, or securities; nor, unless specifically named in this policy in writing, bullion or manuscripts.

(4)   Perils not included. - This insurer shall not be liable for loss by fire or other perils insured against in this policy caused, directly or indirectly, by enemy attack by armed forces, including action taken by military, naval, or air forces in resisting an actual or an immediately impending enemy attack; invasion; insurrection; rebellion; revolution; civil war; usurped power; order of any civil authority except acts of destruction at the time of and for the purpose of preventing the spread of fire, provided that the fire did not originate from any of the perils excluded by this policy; neglect of the insured to use all reasonable means to save and preserve the property at and after a loss, or when the property is endangered by fire in neighboring premises; or for loss by theft.

(5)   Other insurance. - Other insurance may be prohibited or the amount of insurance may be limited by endorsement attached to this policy.

(6)   Conditions suspending or restricting insurance. - Unless otherwise provided in writing added to this policy, this insurer shall not be liable for loss occurring:

a.   While the hazard is increased by any means within the control or knowledge of the insured;

b.   While a described building, whether intended for occupancy by owner or tenant, is vacant or unoccupied beyond a period of 60 consecutive days; or

c.   As a result of explosion or riot, unless fire ensues, and in that event for loss by fire only.

(7)   Other perils or subjects. - Any other peril to be insured against or subject of insurance to be covered in this policy shall be by endorsement in writing on this policy or added to this policy.

(8)   Added provisions. - The extent of the application of insurance under this policy and of the contribution to be made by this insurer in case of loss, and any other provision or agreement not inconsistent with the provisions of this policy, may be provided for in writing added to this policy; provided, however, no provision may be waived except such as by the terms of this policy is subject to change.

(9)   Waiver provisions. - No permission affecting this insurance shall exist, or waiver of any provision be valid, unless granted in this policy or expressed in writing added to this policy. No provision, stipulation, or forfeiture shall be held

to be waived by any requirement or proceeding on the part of this insurer relating to appraisal or to any examination provided for in this policy.

(10) Cancellation of policy. - This policy shall be cancelled at any time at the request of the insured, in which case this insurer shall, upon demand and surrender of this policy, refund the excess of paid premium above any short rates for the expired time. This policy may be cancelled at any time by this insurer by giving to the insured a five days' written notice of cancellation with or without tender of the excess of paid premium above the pro rata premium for the expired time, which excess, if not tendered, shall be refunded on demand. Notice of cancellation shall state that said excess premium (if not tendered) will be refunded on demand.

(11) Mortgagee interests and obligations. - If loss is made payable, in whole or in part, to a designated mortgagee not named in this policy as the insured, such interest in this policy may be cancelled by giving to such a mortgagee a ten days' written notice of cancellation. If the insured fails to render proof of loss, the mortgagee, upon notice, shall render proof of loss as specified in this policy within 60 days thereafter and shall be subject to the provisions of this policy relating to appraisal and time of payment and of bringing suit. If this insurer claims that no liability existed as to the mortgagor or owner, it shall, to the extent of payment of loss to the mortgagee, be subrogated to all the mortgagee's rights of recovery, but without impairing the mortgagee's right to sue; or this insurer may pay off the mortgage debt and require an assignment of that debt and of the mortgage. Other provisions relating to the interests and obligations of the mortgagee may be added to this policy by agreement in writing.

(12) Pro rata liability. - This insurer shall not be liable for a greater proportion of any loss than the amount insured by this policy bears to all insurance covering the property against the peril involved, whether collectible or not.

(13) Requirements in case loss occurs. - The insured shall give immediate written notice to this insurer of any loss, protect the property from further damage, forthwith separate the damaged and undamaged personal property, put it in the best possible order, and furnish a complete inventory of the destroyed, damaged, and undamaged property, showing in detail quantities, costs, actual cash value, and amount of loss claimed. Within 60 days after the loss, unless that time is extended in writing by this insurer, the insured shall render to this insurer a proof of loss, signed and sworn to by the insured, stating the knowledge and belief of the insured as to the following: the time and origin of the loss, the interest of the insured and of all others in the property, the actual

cash value of each item of the property and the amount of loss to the property, all encumbrances on the property, all other contracts of insurance, whether valid or not, covering any of the property, any changes in the title, use, occupation, location, possession, or exposures of the property since the issuing of this policy, by whom and for what purpose any building described in this policy and the several parts of the building were occupied at the time of loss and whether or not it then stood on leased ground, and shall furnish a copy of all the descriptions and schedules in all policies and, if required, verified plans and specifications of any building, fixtures, or machinery destroyed or damaged. The insured, as often as may be reasonably required, shall exhibit to any person designated by this insurer all that remains of any property described in this policy, and submit to examinations under oath by any person named by this insurer, and subscribe the same; and, as often as may be reasonably required, shall produce for examination all books of account, bills, invoices, and other vouchers, or certified copies of them if originals are lost, at such reasonable time and place as may be designated by this insurer or its representative, and shall permit extracts and copies of them to be made.

(14)   Appraisal. - If the insured and this insurer fail to agree as to the actual cash value or the amount of loss, then, on the written demand of either, each shall select a competent and disinterested appraiser and notify the other of the appraiser selected within 20 days after the demand. The appraisers shall first select a competent and disinterested umpire; and failing for 15 days to agree upon a competent and disinterested umpire, on the request of the insured or this insurer, a competent and disinterested umpire shall be selected by a judge of a court of record in the state in which the property covered is located. The appraisers shall then appraise the loss, stating separately actual cash value and loss to each item; and, failing to agree, shall submit only their differences to the umpire. An award in writing, so itemized, of any two when filed with this insurer shall determine the amount of actual cash value and loss. Each appraiser shall be paid by the party selecting him and the expenses of appraisal and umpire shall be paid by the parties equally.

(15)   Company's options. - It shall be optional with this insurer to take all, or any part, of the property at the agreed or appraised value and also to repair, rebuild, or replace the property destroyed or damaged with other of like kind and quality within a reasonable time, on giving notice of its intention so to do within 30 days after the receipt of the proof of loss required in this policy.

(16)   Abandonment. - There can be no abandonment to this insurer of any property.

(17) When loss payable. - The amount of loss for which this insurer may be liable shall be payable 60 days after proof of loss, as provided in this policy, is received by this insurer and ascertainment of the loss is made either by written agreement between the insured and this insurer or by the filing with this insurer of an award as provided in this policy.

(18) Suit. - No suit or action on this policy for the recovery of any claim shall be sustainable in any court of law unless all the requirements of this policy have been complied with and unless commenced within three years after inception of the loss.

(19) Subrogation. - This insurer may require from the insured an assignment of all rights of recovery against a party for loss to the extent that payment therefor is made by this insurer. (2009-171, s. 1.)

§ 58-44-20. Standard policy; permissible variations.

With the exception of policies covering (i) automobile fire, theft, comprehensive, and collision or (ii) marine and inland marine insurance, no fire insurance company shall issue fire insurance policies on property in this State other than those containing the provisions set forth in G.S. 58-44-16 except as follows:

(1) A company may print on or in its policies the date of incorporation, the amount of its paid-up capital stock, the names of its officers, and to the words at the top of the back of said policy, "Standard Fire Insurance Policy for" may be added after or before the words "North Carolina" the names of any states or political jurisdiction in which the said policy form may be standard when the policy is used.

(2) A company may print in its policies or use in its policies written or printed forms of description and specification of the property insured.

(3) A company may write or print upon the margin or across the face of a policy, in unused spaces or upon separate slips or riders to be attached thereto, provisions adding to or modifying those contained in the standard form, and all such slips, riders, and provisions must be signed by an officer or agent of the company so using them. Provided, however, such provisions shall not have the effect of making the provisions of the standard policy form more restrictive

except for such restrictions as are provided for in the charter or bylaws of a domestic mutual fire insurance company doing business in no more than three adjacent counties of the State and chiefly engaged in writing policies of insurance on rural properties upon an assessment or nonpremium basis, provided all such restrictions contained in the charter and bylaws of such domestic mutual fire insurance company shall be actually included within the printed terms of the policy contract so affected as a condition precedent to their being effective and binding on any policyholder. The iron safe or any similar clause requiring the taking of inventories, the keeping of books and producing the same in the adjustment of any loss, shall not be used or operative in the settlement of losses on buildings, furniture and fixtures, or any property not subject to any change in bulk and value.

(4) Binders or other contracts for temporary insurance may be made, orally or in writing, for a period which shall not exceed 60 days, and shall be deemed to include all the terms of such standard fire insurance policy and all such applicable endorsements, approved by the Commissioner, as may be designated in such contract of temporary insurance; except that the cancellation clause of such standard fire insurance policy, and the clause thereof specifying the hour of the day at which the insurance shall commence, may be superseded by the express terms of such contract of temporary insurance.

(5) Two or more companies authorized to do in this State the business of fire insurance, may, with the approval of the Commissioner, issue a combination standard form of fire insurance policy which shall contain the following provisions:

a. A provision substantially to the effect that the insurers executing such policy shall be severally liable for the full amount of any loss or damage, according to the terms of the policy, or for specified percentages or amounts thereof, aggregating the full amount of such insurance under such policy.

b. A provision substantially to the effect that service of process, or of any notice or proof of loss required by such policy, upon any of the companies executing such policy, shall be deemed to be service upon all such insurers.

(6) Appropriate forms of supplemental contract or contracts or extended coverage endorsements and other endorsements whereby the interest in the property described in such policy shall be insured against one or more of the perils which the company is empowered to assume, in addition to the perils covered by said standard fire insurance policy may be approved by the

Commissioner, and their use in connection with a standard fire insurance policy may be authorized by him. In his discretion the Commissioner may authorize the printing of such supplemental contract or contracts or extended coverage endorsements and other endorsements in the substance of the form of the standard fire insurance policy. The first page of the policy may in form approved by the Commissioner be arranged to provide space for listing of amounts of insurance, rates and premiums, description of construction, occupancy and location of property covered for the basic coverages insured under the standard form of policy and for additional coverages or perils insured under endorsements attached or printed therein, and such other data as may be conveniently included for duplication on daily reports for office records.

(7) A company may print on or in its policy, with the approval of the Commissioner, any provisions which it is required by law to insert in its policies not in conflict with the substance of provisions of such standard form. Such provisions shall be printed apart from the other provisions, agreements, or conditions of the policy, under a separate title, as follows: "Provisions Required by Law to Be Inserted in This Policy." (1899, c. 54, s. 43; 1901, c. 391, s. 4; Rev., s. 4759; 1907, c. 800, s. 1; 1915, c. 109, s. 10; C.S., s. 6436; 1925, c. 70, s. 5; 1945, c. 378; 1949, c. 418; 1951, c. 767; c. 781, s. 5; 1955, c. 807, s. 3; 1979, c. 755, ss. 5-7; 2009-171, s. 4.)

§ 58-44-25. Optional provisions as to loss or damage from nuclear reaction, nuclear radiation or radioactive contamination.

Insurers issuing the standard fire insurance policy pursuant to G.S. 58-44-16, or any permissible variation of that policy, and policies issued pursuant to G.S. 58-44-20 and Article 36 of this Chapter, are authorized to affix to the policy or include in the policy a written statement that the policy does not cover loss or damage caused by nuclear reaction, nuclear radiation, or radioactive contamination, all whether directly or indirectly resulting from an insured peril under the policy; provided, however, that nothing in this section shall be construed to prohibit the attachment to any such policy of an endorsement or endorsements specifically assuming coverage for loss or damage caused by nuclear reaction, nuclear radiation, or radioactive contamination. (1963, c. 1148; 1987, c. 864, s. 7; 2009-171, s. 3.)

§ 58-44-30. Notice by insured or agent as to increase of hazard, unoccupancy and other insurance.

If notice in writing signed by the insured, or his agent, is given before loss or damage by any peril insured against under the standard fire insurance policy to the agent of the company of any fact or condition stated in G.S. 58-44-16, it is equivalent to an agreement in writing added to the policy and has the force of the agreement in writing referred to in the standard fire insurance policy with respect to the liability of the company and the waiver; but this notice does not affect the right of the company to cancel the policy as stipulated in the policy. (1899, c. 54, s. 43; Rev., s. 4761; 1907, c. 578, s. 1; 1915, c. 109, s. 11; C.S., s. 6438; 1929, c. 60, s. 1; 1945, c. 378; 2009-171, s. 2.)

§ 58-44-35. Judge to select umpire.

Any resident judge of the superior court of the district in which the property insured is located is designated as the judge of the court of record to select the umpire referred to in the standard form of policy as set forth in G.S. 58-44-16(f)(14). The judge may not select the umpire until all of the following conditions have been met:

(1)   Proof of notice to all parties of record has been filed with the court, and at least 15 days have passed since the filing of the proof of notice.

(2)   Upon the request of any party of record, the judge has conducted a hearing. The hearing by the judge shall be governed by the practice for hearings in other civil actions before a judge without a jury and shall be limited to the issue of umpire selection. (1945, c. 378; 2013-199, s. 23.)

§ 58-44-40. Effect of failure to give notice of encumbrance.

No policy of insurance issued upon any property shall be held void because of the failure to give notice to the company of a mortgage or deed of trust existing thereon or thereafter placed thereon, except during the life of the mortgage or deed of trust. (1915, c. 109, s. 4; C.S., s. 6440.)

§ 58-44-45. Policy issued to husband or wife on joint property.

Any policy of fire insurance issued to husband or wife, on buildings and household furniture owned by the husband and wife, either by entirety, in common, or jointly, either name of one of the parties in interest named as the insured or beneficiary therein, shall be sufficient and the policy shall not be void for failure to disclose the interest of the other, unless it appears that in the procuring of the issuance of such policy, fraudulent means or methods were used by the insured or owner thereof. (1945, c. 378.)

§ 58-44-50. Bar to defense of failure to render timely proof of loss.

In any action brought to enforce an insurance policy subject to the provisions of this Article, any party claiming benefit under the policy may reply to the pleading of any other party against whom liability is sought which asserts as a defense, the failure to render timely proof of loss as required by the terms of the policy that such failure was for good cause and that the failure to render timely proof of loss has not substantially harmed the party against whom liability is sought in his ability to defend. The issues raised by such reply shall be determined by the jury if jury trial has been demanded. (1973, c. 1391.)

§ 58-44-55. Farmowners' and other property policies; ice, snow, or sleet damage.

Under any policy of farmowners' or other property insurance that insures against all direct loss by fire, lightning, or other perils that may be delivered or issued for delivery in this State with respect to any farm dwellings, appurtenant private structures, barns, or other farm buildings or farm structures located in this State, coverage shall be available for inclusion therein or supplemental thereto to include direct loss caused by weight of ice, snow, or sleet that results in physical damage to such buildings or structures, and shall be offered to all insureds requesting these policies. (1981, c. 550, s. 1.)

§ 58-44-60. Notice to property insurance policyholder about flood, earthquake, mudslide, mudflow, landslide, and windstorm or hail insurance coverage.

(a) Every insurer that sells residential or commercial property insurance policies that do not provide coverage for the perils of flood, earthquake, mudslide, mudflow, landslide, or windstorm or hail shall, upon the issuance and renewal of each policy, identify to the policyholder which of these perils are not covered under the policy. The insurer shall print the following warning, citing which peril is not covered, in Times New Roman 16-point font or other equivalent font and include it in the policy on a separate page immediately before the declarations page:

"WARNING: THIS PROPERTY INSURANCE POLICY DOES NOT PROTECT YOU AGAINST LOSSES FROM [FLOODS], [EARTHQUAKES], [MUDSLIDES], [MUDFLOWS], [LANDSLIDES], [WINDSTORM OR HAIL]. YOU SHOULD CONTACT YOUR INSURANCE COMPANY OR AGENT TO DISCUSS YOUR OPTIONS FOR OBTAINING COVERAGE FOR THESE LOSSES. THIS IS NOT A COMPLETE LISTING OF ALL OF THE CAUSES OF LOSSES NOT COVERED UNDER YOUR POLICY. YOU SHOULD READ YOUR ENTIRE POLICY TO UNDERSTAND WHAT IS COVERED AND WHAT IS NOT COVERED."

(b) As used in this section, "insurer" includes an entity that sells property insurance under Articles 21, 45, or 46 of this Chapter. (2006-145, s. 2; 2007-300, s. 5; 2012-162, s. 5.)

Part 2. Mediation of Emergency or Disaster-Related Property Insurance Claims.

§ 58-44-70. Purpose and scope.

(a) This Part provides for a nonadversarial alternative dispute resolution procedure for a facilitated claim resolution conference prompted by the critical need for effective, fair, and timely handling of insurance claims arising out of damages to residential property as the result of an event for which there is a state of disaster declared within 60 days of the event. This Part applies only (i) if a state of disaster has been proclaimed for the State or for an area within the State by the Governor or by a resolution of the General Assembly under G.S. 166A-19.21 or (ii) if the President of the United States has issued a major disaster declaration for the State or for an area within the State under the

Robert T. Stafford Disaster Relief and Emergency Assistance Act, 42 U.S.C. § 5121, et seq., as amended; and (iii) if the Commissioner issues an order establishing the mediation procedure authorized by this Part.

(b)   The procedure authorized by this Part is available to all first-party claimants who have insurance claims resulting from damage to residential property occurring in this State. This Part does not apply to commercial insurance, motor vehicle insurance, or to liability coverage contained in property insurance policies.

(c)   The Commissioner may designate a person, either within the Department or outside of the Department, as the Administrator or other functionary to carry out any of the Commissioner's duties under this Part. (2006-145, s. 1; 2007-300, s. 1; 2012-12, s. 2(m); 2013-199, s. 22(d).)

§ 58-44-75. Definitions.

As used in this Part:

(1)   Administrator. - The Commissioner or the Commissioner's designee; and the term is used interchangeably with regard to the Commissioner's duties under this Part.

(2)   Repealed by Session Laws 2013-199, s. 22(e), effective June 26, 2013.

(3)   Disputed claim. - Any matter on which there is a dispute as to the cause of loss or amount of loss, for which the insurer has denied payment, in part or whole, with respect to claims arising from a disaster. Unless the parties agree to mediate a disputed claim involving a lesser amount, a "disputed claim" involves the insured requesting one thousand five hundred dollars ($1,500) or more to settle the dispute, or the difference between the positions of the parties is one thousand five hundred dollars ($1,500) or more. "Disputed claim" does not include a dispute with respect to which the insurer has reported allegations of fraud, based on a referral to the insurer's special investigative unit, to the Commissioner. A disputed claim does not include one in which there has been a denial of coverage for the loss because of exclusions in the policy, terms in the policy, conditions in the policy, or nonexistence of the policy at the time of the loss.

(4) Mediation. - As defined in G.S. 7A-38.1(b)(2).

(5) Mediator. - A neutral person who acts to encourage and facilitate a resolution of a claim.

(6) Party or parties. - The insured and his or her insurer, including a surplus lines insurer and the underwriting associations in Articles 45 and 46 of this Chapter, when applicable. (2006-145, s. 1; 2012-12, s. 2(n); 2013-199, s. 22(e).)

§ 58-44-80. Notification of right to mediate.

(a) Insurers shall notify their insureds in this State who have claimed damage to their residential properties as a result of a disaster of their right to mediate disputed claims. This requirement applies to all disputed claims, including instances where checks have been issued by the insurer to the insured.

(b) The insurer shall mail the notice described in subsection (a) of this section to an insured within five days after the time the insured or the Administrator notifies the insurer of a dispute regarding the insured's claim. The following apply:

(1) If the insurer has not been notified of a disputed claim before the time an insurer notifies the insured that a claim has been denied in whole or in part, the insurer shall mail a notice of the right to mediate to the insured in the same mailing as the notice of denial.

(2) The insurer is not required to send a notice of the right to mediate if a claim is denied because the amount of the claim is less than the insured's deductible.

(3) The mailing that contains the notice of the right to mediate shall include any consumer brochure on mediation developed by the Commissioner.

(4) Notification shall be in writing and shall be legible, conspicuous, and printed in at least 12-point type.

(5) The first paragraph of the notice shall contain the following statement: "The General Assembly of North Carolina has enacted a law to facilitate fair and timely handling of residential property insurance claims arising out of disasters. The law gives you the right to attend a mediation conference with your insurer in order to settle any dispute you have with your insurer about your claim. An independent mediator, who has no connection with your insurer, will be in charge of the mediation conference."

(c) The notice shall also:

(1) Include detailed instructions on how the insured is to request mediation, including name, address, and phone and fax numbers for requesting mediation through the Administrator.

(2) Include the insurer's address and phone number for requesting additional information.

(3) State that the Administrator will select the mediator. (2006-145, s. 1; 2007-300, s. 2.)

§ 58-44-85. Request for mediation.

(a) If an insured requests mediation before receipt of the notice of the right to mediate or if the date of the notice cannot be established, the insurer shall be notified by the Administrator of the existence of the dispute before the Administrator processes the insured's request for mediation. An insured must request mediation within 60 days after the denial of the claim; failure to request mediation within this time period shall only bar the right to demand mediation; it shall not prejudice any other legal right or remedy of the insured nor prohibit the insurer from voluntarily accepting the request for mediation.

(b) If an insurer receives a request for mediation, the insurer shall electronically transmit the request to the Administrator within three business days after receipt of the request. If the Department receives any requests, it shall electronically transmit those requests to the Administrator within three business days after receipt. The Administrator shall notify the insurer within 48 hours after receipt of a request that has been filed with the Department.

(c) In the insured's request for mediation, the insured shall provide the following information, if known:

(1) Name, address, and daytime telephone number of the insured and location of the property if different from the address given.

(2) The claim and policy number for the insured.

(3) A brief description of the nature of the dispute.

(4) The name of the insurer and the name, address, and phone number of the contact person for scheduling mediation.

(5) Information with respect to any other policies of insurance that may provide coverage of the insured property for named perils such as flood, earthquake, or windstorm. (2006-145, s. 1.)

§ 58-44-90. Mediation fees.

(a) The fees of the mediator and of the Administrator as established by the Commissioner shall be borne by the insurer. All other mediation costs, fees, or expenses shall be borne by the party incurring such costs, fees, or expenses unless otherwise provided in a settlement agreement.

(b) The Commissioner may establish fee schedules, through emergency rules, for fees to be paid to the Administrator, the mediator, and for timely and untimely mediation cancellations. (2006-145, s. 1.)

§ 58-44-95. Scheduling of mediation; qualification of mediator.

(a) The Administrator shall select a mediator and schedule the mediation conference.

(b) In order to be approved, a mediator must be certified by the Dispute Resolution Commission under G.S. 7A-38.2. (2006-145, s. 1; 2007-300, s. 3.)

§ 58-44-100. Conduct of the mediation conference.

(a) The Commissioner may adopt rules, in addition to the provisions of this section and that are not in conflict with G.S. 7A-38.1 or the Rules Implementing Statewide Mediated Settlement Conferences in Superior Court Civil Actions adopted by the Supreme Court of North Carolina pursuant to G.S. 7A-38.1 and G.S. 7A-38.2, for the conduct of mediation conferences under this Part. The rules adopted by the Commissioner shall include a requirement of the mediator to advise the parties of the mediation process and their rights and duties in the process.

(b) Repealed by Session Laws 2007-300, s. 4, effective October 1, 2007, and applicable to policies issued or renewed on or after that date.

(c) The mediator shall terminate the negotiations if the mediator determines that either party is unable or unwilling to participate meaningfully in the process or upon mutual agreement of the parties.

(d) Repealed by Session Laws 2007-300, s. 4, effective October 1, 2007, and applicable to policies issued or renewed on or after that date.

(e) The representative of the insurer attending the conference shall:

(1) Bring, in paper or electronic medium, a copy of the policy and the entire claims file to the conference.

(2) Know the facts and circumstances of the claim and be knowledgeable of the provisions of the policy.

(f) An insurer will be deemed to have failed to appear if the insurer's representative lacks authority to settle within the limits of the policy.

(g) The mediator shall be in charge of the conference and shall establish and describe the procedures to be followed. The mediator shall conduct the conference in accordance with the Standards of Professional Conduct for Mediators adopted by the Supreme Court of North Carolina and, where not inconsistent, with the Rules Implementing Statewide Mediated Settlement Conferences in Superior Court Civil Actions adopted by the Supreme Court of North Carolina pursuant to G.S. 7A-38.1 and G.S. 7A-38.2. The Commissioner may refer any matter regarding the conduct of any mediator to the North Carolina Dispute Resolution Commission.

(h) All statements made and documents produced at a settlement conference shall be deemed settlement negotiations in anticipation of litigation. The provisions of G.S. 7A-38.1(j), (l), and (m) apply and are incorporated into this Part by reference. If the Commissioner or an employee or designee of the Commissioner attends a settlement conference, the Commissioner, employee, or designee shall not be compelled to testify about what transpired at the settlement conference or about any other matter in connection with the settlement conference.

(i) A party may move to disqualify a mediator for good cause at any time. The request shall be directed to the Administrator if the grounds are known before the mediation conference. Good cause consists of conflict of interest between a party and the mediator, inability of the mediator to handle the conference competently, or other reasons that would reasonably be expected to impair the conference. (2006-145, s. 1; 2007-300, s. 4.)

§ 58-44-105. Post mediation.

(a) Within five days after the conclusion of the conference, the mediator shall file with the Administrator a mediator's status report, on a form prescribed by the Administrator, indicating whether or not the parties reached a settlement.

(b) Mediation is nonbinding unless all the parties specifically agree otherwise in writing.

(c) If the parties reach a settlement, the mediator shall include a copy of the settlement agreement with the status report. Within three business days after the conclusion of the conference, the insurer shall disburse the settlement funds in accordance with the terms of the settlement agreement. The insured has three business days after receipt of the settlement funds within which to notify the Commissioner and the insurer of the insured's decision to rescind the settlement agreement, as long as the insured has not received the settlement funds by electronic means or has not cashed or deposited any check or draft disbursed to the insured in payment of the settlement funds.

(d)   If a settlement agreement is reached and is not rescinded, it shall act as a release of all specific claims that were presented in the conference. Any subsequent claim under the policy shall be presented as a separate claim. (2006-145, s. 1.)

§ 58-44-110. Nonparticipation in mediation program.

If the insured decides not to participate in this program or if the parties are unsuccessful at resolving the claim, the insured may choose to proceed under the appraisal process set forth in the insurance policy, by litigation, or by any other dispute resolution procedure available under North Carolina law. (2006-145, s. 1.)

§ 58-44-115. Commissioner's review.

If the insured rescinds a settlement agreement in accordance with G.S. 58-44-105(c), the Commissioner may review the settlement agreement to determine if the agreement was fair to the parties to the agreement. If the Commissioner, upon review and within 10 business days after receiving notice of the rescission, deems that it was fair to the parties, the insured, upon notice from the Commissioner, may withdraw the rescission within five business days after receipt of notice from the Commissioner and reinstate the settlement agreement as if no rescission had taken place. The Commissioner's review and findings shall not be offered or accepted as evidence in any subsequent proceedings. (2006-145, s. 1.)

§ 58-44-120. Relation to Administrative Procedure Act.

The applicable provisions of Chapter 150B of the General Statutes shall govern issues relating to mediation that are not addressed in this Part. The provisions of this Part shall govern in the event of any conflict with Chapter 150B of the General Statutes. (2006-145, s. 1.)

Article 44A.

Portable Electronics Insurance.

§ 58-44A-1. Definitions.

As used in this Article, the following definitions apply:

(1) Customer. - A person who purchases portable electronics or services.

(2) Enrolled customer. - A customer who elects coverage under a portable electronics insurance policy issued to a vendor of portable electronics.

(3) Location. - Any physical location in the State of North Carolina or any Web site, call center site, or similar location directed to residents of the State of North Carolina.

(4) Portable electronics. - Electronic devices that are portable in nature, their accessories, and services related to the use of the device.

(5) Portable electronics insurance. - Insurance providing coverage for the repair or replacement of portable electronics which may provide coverage for portable electronics against any one or more of the following causes of loss: (i) loss, (ii) theft, and (iii) inoperability due to mechanical failure, malfunction, damage, or other similar causes of loss. The term does not include the following:

a. A service contract or extended warranty providing coverage limited to the repair, replacement, or maintenance of property for the operational or structural failure of the property due to a defect in materials, workmanship, accidental damage from handling, power surges, or normal wear and tear.

b. A policy of insurance covering a seller's or a manufacturer's obligations under a warranty.

c. A homeowner's, renter's, private passenger automobile, commercial multiperil, or similar policy.

(6) Portable electronics transaction. - Either of the following:

a. The sale or lease of portable electronics by a vendor to a customer.

b. The sale of a service related to the use of portable electronics by a vendor to a customer.

(7) Supervising entity. - A business entity that is a licensed insurer or insurance producer.

(8) Vendor. - A person in the business of engaging in portable electronics transactions directly or indirectly. (2011-225, s. 1.)

§ 58-44A-5. Licensure of vendors.

(a) A vendor is required to hold a limited lines license to sell or offer coverage under a policy of portable electronics insurance.

(b) A limited lines license issued under this section shall authorize any employee or authorized representative of the vendor to sell or offer coverage under a policy of portable electronics insurance to a customer at each location at which the vendor engages in portable electronics transactions.

(c) Notwithstanding any other provision of law, a license issued pursuant to this section shall authorize the licensee and its employees or authorized representatives to engage in those activities that are permitted in this section. (2011-225, s. 1.)

§ 58-44A-10. Requirements for sale of portable electronics insurance.

(a) At every location where portable electronics insurance is offered to customers, brochures or other written materials shall be made available to a prospective customer. Those materials shall do the following:

(1) Disclose that portable electronics insurance may provide a duplication of coverage already provided by a customer's homeowner's insurance policy, renter's insurance policy, or other source of coverage.

(2) State that the enrollment by the customer in a portable electronics insurance program is not required in order to purchase or lease portable electronics or services.

(3) Summarize the material terms of the insurance coverage, including:

a. The identity of the insurer.

b. The identity of the supervising entity.

c. The amount of any applicable deductible and how it is to be paid.

d. Benefits of the coverage.

e. Key terms and conditions of coverage, such as whether portable electronics may be repaired or replaced with similar make and model reconditioned or nonoriginal manufacturer parts or equipment.

(4) Summarize the process for filing a claim, including a description of how to return portable electronics and the maximum fee applicable in the event the enrolled customer fails to comply with any equipment return requirements.

(5) State that the enrolled customer may cancel enrollment for coverage under a portable electronics insurance policy at any time and the person paying the premium shall receive a refund of any applicable unearned premium.

(b) Portable electronics insurance may be offered on a month-to-month or other periodic basis as a group or master commercial inland marine policy issued to a vendor of portable electronics for its enrolled customers.

(c) Eligibility and underwriting standards for customers electing to enroll in coverage shall be established for each portable electronics insurance program.

(d) The terms of the termination or modification of coverage under a policy of portable electronic insurance offered in compliance with this section shall be as set forth in the policy. (2011-225, s. 1.)

§ 58-44A-15. Authority of vendors of portable electronics.

(a) The employees and authorized representatives of vendors may sell or offer portable electronics insurance to customers and shall not be subject to licensure as an insurance producer under this Chapter provided that the following are true:

(1) The vendor obtains a limited lines license to authorize its employees or authorized representatives to sell or offer portable electronics insurance pursuant to this section.

(2) The insurer issuing the portable electronics insurance either directly supervises or appoints a supervising entity to supervise the administration of the program, including development of a training program for employees and authorized representatives of the vendors. The training required by this subdivision shall comply with the following:

a. The training shall be delivered to employees and authorized representatives of a vendor who are directly engaged in the activity of selling or offering portable electronics insurance.

b. The training may be provided in electronic form. If conducted in an electronic form, the supervising entity shall implement a supplemental education program regarding portable electronics insurance that is conducted and overseen by licensed employees of the supervising entity.

c. Each employee and authorized representative shall receive basic instruction about the portable electronics insurance offered to customers and the disclosures required under G.S. 58-44A-10.

(3) No employee or authorized representative of a vendor of portable electronics shall advertise, represent, or otherwise hold himself or herself out as a non-limited lines licensed insurance producer.

(b) The charges for portable electronics insurance coverage may be billed and collected by the vendor of portable electronics. Any charge to the enrolled customer for coverage that is not included in the cost associated with the purchase or lease of portable electronics or related services shall be separately itemized on the enrolled customer's bill. If the portable electronics insurance coverage is included with the purchase or lease of portable electronics or related services, the vendor shall clearly and conspicuously disclose to the enrolled customer that the portable electronics insurance coverage is included with the portable electronics or related services. Vendors billing and collecting such charges shall not be required to maintain such funds in a segregated account, provided that the vendor is authorized by the insurer to hold such funds in an alternative manner and remits such amounts to the supervising entity within 60 days of receipt. All funds received by a vendor from an enrolled customer for the sale of portable electronics insurance shall be considered funds held in trust by the vendor in a fiduciary capacity for the benefit of the insurer. Vendors may receive compensation for billing and collection services in accordance with G.S. 58-33-85. (2011-225, s. 1.)

§ 58-44A-20. Suspension or revocation of license.

If a vendor of portable electronics or its employee or authorized representative violates any provision of this section, the Commissioner may do any of the following:

(1) Revoke or suspend a limited lines license issued under this Part [Article] in accordance with the provisions of G.S. 58-33-46.

(2) After notice and hearing, impose other penalties, including suspending the transaction of insurance at specific locations where violations of this Article have occurred, as the Commissioner deems necessary and reasonable to carry out the purpose of this Article. (2011-225, s. 1.)

§ 58-44A-25. Application for license.

The prerequisites for issuance of a limited lines license under this Article are the filing with the Commissioner of the following:

(1) A license application, signed by an officer of the applicant, for the limited lines license in such form or forms, and supplements thereto, and containing such information, as the Commissioner may prescribe.

(2) A certificate by the insurer that is to be named in such limited lines license, stating that it has satisfied itself that the named applicant is trustworthy and competent to act as its insurance agent for this limited purpose and that the insurer will appoint such applicant to act as the agent in reference to the kinds of insurance as are permitted by this section, if the limited lines license applied for

is issued by the Commissioner. Such certificate shall be subscribed to by an officer or managing agent of such insurer and affirmed as true under the penalties of perjury. (2011-225, s. 1.)

Article 45.

Essential Property Insurance for Beach Area Property.

§ 58-45-1. Declarations and purpose of Article.

(a) It is hereby declared by the General Assembly of North Carolina that an adequate market for essential property insurance is necessary to the economic welfare of the beach and coastal areas of the State of North Carolina and that without such insurance the orderly growth and development of those areas would be severely impeded; that furthermore, adequate insurance upon property in the beach and coastal areas is necessary to enable homeowners and commercial owners to obtain financing for the purchase and improvement of their property; and that while the need for such insurance is increasing, the market for such insurance is not adequate and is likely to become less adequate in the future; and that the present plans to provide adequate insurance on property in the beach and coastal areas, while deserving praise, have not been sufficient to meet the needs of this area. It is further declared that the State has an obligation to provide an equitable method whereby every licensed insurer writing essential property insurance in North Carolina is required to meet its public responsibility instead of shifting the burden to a few willing and public-spirited insurers. It is the purpose of this Article to accept this obligation and to provide a mandatory program to assure an adequate market for essential property insurance in the beach and coastal areas of North Carolina.

(b) The General Assembly further declares that it is its intent in creating and, from time to time, amending this Article that the market provided by this Article not be the first market of choice, but the market of last resort.

(c) It is the intent of the General Assembly that except for North Carolina gross premium taxes and the fire and lightning tax, the activities of the Association be exempt from State and federal taxation to the fullest extent permitted by law. (1967, c. 1111, s. 1; 1969, c. 249; 1979, c. 601, s. 1; 1997-498, s. 9; 2009-472, s. 1.)

§ 58-45-5. Definition of terms.

As used in this Article, unless the context clearly otherwise requires:

(1) Association. - The North Carolina Insurance Underwriting Association established under this Article.

(2) Beach area. - All of that area of the State of North Carolina south and east of the inland waterway from the South Carolina line to Fort Macon (Beaufort Inlet); thence south and east of Core, Pamlico, Roanoke and Currituck sounds to the Virginia line, being those portions of land generally known as the Outer Banks.

(2a) Catastrophe recovery charge. - Any charge collected by member insurers from policyholders statewide, including any charge collected by the Association and Fair Plan from their policyholders, upon issuance or renewal of residential and commercial property insurance policies, other than National Flood Insurance policies, after a deficit event has occurred as provided in G.S. 58-45-47. The amount of the catastrophe recovery charge collected in a particular year shall not exceed an aggregate amount of ten percent (10%) of policy premium. The catastrophe recovery charge shall be limited to the recovery of losses resulting from claims for property damage, allocated loss expenses, and actual costs and expenses directly resulting from the catastrophe recovery charge plan.

(2b) Coastal area. - All of that area of the State of North Carolina comprising the following counties: Beaufort, Brunswick, Camden, Carteret, Chowan, Craven, Currituck, Dare, Hyde, Jones, New Hanover, Onslow, Pamlico, Pasquotank, Pender, Perquimans, Tyrrell, and Washington. "Coastal area" does not include the portions of these counties that lie within the beach area.

(2c) Coastal Property Insurance Pool. - The name of which was formerly known as "the Beach Plan" and which is governed by the North Carolina Insurance Underwriting Association. All references to "the Beach Plan" shall mean the Coastal Property Insurance Pool, which is the market of last resort provided by the Association to the beach area and the coastal area.

(3) Repealed by Session Laws 1991, c. 720, s. 6.

(3a) Crime insurance. - Insurance against losses resulting from robbery, burglary, larceny, and similar crimes, as more specifically defined and limited in the various crime insurance policies, or their successor forms of coverage, approved by the Commissioner and issued by the Association. Such policies shall not be more restrictive than those issued under the Federal Crime Insurance Program authorized by Public Law 91-609.

(3b) Directors. - The Board of Directors of the Association.

(4) Essential property insurance. - Insurance against direct loss to property as defined in the standard statutory fire policy and extended coverage, vandalism and malicious mischief endorsements thereon, or their successor forms of coverage, as approved by the Commissioner.

(5) Insurable property. - Real property at fixed locations in the beach and coastal area, including travel trailers when tied down at a fixed location, or the tangible personal property located therein, but shall not include insurance on motor vehicles; which property is determined by the Association, after inspection and under the criteria specified in the plan of operation, to be in an insurable condition. However, any one and two family dwellings built in substantial accordance with the Federal Manufactured Home Construction and Safety Standards, any predecessor or successor federal or State construction or safety standards, and any further construction or safety standards promulgated by the association and approved by the Commissioner, or the North Carolina Uniform Residential Building Code and any structure or building built in substantial compliance with the North Carolina State Building Code, including the design-wind requirements, which is not otherwise rendered uninsurable by reason of use or occupancy, shall be an insurable risk within the meaning of this Article. However, none of the following factors shall be considered in determining insurable condition: neighborhood, area, location, environmental hazards beyond the control of the applicant or owner of the property. Also, any structure begun on or after January 1, 1970, not built in substantial compliance with the Federal Manufactured Home Construction and Safety Standards, any predecessor or successor federal or State construction or safety standards, and any further construction or safety standards promulgated by the association and approved by the Commissioner, or the North Carolina Uniform Residential Building Code or the North Carolina State Building Code, including the design-wind requirements therein, shall not be an insurable risk. The owner or applicant

shall furnish with the application proof in the form of a certificate from a local building inspector, contractor, engineer or architect that the structure is built in substantial accordance with the Federal Manufactured Home Construction and Safety Standards, any predecessor or successor federal or State construction or safety standards, and any further construction or safety standards promulgated by the association and approved by the Commissioner, or the North Carolina Uniform Residential Building Code or the North Carolina State Building Code; however, an individual certificate shall not be necessary where the structure is located within a political subdivision which has certified to the Association on an annual basis that it is enforcing the North Carolina Uniform Residential Building Code or the North Carolina State Building Code and has no plans to discontinue enforcing these codes during that year.

(6) Repealed by Session Laws 1995 (Regular Session, 1996), c. 592, s. 2.

(6a) Named storm. - A weather-related event involving wind that has been assigned a formal name by the National Hurricane Center, National Weather Service, World Meteorological Association, or any other generally recognized scientific or meteorological association that provides formal names for public use and reference. A named storm includes hurricanes, tropical depressions, and tropical storms.

(6b) Net direct premiums. - Gross direct premiums (excluding reinsurance assumed and ceded) written on property in this State for essential property insurance, farmowners insurance, homeowners insurance, and the property portion of commercial multiple peril insurance policies as computed by the Commissioner, less:

a. Return premiums on uncancelled contracts;

b. Dividends paid or credited to policyholders; and

c. The unused or unabsorbed portion of premium deposits.

(6c) Nonrecoupable assessment. - Any assessment levied on and payable by members of the Association that is not directly recoverable from policyholders. Prospective exposure to nonrecoupable assessments shall be considered as an appropriate factor in the making of rates by the North Carolina Rate Bureau.

(7) Plan of operation. - The plan of operation of the Association approved or promulgated by the Commissioner under this Article.

(8) Voluntary market. - Insurance written voluntarily by companies other than through this Article or Article 46 of this Chapter.

(9) Voluntary market rates. - Property insurance rates determined or permitted under Article 36, 40, or 41 of this Chapter. (1967, c. 1111, s. 1; 1969, c. 249; 1979, c. 601, ss. 2, 3; 1985, c. 516, s. 1; 1985 (Reg. Sess., 1986), c. 1027, ss. 21, 25; 1987 (Reg. Sess., 1988), c. 975, ss. 18, 19; 1991, c. 720, ss. 4, 6; 1991 (Reg. Sess., 1992), c. 784, s. 4; 1995 (Reg. Sess., 1996), c. 592, s. 2; 1997-498, s. 1; 2009-472, s. 1.)

§ 58-45-6. Persons who can be insured by the Association.

As used in this Article, "person" includes the State of North Carolina and any county, city, or other political subdivision of the State of North Carolina. (2000-122, s. 5; 2002-187, s. 1.4.)

§ 58-45-10. North Carolina Insurance Underwriting Association created.

There is hereby created the North Carolina Insurance Underwriting Association, consisting of all insurers authorized to write and engage in writing within this State, on a direct basis, essential property insurance, except town and county mutual insurance associations and assessable mutual companies as authorized by G.S. 58-7-75(5)b, 58-7-75(5)d, and 58-7-75(7)b and except an insurer who only writes insurance in this State on property exempted from taxation by the provisions of G.S. 105-278.1 through G.S. 105-278.8. Every such insurer shall be a member of the Association and shall remain a member of the Association so long as the Association is in existence as a condition of its authority to continue to transact the business of insurance in this State. (1967, c. 1111, s. 1; 1969, c. 249; 1971, c. 1067, s. 2; 1987 (Reg. Sess., 1988), c. 975, s. 20; 1998-211, s. 6.)

§ 58-45-15. Powers and duties of Association.

The Association shall, pursuant to the provisions of this Article and the plan of operation, and with respect to the insurance coverages authorized in this Article, have the power on behalf of its members:

(1)   To cause to be issued policies of insurance to applicants.

(2)   To assume reinsurance from its members.

(3)   To cede reinsurance to its members and to purchase reinsurance in behalf of its members.

(4)   To pledge the proceeds of assessments, projected reinsurance recoveries, other recoverables, and any other funds available to the Association as the source of revenue for and to secure lines of credit or other borrowings or financing arrangements necessary to fund any actual, projected, or future deficits of the Association, including borrowing from member companies.

(5)   To publish in the North Carolina Register all homeowners' rate filings with the Department of Insurance. (1967, c. 1111, s. 1; 1969, c. 249; 1999-114, s. 7; 2009-472, s. 1.)

§ 58-45-20. Temporary directors of Association.

Within 10 days after April 17, 1969, the Commissioner shall appoint a temporary board of directors of this Association, which shall consist of 11 representatives of members of the Association. Such temporary board of directors shall prepare and submit a plan of operation in accordance with G.S. 58-45-30 and shall serve until the permanent board of directors shall take office in accordance with said plan of operation. (1967, c. 1111, s. 1; 1969, c. 249.)

§ 58-45-25. Each member of Association to participate in nonrecoupable assessments.

(a)   Subject to the limitations contained in G.S. 58-45-47, each member of the Association shall participate in the nonrecoupable assessments levied by the Association in the proportion that its net direct premium written in this State during the preceding calendar year for residential and commercial properties outside of the beach and coastal areas bears to the aggregate net direct premiums written in this State during the preceding calendar year for residential and commercial properties outside of the beach and coastal areas by all members of the Association, as certified to the Association by the Commissioner. The Commissioner shall certify each member's participation after review of annual statements and any other reports and data necessary to determine participation and may obtain any necessary information or data from any member of the Association for this purpose. Any insurer that is authorized to write and that is engaged in writing any insurance, the writing of which requires the insurer to be a member of the Association under G.S. 58-45-10, shall become a member of the Association on the first day of January after authorization. The determination of the insurer's participation in the Association shall be made as of the date of membership of the insurer in the same manner as for all other members of the Association.

(b) All member companies shall receive credit each year for essential property insurance, farmowners insurance, homeowners insurance, and the property portion of commercial multiple peril policies voluntarily written in the beach and coastal areas in accordance with guidelines and procedures to be submitted by the Directors to the Commissioner for approval. Such credits also shall apply to any nonrecoupable assessments levied pursuant to G.S. 58-45-47. The participation of each member company in the nonrecoupable assessments levied by the Association shall be reduced accordingly; provided, no credit shall be given where coverage for the peril of wind has been excluded. The guidelines and procedures for granting credit shall encourage and assist each member company to voluntarily write these coverages in the beach and coastal areas for commercial and residential properties.

(b1) The accumulated surplus of the Association shall be retained from year to year and used to pay losses, reinsurance costs, and other operating expenses as necessary. No member company shall be entitled to the distribution of any portion of the Association's surplus, except pursuant to judgments entered prior to August 26, 2009.

(b2) The premiums, surplus, assessments, investment income, and other revenue of the Association are funds received for the sole purpose of providing insurance coverage, paying claims for Association policyholders, purchasing reinsurance, securing and repaying debt obligations issued by the Association, and conducting all other activities of the Association, as required or permitted by this Article. Accumulated surplus shall not be removed from the Association or used for other purposes except pursuant to judgments entered prior to August 26, 2009.

(c)   The North Carolina Insurance Underwriting Association shall use the "take out" program, as filed with and approved by the Commissioner, in the coastal area. (1967, c. 1111, s. 1; 1969, c. 249; 1991, c. 720, s. 58; 1995 (Reg. Sess., 1996), c. 592, s. 1; 1997-498, s. 2; 2009-472, s. 1.)

§ 58-45-30. Directors to submit plan of operation to Commissioner; review and approval; amendments; appeal from Commissioner to superior court.

(a)   The Directors shall submit to the Commissioner for his review and approval, a proposed plan of operation. The plan shall set forth the number, qualifications, terms of office, and manner of election of the members of the board of directors, and shall grant proper credit annually to each member of the Association for essential property insurance, farmowners, homeowners insurance, and the property portion of commercial multiple peril policies voluntarily written in the beach and coastal areas and shall provide for the efficient, economical, fair and nondiscriminatory administration of the Association and for the prompt and efficient provision of essential property insurance in the beach and coastal areas of North Carolina to promote orderly community development in those areas and to provide means for the adequate maintenance and improvement of the property in those areas. The plan may include the establishment of necessary facilities; management of the Association; the assessment of members to defray losses and expenses; underwriting standards; procedures for the acceptance and cession of reinsurance; procedures for determining the amounts of insurance to be provided to specific risks; time limits and procedures for processing applications for insurance; and any other provisions that are considered necessary by the Commissioner to carry out the purposes of this Article.

(b)   The proposed plan and any amendments thereto shall be filed with the Commissioner and approved by him if he finds that such plan fulfills the purposes provided by G.S. 58-45-1. In the review of the proposed plan the Commissioner may, in his discretion, consult with the directors of the Association and may seek any further information which he deems necessary to his decision. If the Commissioner approves the proposed plan, he shall certify such approval to the directors and the plan shall become effective 10 days after such certification. If the Commissioner disapproves all or any part of the proposed plan of operation he shall return the same to the directors with his written statement for the reasons for disapproval and any recommendations he may wish to make. The directors may alter the plan in accordance with the Commissioner's recommendation or may within 30 days from the date of disapproval return a new plan to the Commissioner. Should the directors fail to submit a plan that meets the requirements of this Article or accept the recommendations of the Commissioner within 30 days after his disapproval of the plan, the Commissioner shall promulgate and place into effect a plan of operation that meets the requirements of this Article certifying the same to the directors of the Association. Any such plan promulgated by the Commissioner shall take effect 10 days after certification to the directors.

(c) The directors of the Association may, subject to the approval of the Commissioner, amend the plan of operation at any time. The Commissioner may review the plan of operation at any time the Commissioner deems expedient or prudent, but not less than once in each calendar year. After review of the plan the Commissioner may amend the plan after consultation with the directors and upon certification to the directors of the amendment. Any order of the Commissioner with respect to the proposed plan of operation or any amendments thereto shall be subject to review upon petition by the Association as provided by G.S. 58-2-75.

(d) As used in this subsection, "homeowners' insurance policy" means a multiperil policy providing full coverage of residential property similar to the coverage provided under an HO-2, HO-3, HO-4, or HO-6 policy under Article 36 of this Chapter. The Association shall issue, for principal residences, homeowners' insurance policies approved by the Commissioner. Homeowners' insurance policies shall be available to persons who reside in the beach and coastal areas who meet the Association's underwriting standards and who are unable to obtain homeowners' insurance policies from insurers that are authorized to transact and are actually writing homeowners' insurance policies in this State. The Association shall file for approval by the Commissioner underwriting standards to determine whether property is insurable. The standards shall reflect underwriting standards commonly used in the voluntary homeowners' insurance business. The terms and conditions of the homeowners' insurance policies available under this subsection shall not be more favorable than those of homeowners' insurance policies available in the voluntary market in beach and coastal counties.

(e) The Association shall, subject to the Commissioner's approval or modification, provide in the plan of operation for coverage for appropriate classes of manufacturing risks.

(f) As used in this section, "plan of operation" includes all written rules, practices, and procedures of the Association, except for staffing and personnel matters. (1967, c. 1111, s. 1; 1969, c. 249; 1986, Ex. Sess., c. 7, s. 8; 1987, c. 731, s. 1; c. 864, s. 41; 1991, c. 720, s. 59; 1991 (Reg. Sess., 1992), c. 784, s. 5; 1997-498, s. 3; 2002-185, s. 2; 2003-158, ss. 1, 3.1; 2009-472, s. 1.)

§ 58-45-35. Persons eligible to apply to Association for coverage; contents of application.

(a) Any person having an insurable interest in insurable property, may, on or after the effective date of the plan of operation, be entitled to apply to the Association for such coverage and for an inspection of the property. A broker or agent authorized by the applicant may apply on the applicant's behalf. Each application shall contain a statement as to whether or not there are any unpaid premiums due from the applicant for essential property insurance on the property.

The term "insurable interest" as used in this subsection shall include any lawful and substantial economic interest in the safety or preservation of property from loss, destruction or pecuniary damage.

(b) If the Association determines that the property is insurable and that there is no unpaid premium due from the applicant for prior insurance on the property, the Association, upon receipt of the premium, or part of the premium, as is prescribed in the plan of operation, shall cause to be issued a policy of essential property insurance and shall offer additional extended coverage, optional perils endorsements, business income and extra expense coverage, crime insurance, separate policies of windstorm and hail insurance, or their successor forms of coverage, for a term of one year or three years. Short term policies may also be issued. Any policy issued under this section shall be renewed, upon application, as long as the property is insurable property.

(b1) If the Association determines that the property, for which application for a homeowners' policy is made, is insurable, that there is no unpaid premium due from the applicant for prior insurance on the property, and that the underwriting guidelines established by the Association and approved by the Commissioner are met, the Association, upon receipt of the premium, or part of the premium, as is prescribed in the plan of operation, shall cause to be issued a homeowners' insurance policy.

(c) If the Association, for any reason, denies an application and refuses to cause to be issued an insurance policy on insurable property to any applicant or takes no action on an application within the time prescribed in the plan of operation, the applicant may appeal to the Commissioner and the Commissioner, or the Commissioner's designee from the Commissioner's staff, after reviewing the facts, may direct the Association to issue or cause to be issued an insurance policy to the applicant. In carrying out the Commissioner's duties under this section, the Commissioner may request, and the Association shall provide, any information the Commissioner deems necessary to a determination concerning the reason for the denial or delay of the application.

(d) An agent who is licensed under Article 33 of this Chapter as an agent of a company which is a member of the Association established under this Article shall not be deemed an agent of the Association. The foregoing notwithstanding, an agent of a company which is a member of the Association shall have the authority, subject to the underwriting guidelines established by the Association, to temporarily bind coverage with the Association. The Association shall establish rules and procedures, including any limitations for binding authority, in the plan of operation.

Any unearned premium on the temporary binder shall be returned to the policyholder if the Association refuses to issue a policy. Nothing in this section shall prevent the Association from suspending binding authority in accordance with its plan of operation.

(e) Policies of windstorm and hail insurance provided for in subsection (b) of this section are available only for risks in the beach and coastal areas for which essential property insurance has been written by licensed insurers. Whenever such other essential property insurance written by licensed insurers includes replacement cost coverage, the Association shall also offer replacement cost coverage. In order to be eligible for a policy of windstorm and hail insurance, the applicant shall provide the Association, along with the premium payment for the windstorm and hail insurance, a certificate that the essential property insurance is in force. The policy forms for windstorm and hail insurance shall be filed by the Association with the Commissioner for the Commissioner's approval before they may be used. Catastrophic losses, as determined by the Association and approved by the Commissioner, that are covered under the windstorm and hail coverage in the beach and coastal areas shall be adjusted by the licensed insurer that issued the essential property insurance and not by the Association. The Association shall reimburse the insurer for reasonable expenses incurred by the insurer in adjusting windstorm and hail losses. (1967, c. 1111, s. 1; 1969, c. 249; 1985, c. 516, s. 2; 1985 (Reg. Sess., 1986), c. 1027, s. 22; 1987, c. 421, ss. 1, 2; c. 629, s. 11; c. 864, s. 24; 1987 (Reg. Sess., 1988), c. 975, ss. 21-23; 1989, c. 376; c. 485, s. 26; 1991, c. 720, s. 25; 1991 (Reg. Sess., 1992), c. 784, s. 1; 1995, c. 517, s. 28; 1995 (Reg. Sess., 1996), c. 740, s. 1; 1997-498, ss. 5, 6; 2001-421, s. 4.1; 2002-185, s. 4.1; 2003-158, s. 2.)

§ 58-45-36. Temporary contracts of insurance.

Consistent with G.S. 58-45-35(d), the Association shall be temporarily bound by a written temporary binder of insurance issued by any duly licensed insurance agent or broker. Coverage shall be effective upon payment to the agent or broker of the entire premium or part of the premium, as prescribed by the Association's plan of operation. Nothing in this section shall impair or restrict the rights of the Association under G.S. 58-45-35(b) to decline to issue a policy based upon a lack of insurability as determined by the Association or the existence of an unpaid premium due from the applicant. (2002-185, s. 4.2.)

§ 58-45-40. Association members may cede insurance to Association.

Any member of the Association may cede to the Association essential property insurance written on insurable property, to the extent, if any, and on the terms and conditions set forth in the plan of operation. (1967, c. 1111, s. 1; 1969, c. 249.)

§ 58-45-41. Coverage limits.

(a) The Association shall cause to be issued insurance up to the reasonable value of the insurable property, subject to a maximum of seven hundred fifty thousand dollars ($750,000) on habitational property. The above limits on habitational property shall apply to the value of the building only. Insurance issued by the Association for commercial property shall not exceed three million dollars ($3,000,000) on any freestanding structure or any building unit within multiple firewall divisions, provided the aggregate insurance on structures with multiple firewall divisions shall not exceed six million dollars ($6,000,000) on all interest at one risk.

(b) Contents of habitational property can be insured up to forty percent (40%) of the building value. The Association shall ensure that rates accurately reflect the maximum limits for contents coverage and any reduction in contents coverage limits for habitational property.

(c) If the value of the property exceeds the maximum coverage limits as described in this section, the Association shall not issue coverage without the insured's purchase of excess coverage to the full value of the property insured. (2009-472, s. 1.)

§ 58-45-45. Rates, rating plans, rating rules, and forms applicable.

(a) Rates shall not be excessive, inadequate, or unfairly discriminatory. Except as provided in subsections (a1), (a2), and (b) of this section, rates, rating plans, rating rules, and forms applicable to the insurance written by the Association shall be in accordance with the most recent manual rates or adjusted loss costs and forms that are legally in effect in the State. Except as provided in subsection (c) of this section, no special surcharge, other than those presently in effect, may be applied to the property insurance rates of properties located in the beach and coastal areas.

(a1) The Association's rates shall be the North Carolina Rate Bureau Manual Rates plus a surcharge of five percent (5%) of the applicable North Carolina Rate Bureau Manual Rate for wind and hail coverage and a surcharge of fifteen percent (15%) of the applicable North Carolina Rate Bureau Manual Rate for homeowners' insurance including wind and hail coverage. It is the intent of the General Assembly that these surcharges ensure that the Coastal Property Insurance Pool is the market of last resort over and above the manual rate.

(a2) (See Editor's note) The Association shall offer a deductible for named storm wind and hail losses of one percent (1%) of the insured value of the property for all policies and may offer any other deductible options provided by the North Carolina Rate Bureau, so long as the deductible is not lower than one percent (1%) of the insured value of the property applicable to named storm wind and hail losses.

(b) The rates, rating plans, and rating rules for the separate policies of windstorm and hail insurance described in G.S. 58-45-35(b) shall be filed by the Association with the Commissioner for the Commissioner's approval, disapproval, or modification. The provisions of Articles 40 and 41 of this Chapter shall govern the filings. Policy deductible plans, consistent with G.S. 58-45-1(b), may be filed by the Association with the Commissioner for the Commissioner's approval, disapproval, or modification.

(c) Repealed by Session Laws 2009-472, s. 1.

(d) When the Association files rates, classification plans, rating plans, rating systems, or surcharges, the procedures of G.S. 58-40-25 through G.S. 58-40-45 shall apply, and the appeal procedures of G.S. 58-2-80 and G.S. 58-2-85 shall apply to filings under this section, except as otherwise provided.

(e) The Association shall file no later than May 1, 2010, a schedule of credits for policyholders based on the presence of mitigation and construction features and on the condition of buildings that it insures. The Association shall develop rules applicable to the operation of the schedule and the mitigation program with approval by the Commissioner. The schedule shall not be unfairly discriminatory and shall be reviewed by the Association annually, with the results included as part of the Association's annual report to the Commissioner.

(f) The Association shall file not later than May 1, 2010, with the Commissioner an installment plan for premium payments and shall accept other methods of payment that are the same as those filed by the North Carolina Rate Bureau. The Association shall collect an installment fee if premiums are paid other than on an annual basis.

(g) The Association shall consider the purchase of reinsurance each calendar year in order to maintain the ability to pay losses and expenses from a named storm or combination of named storms. (1967, c. 1111, s. 1; 1969, c. 249; 1979, c. 601, s. 4; 1987 (Reg. Sess., 1988), c. 975, s. 24; 1991 (Reg. Sess., 1992), c. 784, s. 2; 1997-498, ss. 7, 8; 1999-114, s. 7.1; 2003-158, s. 3; 2009-472, s. 1.)

§ 58-45-46. Unearned premium, loss, and loss expense reserves.

The Association shall make provisions for reserving unearned premiums and reserving for losses, including incurred but not reported losses, and loss expenses, in accordance with G.S. 58-3-71, 58-3-75, and 58-3-81. (2002-185, s. 5.1.)

§ 58-45-47. Deficit event.

(a) In the event of losses and expenses to the Association exceeding available surplus, reinsurance, and other sources of funding of Association losses, the Association is authorized to issue a nonrecoupable assessment upon its members in accordance with its Plan of Operation. Member assessments shall not exceed one billion dollars ($1,000,000,000) for losses incurred from any event or series of events that occur in a given calendar year, regardless of when such assessments are actually levied on or collected from member companies.

(b) When the Association knows that it has incurred losses and loss expenses in a particular calendar year that will exceed the combination of available surplus, reinsurance, and other sources of funding, including permissible member company assessments, then the Association shall immediately give notice to the Commissioner that a deficit event has occurred.

(c) Upon a determination by the Association that a deficit event has occurred, the Association shall determine, in its discretion, the appropriate means of financing the deficit, which may include, but is not limited to, the purchase of reinsurance, arranging lines of credit, or other forms of borrowing or financing. If the Association determines that the member companies have paid one billion dollars ($1,000,000,000) in nonrecoupable assessments for losses and expenses incurred in any given year pursuant to subsection (a) of this section, the Association may, subject to the verification by the Commissioner that the dollar value of losses and expenses has reached the level necessary for a catastrophe recovery charge, authorize member companies to impose a catastrophe recovery charge on their residential and commercial property insurance policyholders statewide. Catastrophe recovery charges shall be charged as a uniform percentage of written premiums as prescribed by the Commissioner and shall not exceed an aggregate amount of ten percent (10%) of the annual policy premium on any one policy of insurance. Catastrophe recovery charges collected under this section shall be transferred directly to the Association on a periodic basis as determined by the Association and ordered by the Commissioner. The Association and the FAIR Plan also shall charge their policyholders a catastrophe recovery charge as provided in this section.

(d) The catastrophe recovery charge shall be clearly identified to policyholders on the premium statement, declarations page, or by other appropriate electronic or written method. The identification shall refer to the post-catastrophe loss for which the charge was imposed. Any such catastrophe recovery charge shall not be considered premium for any purpose, including premium taxes or commissions, except that failure to pay the catastrophe recovery charge shall be treated as failure to pay premium and shall be grounds for termination of insurance. The identified catastrophe recovery charge shall be accompanied by an explanation of the charge and shall appear on the medium by which the charge is conveyed to the policyholder. The explanatory language shall be prescribed by the Commissioner.

(e) The Association shall report quarterly to the Commissioner providing all financial information for each catastrophe recovery charge authorized by this section, including total catastrophe recovery charge funds recovered to date and any information reasonably requested by the Commissioner.

(f) The Association shall recalculate the catastrophe recovery charge amount annually and, subject to procedure approved by the Commissioner, adjust the charge percentage as needed.

(g) The catastrophe recovery charge amount shall continue until financing of the deficit event has been paid in full. Upon order of cessation, any catastrophe recovery charge amounts collected by member companies, the Association or the FAIR Plan that exceed amounts necessary for payment of the debt shall be remitted to the Association and added to the surplus for the purposes of offsetting future Association losses or expenses.

(h) Nothing contained in this section prohibits the Association from entering into any financing arrangements for the purpose of financing a deficit, provided that the pledge of catastrophe recovery charge amounts under such financing agreements shall not result in the actual levying of any catastrophe recovery charge until after the Association has incurred a deficit and until after the Commissioner has approved implementation of the Association's catastrophe recovery charge plan. (2009-472, s. 1.)

§ 58-45-50. Appeal from acts of Association to Commissioner; appeal from Commissioner to superior court.

(a) Any person or any insurer who may be aggrieved by an act, ruling, or decision of the Association other than an act, ruling, or decision relating to (i) the cause or amount of a claimed loss or (ii) the reasonableness of expenses incurred by an insurer in adjusting windstorm and hail losses, may, within 30 days after the ruling, appeal to the Commissioner. Any hearings held by the Commissioner under the appeal shall be in accordance with rules adopted by the Commissioner: Provided, however, the Commissioner is authorized to appoint a member of the Commissioner's staff as deputy commissioner for the purpose of hearing those appeals and a ruling based upon the hearing shall have the same effect as if heard by the Commissioner. All persons or insureds aggrieved by any order or decision of the Commissioner may appeal as is provided in G.S. 58-2-75.

(b) No later than 10 days before each hearing, the appellant shall file with the Commissioner or the Commissioner's designated hearing officer and shall serve on the appellee a written statement of the appellant's case and any evidence that the appellant intends to offer at the hearing. No later than five days before the hearing, the appellee shall file with the Commissioner or the designated hearing officer and shall serve on the appellant a written statement of the appellee's case and any evidence that the appellee intends to offer at the hearing. Each hearing shall be recorded and may be transcribed. If the matter is between an insurer and the Association, the cost of the recording and transcribing shall be borne equally by the appellant and appellee; provided that upon any final adjudication the prevailing party shall be reimbursed for his share of such costs by the other party. If the matter is between an insured and the Association, the cost of transcribing shall be borne equally by the appellant and appellee; provided that the Commissioner may order the Association to pay recording or transcribing costs for which the insured is financially unable to pay. Each party shall, on a date determined by the Commissioner or the designated hearing officer, but not sooner than 15 days after delivery of the completed transcript to the party, submit to the Commissioner or the designated hearing officer and serve on the other party, a proposed order. The Commissioner or the designated hearing officer shall then issue an order. (1967, c. 1111, s. 1; 1969, c. 249; 1985, c. 516, s. 3; 1989 (Reg. Sess., 1990), c. 1069, s. 18; 1991, c. 720, s. 4; 1999-219, s. 1.2; 2001-421, s. 4.2.)

§ 58-45-55. Reports of inspection made available.

All reports of inspection performed by or on behalf of the Association shall be made available to the members of the Association, applicants, agent or broker, and the Commissioner. (1967, c. 1111, s. 1; 1969, c. 249.)

§ 58-45-60. Association and Commissioner immune from liability.

There shall be no liability on the part of and no cause of action of any nature shall arise against any member insurer, the Association or its agents or employees, the board of directors, or the Commissioner or his representatives for any action taken by them in good faith in the performance of their powers and duties under this Article. (1967, c. 1111, s. 1; 1969, c. 249; 1991, c. 720, s. 4; 1999-114, s. 5.)

§ 58-45-65. Association to file annual report with Commissioner.

The Association shall file in the office of the Commissioner on an annual basis on or before January 1 a statement which shall summarize the transactions, conditions, operations and affairs of the Association during the preceding year. Such statement shall contain such matters and information as are prescribed by the Commissioner and shall be in such form as is approved by him. The Commissioner may at any time require the Association to furnish to him any additional information with respect to its transactions or any other matter which the Commissioner deems to be material to assist him in evaluating the operation and experience of the Association. (1967, c. 1111, s. 1; 1969, c. 249; 1987 (Reg. Sess., 1988), c. 975, s. 27.)

§ 58-45-65.1. Association to be audited.

The Association shall be audited on an annual basis by an auditor selected by the Commissioner. (2009-472, s. 1.)

§ 58-45-70. Commissioner may examine affairs of Association.

The Commissioner may from time to time make an examination into the affairs of the Association when he deems it to be prudent and in undertaking such examination he may hold a public hearing pursuant to the provisions of G.S. 58-2-50. When making an examination under this section, the Commissioner may retain attorneys, appraisers, independent actuaries, independent certified public accountants, or other professionals and specialists as examiners, the reasonable cost of which shall be borne by the Association. Examinations shall be conducted in accordance with G.S. 58-2-131, 58-2-132, and 58-2-133. (1967, c. 1111, s. 1; 1969, c. 249; 2009-472, s. 1.)

§ 58-45-71. Report of member companies to Commissioner.

Each member company of the Association shall report by February 1 of each year to the Commissioner the amount of homeowners' coverage, including separate coverage for homeowners' wind and hail, written in the preceding calendar year by that member company in the beach area and the coastal area. The report shall include the number and type of homeowners' policies written by the member company in each area, the total amount of homeowners' coverage for each area, any increases and decreases in homeowners' coverage written in each area from the prior year, and other information as prescribed by the Commissioner and in such form as approved by him. (2009-472, s. 1.)

§ 58-45-75. Commissioner authorized to promulgate reasonable rules and regulations.

The Commissioner shall have authority to make reasonable rules and regulations, not inconsistent with law, to enforce, carry out and make effective the provisions of this Article. The Commissioner shall not be liable for any act or omission in connection with the administration of the duties imposed upon him by the provisions of this Article. (1967, c. 1111, s. 1; 1969, c. 249; 1991, c. 720, s. 4.)

§ 58-45-80. Premium taxes to be paid through Association.

All premium taxes due on insurance written under this Article shall be remitted by each insurer to the Association; and the Association, as collecting agent for its member companies, shall forward all such taxes to the Secretary of Revenue as provided in Article 8B of Chapter 105 of the General Statutes. (1985 (Reg. Sess., 1986), c. 928, s. 10; 1995 (Reg. Sess., 1996), c. 747, s. 12.)

§ 58-45-85. Assessment; inability to pay.

(a) If any insurer fails, by reason of insolvency, to pay any assessment as provided in this Article, the amount assessed each insurer shall be immediately recalculated, excluding the insolvent insurer, so that its assessment is assumed and redistributed among the remaining insurers. Any assessment against an insolvent insurer shall not be a charge against any special deposit fund held under the provisions of Article 5 of this Chapter for the benefit of policyholders.

(b) The nonrecoupable assessment of a member insurer may be ordered deferred in whole or in part upon application by the insurer if, in the opinion of the Commissioner or his designee, payment of the assessment would render the insurer insolvent or in danger of insolvency or would otherwise leave the insurer in a condition so that further transaction of the insurer's business would be hazardous to its policyholders. If payment of an assessment against a member insurer is deferred by order of the Commissioner or his designee in whole or in part, the amount by which the assessment is deferred must be assessed against other member insurers in the same manner as provided in this Article. In its order of deferral, or in necessary subsequent orders, the Commissioner or his designee shall prescribe a plan by which the assessment so deferred must be repaid to the Association by the impaired insurer with interest at the six-month treasury bill rate adjusted semiannually. The plan also shall provide for the reimbursement of excess assessments paid by member companies as a result of a deferral of assessments for an impaired insurer. (1991 (Reg. Sess., 1992), c. 784, s. 7; 2009-472, s. 1.)

§ 58-45-90. Open meetings.

The Association is subject to the Open Meetings Act, Article 33C of Chapter 143 of the General Statutes, as amended. (2002-185, s. 7.1.)

§ 58-45-95. Information availability.

Information concerning the Association's activities shall be made fully available upon request provided that no competitive information concerning an individual company's business plans, data, or operations may be disclosed by the Association if such company has properly designated such information as being a trade secret pursuant to G.S. 66-152(3) upon submitting such information to the Association. No confidential information may be disclosed by the Association identifying individual policyholders without such policyholders' consent unless such information is provided pursuant to reasonable rules adopted by the Association permitting such information to be disclosed for the purpose of enhancing the availability of insurance that is written in the voluntary market. (2009-472, s. 1.)

§ 58-45-96. Succession and dissolution.

In the event that a successor organization is created to perform the Association's general functions, the surplus, assets, and liabilities then held by the Association shall be transferred to such successor organization. The pledge or sale of, the lien upon, and the security interest in any rights, revenues, or other assets of the Association created pursuant to any financing arrangements entered into by the Association shall be and remain valid and enforceable on the successor organization, notwithstanding the commencement of any rehabilitation, insolvency, liquidation, bankruptcy, conservatorship, reorganization, or similar proceeding against the Association. No such proceeding shall relieve the Association of its obligation to continue to collect assessments or other revenues pledged pursuant to any financing arrangements. In the event of dissolution, surplus then held shall not be distributed to member insurers. (2009-472, s. 1.)

Article 46.

Fair Access to Insurance Requirements.

§ 58-46-1. Purpose and geographic coverage of Article.

(a) It is the purpose of this Article to provide a program whereby adequate basic property insurance may be made available to property owners having insurable property in the State. It is further the purpose of this Article to encourage the improvement of properties located in the State and to arrest the decline of properties located in the State. It is the intent of the General Assembly in creating and, from time to time, amending this Article that the market provided by this Article not be the first market of choice, but the market of last resort.

(b) This Article shall apply to all geographic areas of the State except the "Beach Area" defined in G.S. 58-45-5(2).

(c) As used in this Article, "crime insurance" means insurance against losses resulting from robbery, burglary, larceny, and similar crimes, as more specifically defined and limited in the various crime insurance policies, or their successor forms of coverage, approved by the Commissioner and issued by the Association. Such policies shall not be more restrictive than those issued under the Federal Crime Insurance Program authorized by Public Law 91-609. (1969, c. 1284; 1985, c. 519, s. 1; 1986, Ex. Sess., c. 7, s. 4; 1985 (Reg. Sess., 1986), c. 1027, s. 24; 1987, c. 731, s. 1; 1987 (Reg. Sess., 1988), c. 975, s. 18; 1997-498, s. 10.)

§ 58-46-2. Persons who can be insured by the Association.

As used in this Article, "person" includes the State of North Carolina and any county, city, or other political subdivision of the State of North Carolina. (2000-122, s. 6; 2002-187, s. 1.5.)

§ 58-46-5. Organization of underwriting association.

All insurers licensed to write and writing property insurance in this State on a direct basis are authorized, subject to the approval and regulation by the Commissioner, to establish and maintain a FAIR Plan (Fair Access to Insurance Requirements) and to establish and maintain an underwriting association and to formulate, and from time to time, to amend the plans and articles of the association and rules and regulations in connection therewith, and to assess and share on a fair and equitable basis all expenses, income and losses incident to such FAIR Plan and underwriting association in a manner consistent with the provisions of this Article. (1969, c. 1284; 1985, c. 519, s. 2.)

§ 58-46-10. Participation in association.

(a) Every insurer authorized to write basic property insurance in this State except town and county mutual insurance associations and assessable mutual companies as authorized by G.S. 58-7-75(5)b, 58-7-75(5)d and 58-7-75(7)b and except an insurer who only writes insurance on property exempted from taxation by the provisions of G.S. 105-278.1 through 105-278.8 shall be required to become and remain a member of the Plan and underwriting association and comply with the requirements thereof as a condition of its authority to transact basic property insurance business in the State of North Carolina.

(b) An agent who is licensed under Article 33 of this Chapter as an agent of a company which is a member of the Association established under this Article shall not be deemed an agent of the Association. (1969, c. 1284; 1971, c. 1067, s. 1; 1985, c. 519, s. 3; 1987, c. 629, s. 12; 1991, c. 720, s. 24.)

§ 58-46-15. Requirements of Plan and authority of Association.

The Association formed pursuant to the provisions of this Article shall have authority on behalf of its members to cause to be issued basic property insurance policies, including coverage for farm risks; and shall offer additional extended coverage, optional perils endorsements, and crime insurance policies, or their successor forms of coverage; to reinsure in whole or in part, any such policies; and to cede any such reinsurance. The Plan adopted, pursuant to the provision of this Article, shall provide, among other things, for the perils to be covered, compensation and commissions, assessments of members, the sharing of expenses, income and losses on an equitable basis, cumulative weighted voting for the board of directors of the Association, the administration of the Plan and Association and any other matter necessary or convenient for the purpose of assuring fair access to insurance requirements. The directors of the Association may, subject to the approval of the Commissioner, amend the plan of operation at any time. The Commissioner may review the plan of operation at any time he deems to be expedient or prudent, but not less than once in each calendar year. After review of such plan the Commissioner may amend the plan after consultation with the directors and upon certification to the directors of such amendment. (1969, c. 1284; 1985, c. 519, s. 4; 1986, Ex. Sess., c. 7, ss. 5, 6; 1985 (Reg. Sess., 1986), c. 1027, s. 23; 1987, c. 864, s. 24; 1987 (Reg. Sess., 1988), c. 975, ss. 25, 29.)

§ 58-46-20. Authority of Commissioner.

(a)   Within 90 days following July 2, 1969, and before August 1, 1969, the directors of the association shall submit to the Commissioner for his review, a proposed FAIR Plan and articles of the association consistent with the provisions of this Article.

(b)   The FAIR Plan and articles of association shall be subject to approval by the Commissioner and shall take effect 10 days after having been approved by him. If the Commissioner disapproves all or any part of the proposed Plan and articles, the directors of the association shall within 30 days submit for review an appropriately revised Plan and articles and if the directors fail to do so, the Commissioner shall thereafter promulgate such Plan and articles not inconsistent with the provisions of this Article.

(c)   The Commissioner may designate the kinds of property insurance policies on principal residences to be offered by the association, including insurance policies under Article 36 of this Chapter, and the commission rates to be paid to agents or brokers for these policies, if he finds, after a hearing held in accordance with G.S. 58-2-50, that the public interest requires the designation. The provisions of Chapter 150B do not apply to any procedure under this subsection, except that G.S. 150B-39 and G.S. 150B-41 shall apply to a hearing under this subsection. Within 30 days after the receipt of notification from the Commissioner of a change in designation pursuant to this subsection, the association shall submit a revised plan and articles of association for approval in accordance with subsection (b) of this section.

(d) As used in this section and in G.S. 58-46-15, "FAIR Plan", "plan of operation", and "articles of association" include all written rules, practices, and procedures of the Association, except for staffing and personnel matters. (1969, c. 1284; 1986, Ex. Sess., c. 7, s. 7; 1987, c. 731, s. 1; 1991, c. 720, s. 4; 1991 (Reg. Sess., 1992), c. 784, s. 6.)

§ 58-46-25. Temporary directors of association.

Within 10 days after July 2, 1969, the Commissioner shall appoint a temporary board of directors of the association, which temporary board of directors may prepare and submit a Plan of operation and articles of association in accordance with G.S. 58-46-20. (1969, c. 1284.)

§ 58-46-30. Appeals; judicial review.

The association shall provide reasonable means, to be approved by the Commissioner, whereby any person or insurer affected by any act or decision of the administrators of the Plan or underwriting association, other than an act or decision relating to the cause or amount of a claimed loss, may be heard in person or by an authorized representative, before the governing board of the association or a designated committee. Any person or insurer aggrieved by any decision of the governing board or designated committee, may be appealed to the Commissioner within 30 days after the date of the ruling or decision. The Commissioner, after a hearing held under rules adopted by the Commissioner, shall issue an order approving or disapproving the act or decision with respect to the matter that is the subject of appeal. The Commissioner may appoint a member of the Commissioner's staff as deputy commissioner for the purpose of hearing the appeals and a ruling based on the hearing has the same effect as if heard by the Commissioner. All persons or insurers or their representatives aggrieved by any order or decision of the Commissioner may appeal as provided in G.S. 58-2-75.

No later than 10 days before each hearing, the appellant shall file with the Commissioner or the designated hearing officer and shall serve on the appellee a written statement of the appellant's case and any evidence that the appellant intends to offer at the hearing. No later than five days before the hearing, the appellee shall file with the Commissioner or the designated hearing officer and shall serve on the appellant a written statement of the appellee's case and any evidence that the appellee intends to offer at the hearing. Each hearing shall be recorded and may be transcribed. If the matter is between an insurer and the Association, the cost of the recording and transcribing shall be borne equally by the appellant and appellee; provided that upon any final adjudication the prevailing party shall be reimbursed for his share of such costs by the other party. If the matter is between an insured and the Association, the cost of transcribing shall be borne equally by the appellant and appellee; provided that the Commissioner may order the Association to pay recording or transcribing costs for which the insured is financially unable to pay. Each party shall, on a date determined by the Commissioner or the designated hearing officer, but not sooner than 15 days after delivery of the completed transcript to the party, submit to the Commissioner or the designated hearing officer and serve on the other party, a proposed order. The Commissioner or the designated hearing officer shall then issue an order. (1969, c. 1284; 1985, c. 519, s. 5; 1989 (Reg. Sess., 1990), c. 1069, s. 19; 1999-219, s. 1.3.)

§ 58-46-35. Reports of inspection made available; immunity from liability.

All reports of inspection performed by or on behalf of the association shall be made available to the members of the association, applicants and the Commissioner. There shall be no liability on the part of and no cause of action of any nature shall arise against any member insurer, the Association or its agents or employees, the board of directors, or the Commissioner or his representatives for any action taken by them in good faith in the performance of their powers and duties under this Article. (1969, c. 1284; 1999-114, s. 6.)

§ 58-46-40. Assessment; inability to pay.

In the event any insurer fails by reason of insolvency to pay any assessment as provided herein, the amount assessed each insurer shall be immediately recalculated excluding therefrom the insolvent insurer so that its assessment is, in effect, assumed and redistributed among the remaining insurers. Such an assessment against an insolvent insurer shall not be a charge against any special deposit fund held under the provisions of Article 5 of this Chapter for the benefit of policyholders. (1969, c. 1284; 1985, c. 519, s. 7; 1991, c. 720, s. 26.)

§ 58-46-41. Unearned premium, loss, and loss expense reserves.

The Association shall make provisions for reserving unearned premiums and reserving for losses, including incurred but not reported losses, and loss expenses, in accordance with G.S. 58-3-71, 58-3-75, and 58-3-81. (2002-185, s. 5.2.)

§ 58-46-45. Premium taxes to be paid through Association.

All premium taxes due on insurance written under this Article shall be remitted by each insurer to the Association; and the Association, as collecting agent for its member companies, shall forward all such taxes to the Secretary of Revenue as provided in Article 8B of Chapter 105 of the General Statutes. (1985 (Reg. Sess., 1986), c. 928, s. 10; 1995 (Reg. Sess., 1996), c. 747, s. 13.)

§ 58-46-50. Annual reports.

On or before January 1 of each year the association shall file with the Commissioner a statement that summarizes the transactions, conditions, operations, and affairs of the association during the preceding year. The statement shall contain such matters and information as are prescribed by the Commissioner and shall be in such form as is approved by him. The Commissioner may at any time require the association to furnish him with any additional information with respect to its transactions or any other matter that the Commissioner deems to be material to assist him in evaluating the operation and experience of the association. (1987 (Reg. Sess., 1988), c. 975, s. 26.)

§ 58-46-55. Rates, rating plans, rating rules, and forms applicable.

The rates, rating plans, rating rules, and forms applicable to the insurance written by the association shall be in accordance with the most recent manual rates or adjusted loss costs and forms that are legally in effect in this State. (1987 (Reg. Sess., 1988), c. 975, s. 28; 1991 (Reg. Sess., 1992), c. 784, s. 3; 2009-472, s. 6.)

§ 58-46-60. Open meetings.

The Association is subject to the Open Meetings Act, Article 33C of Chapter 143 of the General Statutes, as amended. (2002-185, s. 7.2.)

Article 47.

Workers' Compensation Self-Insurance.

§§ 58-47-1 through 58-47-50: Repealed by Session Laws 1997-362, s. 2.

Part 1. Employer Groups.

§ 58-47-60. Definitions.

As used in this part:

(1) "Act" means the Workers' Compensation Act in Article 1 of Chapter 97 of the General Statutes, as amended.

(2) "Affiliate" has the same meaning as in G.S. 58-19-5(1).

(3) "Annual statement filing" means the most recent annual filing made with the Commissioner under G.S. 58-2-165.

(4) "Board" means the board of trustees or other governing body of a group.

(5) "Books and records" means all files, documents, and databases in a paper form, electronic medium, or both.

(6) "Control" means "control" as defined in G.S. 58-19-5(2).

(7) "GAAP financial statement" means a financial statement as defined by generally accepted accounting principles.

(8) "Group" means two or more employers who agree to pool their workers' compensation liabilities under the Act and are licensed under this Part.

(9) "Hazardous financial condition" means that, based on its present or reasonably anticipated financial condition, a person is insolvent or, although not financially impaired or insolvent, is unlikely to be able:

a. To meet obligations for known claims and reasonably anticipated claims; or

b. To pay other obligations in the normal course of business.

(10) "Member" means an employer that participates in a group.

(11) "Qualified actuary" means a member in good standing of the Casualty Actuarial Society or a member in good standing of the American Academy of Actuaries, who has been approved as qualified for signing casualty loss reserve opinions by the Casualty Practice Council of the American Academy of Actuaries, and is in compliance with G.S. 58-2-171.

(12) "Rate" means the cost of insurance per exposure unit, whether expressed as a single number or as a prospective loss cost with an adjustment to account for the treatment of expenses, profit, and variations in loss experience, before any application of individual risk variations based on loss or expense considerations, and does not include minimum premiums.

(13) "Service company" means an entity that has contracted with an employer or group for the purpose of providing any services related to claims adjustment, loss control, or both.

(14) "Third-party administrator" or "TPA" means a person engaged by a board to execute the policies established by the board and to provide day-to-day management of the group. "Third-party administrator" or "TPA" does not mean:

a. An employer acting on behalf of its employees or the employees of one or more of its affiliates.

b. An insurer that is licensed under this Chapter or that is acting as an insurer with respect to a policy lawfully issued and delivered by it and under the laws of a state in which the insurer is licensed to write insurance.

c. An agent or broker who is licensed by the Commissioner under Article 33 of this Chapter whose activities are limited exclusively to the sale of insurance.

d. An adjuster licensed by the Commissioner under Article 33 of this Chapter whose activities are limited to adjustment of claims.

e. An individual who is an officer, a member, or an employee of a board.

(15) "Underwriting" means the process of selecting risks and classifying them according to their degrees of insurability so that the appropriate rates may be assigned. The process also includes rejection of those risks that do not qualify. (1997-362, s. 3; 2001-223, s. 21.1.)

§ 58-47-65. Licensing; qualification for approval.

(a) No group shall self-insure its workers' compensation liabilities under the Act unless it is licensed by the Commissioner under this Part. Any self-insured group that was organized and approved under the North Carolina law before July 1, 1995, and whose authority to self-insure its workers' compensation liabilities under the Act has not terminated after that date, shall not be required to be reapproved to be licensed under this Article.

(b) An applicant for a license shall file with the Commissioner the information required by subsection (f) of this section on a form prescribed by the Commissioner at least 90 days before the proposed licensing date. The applicant shall furnish to the Commissioner satisfactory proof of the proposed group's financial ability, through its members, to comply with the Act. No application is complete until the Commissioner has received all required information.

(c) The group shall comprise two or more employers who are members of and are sponsored by a single bona fide trade or professional association. The association shall (i) comprise members engaged in the same or substantially similar business or profession within the State, (ii) have been incorporated in

North Carolina, (iii) have been in existence for at least five years before the date of application to the Commissioner to form a group, and (iv) submit a written determination from the Internal Revenue Service that it is exempt from taxation under 26 U.S.C. § 501(c). This subsection does not apply to a group that was organized and approved under North Carolina law before July 1, 1995.

(d) Only an applicant whose members' employee base is actuarially sufficient in numbers and provides an actuarially appropriate spreading of risk may apply for a license. The Commissioner shall consider (i) the financial strength and liquidity of the applicant relative to its ability to comply with the Act, (ii) the applicant's criteria and procedures regarding the review and monitoring of members' financial strength, (iii) reliability of the financial information, (iv) workers' compensation loss history, (v) underwriting guidelines, (vi) claims administration, (vii) excess insurance or reinsurance, and (viii) access to excess insurance or reinsurance.

(e) Before issuing a license to any applicant, the Commissioner shall require, in addition to the other requirements provided by law, that the applicant file an affidavit signed by the association's board members that it has not violated any of the applicable provisions of this Part or the Act during the last 12 months, and that it accepts the provisions of this Part and the Act in return for the license.

(f) The license application shall comprise the following information:

(1) Biographical affidavits providing the education, prior occupation, business experience, and other supplementary information submitted for each promoter, incorporator, director, trustee, proposed management personnel, and other persons similarly situated.

(2) A forecast for a five-year period based on the initial capitalization of the proposed group and its plan of operation. The forecast shall be prepared by a certified public accountant, a qualified actuary, or both, be in sufficient detail for a complete analysis to be performed, and be accompanied by a list of the assumptions utilized in making the forecast.

(3) An individual application, under G.S. 58-47-125, of each member applying for coverage in the proposed group on the inception date of the proposed group, with a current GAAP financial statement of each member. The financial statements are confidential, but the Commissioner may use them in any judicial or administrative proceeding.

(4) A breakdown of all forecasted administrative expenses for the proposed group's fiscal year in a dollar amount and as a percentage of the estimated annual premium.

(5) The proposed group's procedures for evaluating the current and continuing financial strength of members.

(6) Evidence of the coverage required by G.S. 58-47-95.

(7) Demonstration provided by the board, satisfactory to the Commissioner, that the proposed group's member employee base is actuarially sufficient in numbers and provides an actuarially appropriate spreading of risk.

(8) An assessment plan under G.S. 58-47-135(a).

(9) A listing of the estimated premium to be developed for each member individually and in total for the proposed group. Payroll data for each of the three preceding years shall be furnished by risk classification.

(10) An executed agreement by each member showing the member's obligation to pay to the proposed group not less than twenty-five percent (25%) of the member's estimated annual premium not later than the first day of coverage afforded by the proposed group.

(11) Composition of the initial board.

(12) An indemnity agreement on a form prescribed by the Commissioner.

(13) Proof, satisfactory to the Commissioner, that either the applicant has within its own organization ample facilities and competent personnel to service its program for underwriting, claims, and industrial safety engineering, or that the applicant will contract for any of these services. If the applicant is to perform any servicing, biographical affidavits of those persons who will be responsible for or performing servicing shall be included with the information in subdivision (1) of this subsection. If a group contracts with a service company or TPA to administer and adjust claims, the group shall provide proof of compliance with the other provisions of this Part.

(14) A letter stipulating the applicant's acceptance of membership in the North Carolina Self-Insurance Security Association under Article 4 of Chapter 97 of the General Statutes.

(15) Any other specific information the Commissioner considers relevant to the organization of the proposed group.

(g) Every applicant shall execute and file with the Commissioner an agreement, as part of the application, in which the applicant agrees to deposit with the Commissioner cash or securities acceptable to the Commissioner. (1997-362, s. 3; 1999-132, s. 13.1; 2003-212, s. 24; 2005-400, s. 19; 2007-127, s. 11.)

§ 58-47-70. License denial; termination; revocation; restrictions.

(a) If the Commissioner denies a license, the Commissioner shall inform the applicant of the reasons for the denial. The Commissioner may issue a license to an applicant that remedies the reasons for a denial within 60 days after the Commissioner's notice. The Commissioner may grant additional time to an applicant to remedy any deficiencies in its application. A request for an extension of time shall be made in writing by the applicant within 30 days after the Commissioner's notice. If the applicant fails to remedy the reasons for the denial, the application shall be withdrawn or denied.

(b) A group shall not terminate its license or cease the writing of renewal business without obtaining prior written approval from the Commissioner. The Commissioner shall not grant the request of any group to terminate its license unless the group has closed or reinsured all of its incurred workers' compensation obligations and has settled all of its other legal obligations, including known and unknown claims and associated expenses.

(c) No group shall transfer its workers' compensation obligations under an assumption reinsurance agreement without complying with Part 2 of Article 10 of this Chapter.

(d) Every group is subject to Article 19 of this Chapter. No group shall merge with another group unless both groups are engaged in the same or a similar type of business. (1997-362, s. 3.)

§ 58-47-75. Reporting and records.

(a) As used in this section:

(1) "Audited financial report" has the same meaning as in the NAIC Model Rule Requiring Annual Audited Financial Reports, as specified in G.S. 58-2-205.

(2) "Duplicate record" means a counterpart produced by the same impression as the original record, or from the same matrix, or by mechanical or electronic rerecording or by chemical reproduction, or by equivalent techniques, such as imaging or image processing, that accurately reproduce the original record.

(3) "Original record" means the writing or recording itself or any counterpart intended to have the same effect by a person executing or issuing it, in the normal and ordinary course of business, or data stored in a computer or similar device, the printout or other output readable by sight, shown to reflect the data accurately. An "original" of a photograph includes the negative or any print from the negative.

(b) Each group shall file with the Commissioner the following:

(1) A statement in accordance with G.S. 58-2-165.

(2) An audited financial report.

(3) Annual payroll information within 90 days after the close of its fiscal year. The report shall summarize the payroll by annual amount paid and by classifications using the rules, classifications, and rates set forth in the most recently approved Workers' Compensation and Employers' Liability Insurance Manual governing audits of payrolls and adjustments of premiums. Each group shall maintain true and accurate payroll records. The payroll records shall be maintained to allow for verification of the completeness and accuracy of the annual payroll report.

(c) Each group shall make its financial statement and audited financial report available to its members upon request.

(d) All records shall be maintained by the group for the years during which an examination under G.S. 58-2-131 has not yet been completed.

(e) All records that are required to be maintained by this section shall be either original or duplicate records.

(f) If only duplicate records are maintained, the following requirements apply:

(1) The data shall be accessible to the Commissioner in legible form, and legible, reproduced copies shall be available.

(2) Before the destruction of any original records, the group in possession of the original records shall:

a. Verify that the records stored consist of all information contained in the original records, and that the original records can be reconstructed therefrom in a form acceptable to the Commissioner; and

b. Implement disaster preparedness or disaster recovery procedures that include provisions for the maintenance of duplicate records at an off-site location.

(3) Adequate controls shall be established with respect to the transfer and maintenance of data.

(g) Each group shall maintain its records under G.S. 58-7-50, G.S. 58-7-55, and the Act.

(h) All books of original entry and corporate records shall be retained by the group or its successor for a period of 15 years after the group ceases to exist. (1997-362, s. 3.)

§ 58-47-80. Assets and invested assets.

Funds shall be held and invested by the board under G.S. 58-7-160, 58-7-162, 58-7-163, 58-7-165, 58-7-167, 58-7-168, 58-7-170, 58-7-172, 58-7-173, 58-7-178, 58-7-179, 58-7-180, 58-7-183, 58-7-185, 58-7-187, 58-7-188, 58-7-192,

58-7-193, 58-7-197, 58-7-200, and 58-19-10. (1997-362, s. 3; 2001-223, s. 21.2; 2003-212, s. 13.)

§ 58-47-85. Surplus requirements.

Every group shall maintain minimum surplus under one of the options in subdivision (1), (2), or (3) of this section:

(1)   Maintain minimum surplus in accordance with Article 12 of this Chapter. A group organized and authorized before the effective date of this section shall comply with this section under the following schedule:

a.   Forty percent (40%) of the surplus, in accordance with Article 12, by January 1, 1999.

b.   Fifty-five percent (55%) of the surplus, in accordance with Article 12, by January 1, 2000.

c.   Seventy percent (70%) of the surplus, in accordance with Article 12, by January 1, 2001.

d.   Eighty-five percent (85%) of the surplus, in accordance with Article 12, by January 1, 2002.

e.   One hundred percent (100%) of the surplus, in accordance with Article 12, by January 1, 2003.

The Commissioner shall not approve any dividend request that results in a surplus that is less than one hundred percent (100%) of the minimum surplus required by Article 12 of this Chapter.

(2)   Maintain minimum surplus at an amount equal to ten percent (10%) of the group's total undiscounted outstanding claim liability, according to the group's annual statement filing, or such other amount as the Commissioner prescribes based on, but not limited to, the financial condition of the group and the risk retained by the group. In addition, the group shall:

a.   Maintain specific excess insurance or reinsurance that provides the coverage limits in G.S. 58-47-95(a). The group shall retain no specific risk greater than five percent (5%) of the group's total annual earned premium according to the group's annual statement filing.

b.   Maintain aggregate excess insurance or reinsurance with a coverage limit being the greater of two million dollars ($2,000,000) or twenty percent (20%) of the group's annual earned premium, according to the group's annual statement filing. The aggregate excess attachment point shall be one hundred ten percent (110%) of the annual earned premium, according to the group's annual statement filing. The required attachment point shall be reduced by each point, or fraction of a point, that a group's expense ratio exceeds thirty percent (30%). Conversely, the required attachment point may be increased by each point, or fraction of a point, that a group's expense ratio is less than thirty percent (30%), but in no event shall the attachment point be greater than one hundred fifteen percent (115%) of the annual earned premium.

c.   Adopt a policy whereby every member:

1.   Pays a deposit to the group of twenty-five percent (25%) of the member's estimated annual earned premium, or another amount that the Commissioner prescribes based on, but not limited to, the financial condition of the group and the risk retained by the group; or

2.   Once every year files with the group the member's most recent year-end balance sheet, which, at a minimum, is compiled by an independent certified public accountant. The balance sheet shall demonstrate that the member's financial position does not show a deficit equity and is appropriate for membership in the group. At the request of the Commissioner, the group shall make these filings available for review. These filings shall be kept confidential; provided that the Commissioner may use that information in any judicial or administrative proceeding.

(3)   Maintain minimum surplus at an amount equal to three hundred thousand dollars ($300,000). The group shall immediately assess its members if, at any time, the group's surplus is less than the minimum surplus amount. In addition, the group shall maintain:

a.   Specific excess insurance or reinsurance that provides coverage limits pursuant to G.S. 58-47-95(a). The group shall retain no specific risk greater than five percent (5%) of the group's total annual earned premium according to the group's annual statement filing.

b. Aggregate excess insurance or reinsurance with a coverage limit being the greater of two million dollars ($2,000,000) or twenty percent (20%) of the group's annual earned premium, according to the group's annual statement filing. The aggregate excess attachment point shall be one hundred ten percent (110%) of the annual earned premium, according to the group's annual statement filing. The required attachment point shall be reduced by each point, or fraction of a point, that a group's expense ratio exceeds thirty percent (30%). Conversely, the required attachment point may be increased by each point, or fraction of a point, that a group's expense ratio is less than thirty percent (30%), but in no event shall the attachment point be greater than one hundred fifteen percent (115%) of the annual earned premium.

The Commissioner may require different levels, or waive the requirement, of specific and aggregate excess loss coverage consistent with the market availability of excess loss coverage, the group's claims experience, and the group's financial condition. (1997-362, s. 3; 1999-132, s. 13.2.)

§ 58-47-90. Deposits.

(a) Each group shall deposit with the Commissioner an amount equal to ten percent (10%) of the group's total annual earned premium, according to the group's annual statement filing, but not less than six hundred thousand dollars ($600,000), or another amount that the Commissioner prescribes based on, but not limited to, the financial condition of the group and the risk retained by the group.

(b) G.S. 58-5-1, 58-5-20, 58-5-25, 58-5-30, 58-5-35, 58-5-40, 58-5-63, 58-5-75, 58-5-80, 58-5-90(a) and (c), 58-5-95, 58-5-110, 58-5-115, and 58-5-120 apply to groups.

(c) A group organized and authorized before January 1, 1998, has until January 1, 2001, to comply with subsection (b) of this section. However, a dividend request shall not be approved by the Commissioner until the group has replaced its surety bonds with the deposit required by subsection (b) of this section.

(d) No judgment creditor, other than a claimant entitled to benefits under the Act, may levy upon any deposits made under this section.

(e) Surety bonds shall be in a form prescribed by the Commissioner and issued by an insurer authorized by the Commissioner to write surety business in North Carolina.

(f) Any surety bond may be exchanged or replaced with another surety bond that meets the requirements of this section if 90 days' advance written notice is provided to the Commissioner. An endorsement to a surety bond shall be filed with the Commissioner within 30 days after its effective date.

(g) If a group ceases to self-insure, dissolves, or transfers its workers' compensation obligations under an assumption reinsurance agreement, the Commissioner shall not release any deposits until the group has fully discharged all of its obligations under the Act. (1997-362, s. 3.)

§ 58-47-95. Excess insurance and reinsurance.

(a) Each group, on or before its effective date of operation and on a continuing basis thereafter, shall maintain specific and aggregate excess loss coverage through an insurance policy or reinsurance contract. Groups shall maintain limits and retentions commensurate with their exposures. A group's retention shall be the lowest retention suitable for groups with similar exposures and annual premium. The Commissioner may require different levels, or waive the requirement, of specific and aggregate excess loss coverage consistent with the market availability of excess loss coverage, the group's claims experience, and the group's financial condition.

(b) Any excess insurance policy or reinsurance contract under this section shall be issued by a licensed insurance company, a licensed captive insurance company, an approved surplus lines insurance company, or an accredited reinsurer, and shall:

(1) Provide for at least 30 days' written notice of cancellation by certified mail, return receipt requested, to the group and to the Commissioner.

(2) Be renewable automatically at its expiration, except upon 30 days' written notice of nonrenewal by certified mail, return receipt requested, to the group and to the Commissioner.

(c) Every group shall provide to the Commissioner evidence of its excess insurance or reinsurance coverage, and any amendments, within 30 days after their effective dates. Every group shall, at the request of the Commissioner, furnish copies of any excess insurance policies or reinsurance contracts and any amendments. (1997-362, s. 3; 2013-116, s. 4.)

§ 58-47-100. Examinations.

G.S. 58-2-131 through G.S. 58-2-134 apply to groups. (1997-362, s. 3; 1999-132, s. 11.7.)

§ 58-47-105. Dividends and other distributions.

(a) Group dividends and other distributions shall be made in accordance with G.S. 58-7-130, 58-8-25(b), and 58-19-30. A group shall be in compliance with this Part before payment of dividends or other distributions to its members. No group shall pay dividends or other distributions to its members until two years after the group's licensing date.

(b) Payment of dividends to the members of any group shall not be contingent upon the maintenance or continuance of membership in the group. (1997-362, s. 3.)

§ 58-47-110. Premium rates.

(a) As used in this section:

(1) "Bureau" means the North Carolina Rate Bureau in Article 36 of this Chapter.

(2) "Expenses" means that portion of a premium rate attributable to acquisition, field supervision, collection expenses, and general expenses, as determined by the group.

(3) "Multiplier" means a group's determination of the expenses, other than loss expense and loss adjustment expense, associated with writing workers' compensation and employers' liability insurance, which shall be expressed as a single nonintegral number to be applied equally and uniformly to the prospective loss costs approved by the Commissioner in making rates for each classification of risks utilized by that group.

(4) "Prospective loss costs" means that portion of a rate that does not include provisions for expenses (other than loss adjustment expenses) or profit and that is based on historical aggregate losses and loss adjustment expenses adjusted through development to their ultimate value and forecasted through trending to a future point in time.

(5) "Supplementary rating information" means any manual or plan of rates, classification, rating schedule, minimum premium, policy fee, rating rule, rate-related underwriting rule, experience rating plan, statistical plan, and any other similar information needed to determine the applicable rate in effect or to be in effect.

(b) Rates and the effective date shall be submitted by the group to the Commissioner for prior approval in the form of a rate filing. The rate filing:

(1) Shall be on a form prescribed by the Commissioner and shall be supported by competent analysis, prepared by an actuary who is a member in good standing of the Casualty Actuarial Society or the American Academy of Actuaries, demonstrating that the resulting rates meet the standards of not being excessive, inadequate, or unfairly discriminatory;

(2) Shall have the final rates and the effective date determined independently and individually by the group;

(3) Shall have manual rates that are the combination of the prospective loss costs and the multiplier;

(4) Shall file any other information that the group considers relevant and shall provide any other information requested by the Commissioner;

(5) Shall be considered complete when the required information and all additional information requested by the Commissioner is received by the Commissioner. When a filing is not accompanied by the information required under this section, the Commissioner shall inform the group within 30 days after

the initial filing that the filing is incomplete and shall note the deficiencies. If information required by a rate filing or requested by the Commissioner is not maintained or cannot be provided, the group shall certify that to the Commissioner;

(6)   May include deviations to the prospective loss cost based on the group's anticipated experience. Sufficient documentation supporting the deviations and the impact of the deviation shall be included in the rate filing. Expense loads, whether variable, fixed, or a combination of variable and fixed, may vary by individual classification or grouping. Each filing that varies the expense load by class shall specify the expense factor applicable to each class and shall include information supporting the justification for the variation;

(7)   Shall include any proposed use of a premium-sized discount program, a schedule rating program, a small deductible credit program or an expense constant or minimum premium, and the use shall be supported in the rate filing; and

(8)   Shall be deemed approved, unless disapproved by the Commissioner in writing, within 60 days after the rate filing is made in its entirety. A group is not required to refile rates previously approved until two years after the effective date of this Part.

(c)   At the time of the rate filing, a group may request to have its approved multiplier remain in effect and continue to use either the prospective loss cost filing in effect at the time of the rate filing or the prospective loss cost filing in effect at the time of the filing, along with all other subsequent prospective loss cost filings, as approved.

(d)   To the extent that a group's manual rates are determined solely by applying its multiplier, as presented and approved in the rate filing, to the prospective loss costs contained in the Bureau's reference filing and printed in the Bureau's rating manual, the group need not develop or file its final rate pages with the Commissioner. If a group chooses to print and distribute final rate pages for its own use, based solely upon the application of its filed prospective loss costs, the group need not file those pages with the Commissioner. If the Bureau does not print the prospective loss costs in its manual, the group shall submit its rates to the Commissioner.

(e)   If a new filing of rules, relativities, and supplementary rating information is filed by the Bureau and approved:

(1) The group shall not file anything with the Commissioner if the group decides to use the revisions as filed, with the effective date as filed together with the prospective loss multiplier on file with the Commissioner.

(2) The group shall notify the Commissioner of its effective date before the Bureau filing's effective date if the group decides to use the revisions as filed but with a different effective date.

(3) The group shall notify the Commissioner before the Bureau filing's effective date if the group decides not to use the revision or revisions.

(4) The group shall file the modification with the Commissioner, for approval, specifying the basis for the modification and the group's proposed effective date if different from the Bureau filing's effective date, if the group decides to use the revision with deviations.

(f) Every group shall adhere to the uniform classification plan and experience rating plan filed by the Bureau.

(g) Groups shall maintain data in accordance with the uniform statistical plan approved by the Commissioner.

(h) Each group shall submit annually a rate certification, signed by an actuary who is a member in good standing of the Casualty Actuarial Society or the American Academy of Actuaries, which states that the group's prospective rates are not excessive, inadequate, or unfairly discriminatory. The certification is to accompany the group's rate filing. If a rate filing is not required, the actuarial rate certification is to be submitted by the end of the calendar year. (1997-362, s. 3.)

§ 58-47-115. Premium payment requirements.

Groups shall collect members' premiums for each policy period in a manner so that at no time the sum of a member's premium payments is less than the total estimated earned premium for that member. (1997-362, s. 3.)

§ 58-47-120. Board; composition, powers, duties, and prohibitions.

(a) Each group shall be governed by a board or other governing body comprising no fewer than three persons, elected for stated terms of office, and subject to the Commissioner's approval. All board members shall be residents of this State or members of the group. At least two-thirds of the board shall comprise employees, officers, or directors of members; provided that the Commissioner may waive this requirement for good cause. The group's TPA, service company, or any owner, officer, employee, or agent of, or any other person affiliated with, the TPA or service company shall not serve as a board member. The board shall ensure that all claims are paid promptly and take all necessary precautions to safeguard the assets of the group.

(b) The board shall be responsible for the following:

(1) Maintaining minutes of its meetings and making the minutes available to the Commissioner.

(2) Providing for the execution of its policies, including providing for day-to-day management of the group and delineating in the minutes of its meetings the areas of authority it delegates.

(3) Designating a chair to facilitate communication between the group and the Commissioner.

(4) Adopting a policy of reimbursement from the assets of the group for out-of-pocket expenses incurred as board members, if so desired.

(c) The board shall not:

(1) Be compensated by the group, TPA, or service company except for out-of-pocket expenses incurred as board members.

(2) Extend credit to members for payment of a premium, except under payment requirements set forth in this Part.

(3) Borrow any money from the group or in the name of the group, except in the ordinary course of business, without first informing the Commissioner of the nature and purpose of the loan and obtaining the Commissioner's approval.

(d)   The board shall adopt bylaws to govern the operation of the group. The bylaws shall comply with the provisions of this section and shall include:

(1)   The method for selecting the board members, including terms of office.

(2)   The method for amending the bylaws and the plans of operation and assessment.

(3)   The method for establishing and maintaining the group.

(4)   The procedures and requirements for dissolving the group.

(e)   Each group shall file a copy of its bylaws with the Commissioner. Any changes to the bylaws shall be filed with the Commissioner no later than 30 days before their effective dates. The Commissioner may order the group to rescind or revoke any bylaw if it violates this section or any other applicable law or administrative rule.

(f)   The board shall adopt and administer a plan of operation to assure the fair, reasonable, and equitable administration of the group. All members shall comply with the plan. The plan shall comply with this section and include:

(1)   Procedures for administering the assets of the group.

(2)   A plan of assessment.

(3)   Loss control services to be provided to the members.

(4)   Rules for payment and collection of premium.

(5)   Basis for dividends.

(6)   Reimbursement of board members.

(7)   Intervals for meetings of the board, which shall be held at least semiannually.

(8)   Procedures for the maintenance of records of all transactions of the group.

(9)   Procedures for the selection of the board members.

(10) Additional provisions necessary or proper for the execution of the powers and duties of the group.

(11) Qualifications for group membership, including underwriting guidelines and procedures to identify any member that is in a hazardous financial condition.

(g) The plan and any amendments become effective upon approval in writing by the Commissioner.

(h) Each year the board shall review:

(1) The performance evaluation of the TPA or service company, if applicable.

(2) Loss control services.

(3) Investment policies.

(4) Delinquent debts.

(5) Membership cancellation procedures.

(6) Admission of new members.

(7) Claims administration and reporting.

(8) Payroll audits and findings.

(9) Excess insurance or reinsurance coverage.

The board's findings from its review shall be documented in the board's minutes.

(i) G.S. 58-7-140 applies to board members. (1997-362, s. 3; 1999-132, s. 13.3.)

§ 58-47-125. Admission and termination of group members.

(a) Prospective group members shall submit applications for membership to the board. The board, a designated employee of the group, or TPA shall approve an application for membership under the bylaws of the group. Members shall have bona fide offices in this State and members' employees shall be primarily engaged in business activities within this State. Members shall receive certificates of coverage from the board on a form acceptable to the Commissioner.

(b) The group shall make available to the Commissioner properly executed applications and indemnity agreements for all members, on forms prescribed by the Commissioner. If the applications and indemnity agreements are not executed properly and maintained, the Commissioner may order the group to cease writing all new business until all of the agreements are executed properly and obtained.

(c) Members may elect to terminate their participation in a group and may be terminated by the group under subsection (d) of this section and the bylaws of the group.

(d) A group may terminate a member's participation in the group on 30 days' written notice to the member. A group may terminate a member's participation in the group for nonpayment of premium on 10 days' written notice to the member. A member may terminate its participation in the group on 10 days' written notice to the group. Notices under this subsection shall be given by certified mail, return receipt requested. No termination by the group is effective until the notice is received by the member. (1997-362, s. 3; 2001-451, s. 3.)

§ 58-47-130. Disclosure.

Every group through its board, TPA, service company, agents, or other representatives shall require, before accepting an application, each applicant for membership to acknowledge in writing that the applicant has received the following:

(1) A document disclosing that the members are jointly and severally liable for the obligations of the group.

(2) A copy of the group's plan of assessment.

(3) The amount of specific and aggregate stop loss or excess insurance or reinsurance carried by the group, the amount and kind of risk retained by the group, and the name and rating of the insurer providing stop loss, excess insurance, or reinsurance. (1997-362, s. 3.)

§ 58-47-135. Assessment plan and indemnity agreement.

(a) Each group shall establish an assessment plan that provides for a reasonable and equitable mechanism for assessing its members. The plan and any amendments shall be approved by the Commissioner. The plan shall include descriptions of the circumstances that initiate an assessment, basis, and allocation to members of the amount being assessed, and collection of the assessment.

(b) The board shall notify the Commissioner of an assessment no fewer than 60 days before an assessment.

(c) The Commissioner shall impose an assessment on members if the board or third-party administrator fails to take action to correct a hazardous financial condition.

(d) Every group shall file an indemnity agreement on a form prescribed by the Commissioner, which jointly and severally binds the members of the group to comply with the provisions of the act and pay obligations imposed by the Act. (1997-362, s. 3.)

§ 58-47-140. Other provisions of this Chapter.

The following provisions of this Chapter apply to workers' compensation self-insurance groups that are subject to this Article:

G.S. 58-1-10, 58-2-45, 58-2-50, 58-2-70, 58-2-100, 58-2-105, 58-2-155, 58-2-161, 58-2-180, 58-2-185, 58-2-190, 58-2-200, 58-3-71, 58-3-81, 58-3-100, 58-3-120, 58-6-25, 58-7-21, 58-7-26, 58-7-30, 58-7-33, 58-7-73, and Articles 13, 19, 30, 33, 34, and 63 of this Chapter. (1997-362, s. 3; 2005-215, s. 15; 2006-226, s. 17.)

Part 2. Third-Party Administrators and Service Companies For Individual And Group Self-insurers.

§ 58-47-150. Definitions.

As used in this Part:

(1) "Books and records" means all files, documents, and databases in a paper form, electronic medium, or both.

(2) "Self-insurer" means a group of employers licensed by the Commissioner under Part 1 of this Article or a single employer licensed by the Commissioner under Article 5 of Chapter 97 of the General Statutes to retain its liability under the Workers' Compensation Act and to pay directly the compensation in the amount and manner and when due as provided for in the Act.

(3) "Service company" means an entity that has contracted with a self-insurer for the purpose of providing any services related to claims adjustment, loss control, or both.

(4) "Third-party administrator" or "TPA" means a person engaged by a self-insurer to execute the policies established by the self-insurer and to provide day-to-day management of the self-insurer. "Third-Party Administrator" and "TPA" does not mean:

a. A self-insurer acting on behalf of its employees or the employees of one or more of its affiliates.

b. An insurer that is licensed under this Chapter or that is acting as an insurer with respect to a policy lawfully issued and delivered by it and under the laws of a state in which the insurer is licensed to write insurance.

c. An agent or broker who is licensed by the Commissioner under Article 33 of this Chapter whose activities are limited exclusively to the sale of insurance.

d. An adjuster licensed by the Commissioner under Article 33 of this Chapter whose activities are limited to adjustment of claims.

e. An individual who is an officer, a member, or an employee of a board.

(5) "Underwriting" means the process of selecting risks and classifying them according to their degrees of insurability so that the appropriate rates may be assigned. The process also includes rejection of those risks that do not qualify. (1997-362, s. 3.)

§ 58-47-155. TPAs and service companies; authority; qualifications.

(a) No person shall act as, offer to act as, or hold himself or herself out as a TPA or a service company with respect to risks located in this State for a self-insurer unless that person complies with this Article.

(b) A TPA or service company shall post with the self-insurer a fidelity bond or other appropriate coverage, issued by an authorized insurer, in a form acceptable to the Commissioner, in an amount commensurate with the risk, and with the governing board of the self-insurer as obligee or beneficiary.

(c) A TPA or service company shall maintain errors and omissions coverage or other appropriate liability insurance in a form acceptable to the Commissioner and in an amount commensurate with the risk. The governing body of the self-insurer shall be obligee or beneficiary of the coverage or insurance.

(d) If the Commissioner determines that a TPA or service company or any other person has not materially complied with this Article or with any rule adopted or order issued under this Article, after notice and opportunity to be heard, the Commissioner may order for each separate violation a civil penalty under G.S. 58-2-70(d).

(e) If the Commissioner finds that because of a material noncompliance that a self-insurer has suffered any loss or damage, the Commissioner may maintain a civil action brought by or on behalf of the self-insurer and its covered members or persons and creditors for recovery of compensatory damages for the benefit of the self-insurer and its covered members or persons and creditors, or for other appropriate relief.

(f)   Nothing in this Article affects the Commissioner's right to impose any other penalties provided for in this Chapter or limits or restricts the rights of covered members or persons, claimants, and creditors.

(g)   If an order of rehabilitation or liquidation of the self-insurer has been entered under Article 30 of this Chapter, and the receiver appointed under that order determines that the TPA or service company or any other person has not materially complied with this Article or any rule adopted or order issued under this Article, and the self-insurer suffered any loss or damage from the noncompliance, the receiver may maintain a civil action for recovery of damages or other appropriate sanctions for the benefit of the self-insurer. (1997-362, s. 3.)

§ 58-47-160. Written agreement; composition; restrictions.

(a)   No person may act as a TPA or service company without a written agreement between the TPA or service company and the self-insurer. The written agreement shall be retained by the self-insurer and the TPA or service company for the duration of the agreement and for five years thereafter. The agreement shall contain all provisions required by this Article, to the extent those requirements apply to the functions performed by the TPA or service company.

(b)   Groups shall file with the Commissioner the written agreement, and any amendments to the agreement, within 30 days after execution. Single employers shall furnish the Commissioner, upon request, the written agreement and any amendments to the agreement. The information required by this section, including any trade secrets, shall be kept confidential; provided that the Commissioner may use that information in any judicial or administrative proceeding instituted against the TPA or service company.

(c)   The written agreement shall set forth the duties and powers of the TPA or service company and the self-insurer. The Commissioner shall disapprove any such written agreement that:

(1)   Subjects the self-insurer to excessive charges for expenses or commission.

(2) Vests in the TPA or service company any control over the management of the affairs of the self-insurer to the exclusion of the governing board of the self-insurer.

(3) Is entered into with any TPA or service company if the person acting as the TPA or service company, or any of the officers or directors of the TPA or service company, is of known bad character or has been affiliated directly or indirectly through ownership, control, management, reinsurance transactions, or other insurance or business relationships with any person known to have been involved in the improper manipulation of assets, accounts, or reinsurance.

(4) Is determined by the Commissioner to contain provisions that are not fair and reasonable to the self-insurer.

(d) The self-insurer, TPA, or service company may, by written notice, terminate the agreement as provided in the agreement. The self-insurer may suspend the underwriting authority of the TPA during the pendency of any dispute regarding the cause for termination of the agreement. The self-insurer shall fulfill any lawful obligations with respect to policies affected by the agreement, regardless of any dispute between the self-insurer and the TPA or service company.

(e) The contract may not be assigned in whole or part by the TPA or service company without prior approval by the governing board of the self-insurer and the Commissioner. (1997-362, s. 3.)

§ 58-47-165. Books and records.

(a) Every TPA or service company shall maintain and make available to the self-insurer complete books and records of all transactions performed on behalf of the self-insurer. The books and records shall be maintained by the self-insurer, TPA, or service company in accordance with G.S. 58-47-180.

(b) The Commissioner shall have access to books and records maintained by a TPA or service company for the purposes of examination, audit, or inspection. The Commissioner shall keep confidential any trade secrets contained in those books and records, including the identity and addresses of the covered members of a self-insurer, except that the Commissioner may use the information in any judicial or administrative proceeding instituted against the TPA or service company.

(c)   The Commissioner may use the TPA or service company as an intermediary in the Commissioner's dealings with the self-insurer if the Commissioner determines that this will result in a more rapid and accurate flow of information from the self-insurer and will aid in the self-insurer's compliance with this Article and the Workers' Compensation Act.

(d)   The self-insurer shall own the books and records generated by the TPA or service company pertaining to the self-insurer's business.

(e)   The self-insurer shall have access to and rights to duplicate all books and records related to its business.

(f)   If the self-insurer and the TPA or service company cancel their agreement, notwithstanding the provisions of subsection (a) of this section, the TPA or service company, shall transfer all books and records to the new TPA, service company, or the self-insurer in a form acceptable to the Commissioner. The new TPA or service company shall acknowledge, in writing, that it is responsible for retaining the books and records of the previous TPA, service company, or the self-insurer as required in subsection (a) of this section. (1997-362, s. 3.)

§ 58-47-170. Payments to TPA or service company.

If a self-insurer uses the services of a TPA, the payment to the TPA of any premiums or charges for insurance by or on behalf of the insured party is considered payment to the self-insurer. The payment of return premiums or claim payments forwarded by the self-insurer to the TPA or service company is not considered payment to the insured party or claimant until the payments are received by the insured party or claimant. This section does not limit any right of the self-insurer against the TPA or service company resulting from the failure of the TPA or service company to make payments to the self-insurer, insured parties, or claimants. (1997-362, s. 3.)

§ 58-47-175. Approval of advertising.

A TPA or service company may use only the advertising pertaining to or affecting the business underwritten by a self-insurer that has been approved in writing by the self-insurer before its use. (1997-362, s. 3.)

§ 58-47-180. Premium collection and payment of claims.

(a) The TPA or service company, at a minimum, shall:

(1) Periodically render an accounting to the self-insurer detailing all transactions performed by the TPA or service company pertaining to the business underwritten, premium or other charges collected, and claims paid by the self-insurer, when applicable.

(2) Deposit all receipts directly into an account maintained in the name of the self-insurer.

(3) Pay claims on drafts or checks of and authorized by the self-insurer.

(4) Not withdraw from the self-insurer's account except for authority limited to pay claims and refund premiums.

(5) Remit return premium, directly from the self-insurer's account, to the person entitled to the return premium.

(b) Any check disbursement authority granted to the TPA or service company may be terminated upon the self-insurer's written notice to the TPA or service company or upon termination of the agreement. The self-insurer may suspend the check disbursement authority during the pendency of any dispute regarding the cause for termination. (1997-362, s. 3.)

§ 58-47-185. Notices; disclosure.

(a) When the services of a TPA are used, the TPA shall provide a written notice approved by the self-insurer to covered members advising them of the identity of, and relationship among, the TPA, the member, and the self-insurer.

(b) When a TPA collects funds, the reason for collection of each item shall be identified to the member and each item shall be shown separately from any premium. Additional charges may not be made for services to the extent the services have been paid for by the self-insurer.

(c) The TPA shall disclose to the self-insurer all charges, fees, and commissions received from all services in connection with the provision of administrative services for the self-insurer, including any fees or commissions paid by self-insurers for obtaining reinsurance.

(d) The TPA or service company shall disclose to the self-insurer the nature of other business in which it is involved. (1997-362, s. 3.)

§ 58-47-190. Compensation.

A TPA or service company shall not enter into any agreement or understanding with a self-insurer that makes the amount of the TPA's or service company's commissions, fees, or charges contingent upon savings affected in the adjustment, settlement, and payment of losses covered by the self-insurer's obligations. This section does not prohibit a TPA or service company from receiving performance-based compensation for providing medical services through a physician-based network or auditing services and does not prevent the compensation of a TPA or service company from being based on premiums or charges collected or the number of claims paid or processed. (1997-362, s. 3.)

§ 58-47-195. Examinations.

TPAs and service companies may be examined under G.S. 58-2-131 through G.S. 58-2-134. (1997-362, s. 3; 1999-132, s. 11.8.)

§ 58-47-200. Unfair trade practices.

TPAs and service companies are subject to Article 63 of this Chapter. (1997-362, s. 3.)

§ 58-47-205. Other requirements.

(a) A TPA or service company, or any owner, officer, employee, or agent of a TPA or service company, or any other person affiliated with or related to the TPA or service company shall not:

(1) Serve as a trustee of a self-insurer.

(2) Make a contribution to the surplus of a self-insurer.

(b) Each TPA or service company shall make available for inspection by the Commissioner copies of all contracts with persons using the services of the TPA. (1997-362, s. 3; 2009-172, s. 4.)

Part 3. Third-Party Administrators for Groups.

§§ 58-47-210 through 58-47-220: Repealed by Session Laws 2001-223, s. 21.3, effective January 1, 2002.

Article 48.

Postassessment Insurance Guaranty Association.

§ 58-48-1. Short title.

This Article shall be known and may be cited as the "Insurance Guaranty Association Act." (1971, c. 670, s. 1.)

§ 58-48-5. Purpose of Article.

The purpose of this Article is to provide a mechanism for the payment of covered claims under certain insurance policies, to avoid excessive delay in payment, and to avoid financial loss to claimants or policyholders because of the insolvency of an insurer, to assist in the detection and prevention of insurer insolvencies, and to provide an association to assess the cost of such protection among insurers. (1971, c. 670, s. 1.)

§ 58-48-10. Scope.

This Article shall apply to all kinds of direct insurance, but shall not be applicable to:

(1) Life, annuity, accident and health or disability insurance;

(2) Mortgage guaranty, financial guaranty or other forms of insurance offering protection against investment risks;

(3) Fidelity or surety bonds, or any other bonding obligations;

(4) Credit insurance, vendors' single interest insurance, collateral protection insurance, or any similar insurance protecting the interests of a creditor arising out of a creditor-debtor transaction;

(5) Insurance of warranties or service contracts;

(6) Title insurance;

(7) Ocean marine insurance;

(8) Repealed by Session Laws 1991 (Regular Session, 1992), c. 802, s. 1.

(9) Any transaction or combination of transactions between a person (including affiliates of such person) and an insurer (including affiliates of such insurer) which involves the transfer of investment or credit risk unaccompanied by transfer of insurance risk;

(10) Insurance written on a retroactive basis to cover known or unknown losses which have resulted from an event with respect to which a claim has already been made, and the claim is known to the insurer at the time the

insurance is bound. (1971, c. 670, s. 1; 1989, c. 206, s. 1; 1991 (Reg. Sess., 1992), c. 802, s. 1.)

§ 58-48-15. Construction.

This Article shall be liberally construed to effect the purpose under G.S. 58-48-5 which shall constitute an aid and guide to interpretation. (1971, c. 670, s. 1.)

§ 58-48-20. Definitions.

As used in this Article:

(1)   "Account" means any one of the three accounts created by G.S. 58-48-25.

(1a)   "Affiliate" means a person who directly, or indirectly, through one or more intermediaries, controls, is controlled by, or is under common control with an insolvent insurer on December 31 of the year next preceding the date the insurer becomes an insolvent insurer.

(2)   "Association" means the North Carolina Insurance Guaranty Association created under G.S. 58-48-25.

(2a)   "Claimant" means any insured making a first party claim or any person instituting a liability claim; provided that no person who is an affiliate of the insolvent insurer may be a claimant.

(3)   Repealed by Session Laws 1991, c. 720, s. 6.

(3a)   "Control" means the possession, direct or indirect, of the power to direct or cause the direction of the management and policies of a person, whether through the ownership of voting securities, by contract, other than a commercial contract for goods or nonmanagement services, or otherwise, unless the power is the result of an official position with or corporate office held by the person. Control shall be presumed to exist if any person, directly or indirectly owns, controls, holds with the power to vote, or holds proxies representing ten percent

(10%) or more of the voting securities of any other person. This presumption may be rebutted by a showing that control does not exist in fact.

(4)   "Covered claim" means an unpaid claim, including one of unearned premiums, which is in excess of fifty dollars ($50.00) and arises out of and is within the coverage and not in excess of the applicable limits of an insurance policy to which this Article applies as issued by an insurer, if such insurer becomes an insolvent insurer after the effective date of this Article and (i) the claimant or insured is a resident of this State at the time of the insured event; or (ii) the property from which the claim arises is permanently located in this State. "Covered claim" shall not include any amount awarded (i) as punitive or exemplary damages; (ii) sought as a return of premium under any retrospective rating plan; or (iii) due any reinsurer, insurer, insurance pool, or underwriting association, as subrogation or contribution recoveries or otherwise. "Covered claim" also shall not include fines or penalties, including attorneys fees, imposed against an insolvent insurer or its insured or claims of any claimant whose net worth exceeds fifty million dollars ($50,000,000) on December 31 of the year preceding the date the insurer becomes insolvent.

(5)   "Insolvent insurer" means (i) an insurer licensed and authorized to transact insurance in this State either at the time the policy was issued or when the insured event occurred and (ii) against whom an order of liquidation with a finding of insolvency has been entered after the effective date of this Article by a court of competent jurisdiction in the insurer's state of domicile or of this State under the provisions of Article 30 of this Chapter, and which order of liquidation has not been stayed or been the subject of a writ of supersedeas or other comparable order.

(6)   "Member insurer" means any person who (i) writes any kind of insurance to which this Article applies under G.S. 58-48-10, including the exchange of reciprocal or interinsurance contracts, and (ii) is licensed and authorized to transact insurance in this State.

(7)   "Net direct written premiums" means direct gross premiums written in this State on insurance policies to which this Article applies, less return premiums thereon and dividends paid or credited to policyholders on such direct business. "Net direct written premiums" does not include premiums on contracts between insurers or reinsurers.

(7a)   "Ocean marine insurance" includes (i) marine insurance as defined in G.S. 58-7-15(20)a., except for inland marine, (ii) marine protection and indemnity insurance as defined in G.S. 58-7-15(21), and (iii) any other form of insurance, regardless of the name, label, or marketing designation of the insurance policy, which insures against maritime perils or risks and other related perils or risks, which are usually insured by traditional marine insurance such as hull and machinery, marine builders' risks, and marine protection and indemnity. The perils and risks insured against include loss, damage, or expense, or legal liability of the insured for loss, damage, or expense, arising out of, or incident to, ownership, operation, chartering, maintenance, use, repair, or construction of any vessel, craft, or instrumentality in use in ocean or inland waterways, including liability of the insured for personal injury, illness, death, or for loss or damage to the property of the insured or another person. "Ocean marine insurance" does not include insurance on vessels or vehicles under five tons gross weight.

(8) "Person" means any individual, corporation, partnership, association or voluntary organization.

(9) "Policyholder" means the person to whom an insurance policy to which this Article applies was issued by an insurer which has become an insolvent insurer.

(10) "Resident" means:

a. An individual domiciled in this State;

b. An individual formerly domiciled in this State at the time the applicable policy was issued or renewed and the term of the policy had not expired at the time of the insured event, and who at the time of the insured event had complied with the laws of the current domicile necessary to allow maintenance in force and effect of the applicable policy; or

c. In the case of a corporation or other entity that is not a natural person, a corporation or entity whose principal place of business is located in this State at the time of the insured event. (1971, c. 670, s. 1; 1985, c. 613, ss. 1-3; 1989, c. 206, s. 2; c. 770, s. 72; 1991, c. 720, s. 6; 1991 (Reg. Sess., 1992), c. 802, s. 2; 1993, c. 452, s. 51; 2003-167, s. 1.)

§ 58-48-25. Creation of the Association.

There is created a nonprofit, unincorporated legal entity to be known as the North Carolina Insurance Guaranty Association. All insurers defined as member insurers in G.S. 58-48-20(6) shall be and remain members of the Association as a condition of their authority to transact insurance in this State. The Association shall perform its functions under a plan of operation established and approved under G.S. 58-48-40 and shall exercise its powers through a board of directors established under G.S. 58-48-30. For purposes of administration and assessment, the Association shall be divided into three separate accounts: (i) the automobile insurance account; (ii) the workers' compensation account; and (iii) the account for all other insurance to which the Article applies. Each person becoming a member insurer after October 1, 1985, shall pay to the Association upon demand a nonrefundable initial membership fee of fifty dollars ($50.00). (1971, c. 670, s. 1; 1985, c. 613, s. 4; 1991 (Reg. Sess., 1992), c. 802, s. 3.)

§ 58-48-30. Board of directors.

(a) The board of directors of the Association shall consist of not less than five nor more than nine persons serving terms as established in the plan of operation. One non-voting member of the board shall be a property and casualty insurance agent authorized to write insurance for a member insurer, and appointed by the Commissioner; and the remaining members shall be selected by member insurers subject to the approval of the Commissioner. Vacancies of the board shall be filled for the remaining period of the term in the same manner as initial appointments. If no members are selected within 60 days after June 25, 1971, the Commissioner may appoint the initial members of the board of directors.

(b) In approving selections to the board, the Commissioner shall consider among other things whether all member insurers are fairly represented.

(c) Members of the board may be reimbursed from the assets of the Association for expenses incurred by them as members of the board of directors. (1971, c. 670, s. 1; 1987, c. 864, s. 60.)

§ 58-48-35. Powers and duties of the Association.

(a) The Association shall:

(1)   Be obligated to the extent of the covered claims existing prior to the determination of insolvency and arising within 30 days after the determination of insolvency, or before the policy expiration date if less than 30 days after the determination, or before the insured replaces the policy or causes its cancellation, if he does so within 30 days of the determination. This obligation includes only the amount of each covered claim that is in excess of fifty dollars ($50.00) and is less than three hundred thousand dollars ($300,000). However, the Association shall pay the full amount of a covered claim for benefits under a workers' compensation insurance coverage, and shall pay an amount not exceeding ten thousand dollars ($10,000) per policy for a covered claim for the return of unearned premium. The Association has no obligation to pay a claimant's covered claim, except a claimant's workers' compensation claim, if:

a.   The insured had primary coverage at the time of the loss with a solvent insurer equal to or in excess of three hundred thousand dollars ($300,000) and applicable to the claimant's loss; or

b.   The insured's coverage is written subject to a self-insured retention equal to or in excess of three hundred thousand dollars ($300,000).

If the primary coverage or the self-insured retention is less than three hundred thousand dollars ($300,000), the Association's obligation to the claimant is reduced by the coverage and the retention. The Association shall pay the full amount of a covered claim for benefits under a workers' compensation insurance coverage to a claimant notwithstanding any self-insured retention, but the Association has the right to recover the amount of the self-insured retention from the employer.

In no event shall the Association be obligated to a policyholder or claimant in an amount in excess of the obligation of the insolvent insurer under the policy from which the claim arises. Notwithstanding any other provision of this Article, a covered claim shall not include any claim filed with the Association after the final date set by the court for the filing of claims against the liquidator or receiver of an insolvent insurer.

(2)   Be deemed the insurer to the extent of the Association's obligation on the covered claims and to such extent shall have all rights, duties, and obligations of the insolvent insurer as if the insurer had not become insolvent. However, the Association has the right but not the obligation to defend an insured who is not a resident of this State at the time of the insured event unless

the property from which the claim arises is permanently located in this State in which instance the Association does have the obligation to defend the matter in accordance with policy.

(3) Allocate claims paid and expenses incurred among the two accounts separately, and assess member insurers separately for each account amounts necessary to pay the obligation of the Association under subsection (a) above subsequent to an insolvency, the expenses of handling covered claims subsequent to an insolvency, the cost of examinations under G.S. 58-48-60 and other expenses authorized by this Article. The assessments of each member insurer shall be in the proportion that the net direct written premiums of the member insurer for the preceding calendar year on the kinds of insurance in the account bears to the net direct written premiums of all member insurers for the preceding calendar year on the kinds of insurance in the account; provided, for purposes of assessment only, premiums otherwise reportable by a servicing insurer under any plan of operation approved by the Commissioner of Insurance under Articles 45 or 46 of this Chapter shall not be deemed to be the net direct written premiums of such servicing insurer or association, but shall be deemed to be the net direct written premiums of the individual insurers to the extent provided for in any such plan of operation. Each member insurer shall be notified of the assessment not later than 30 days before it is due. No member insurer may be assessed in any year on any account an amount greater than two percent (2%) of that member insurer's net direct written premiums for the preceding calendar year on the kinds of insurance in the account. If the maximum assessment, together with the other assets of the Association in any account, does not provide in any one year in any account an amount sufficient to make all necessary payments from that account, the funds available shall be prorated and the unpaid portion shall be paid as soon thereafter as funds become available. The Association may exempt or defer, in whole or in part, the assessment of any member insurer, if the assessment would cause the member insurer's financial statement to reflect amounts of capital or surplus less than the minimum amounts required for a license by any jurisdiction in which the member insurer is authorized to transact insurance. Each member insurer may set off against any assessment, authorized payments made on covered claims and expenses incurred in the payment of such claims by the member insurer if they are chargeable to the account for which the assessment is made.

(4) Investigate claims brought against the Association and adjust, compromise, settle, and pay covered claims to the extent of the Association's obligation and deny all other claims and may review settlements, releases and judgments to which the insolvent insurer or its insureds were parties to

determine the extent to which such settlements, releases and judgments may be properly contested.

(5) Notify such persons as the Commissioner directs under G.S. 58-48-45(b)(1).

(6) Handle claims through its employees or through one or more insurers or other persons designated as servicing facilities. Designation of a servicing facility is subject to the approval of the Commissioner, but such designation may be declined by a member insurer.

(7) Reimburse each servicing facility for obligations of the Association paid by the facility and for expenses incurred by the facility while handling claims on behalf of the Association and shall pay the other expenses of the Association authorized by this Article.

(b) The Association may:

(1) Employ or retain such persons as are necessary to handle claims and perform other duties of the Association.

(2) Borrow funds necessary to effect the purposes of this Article in accord with the plan of operation.

(3) Sue or be sued.

(4) Negotiate and become a party to such contracts as are necessary to carry out the purpose of this Article.

(5) Perform such other acts as are necessary or proper to effectuate the purpose of this Article.

(6) Refund to the member insurers in proportion to the contribution of each member insurer to that account that amount by which the assets of the account exceed the liabilities if, at the end of any calendar year, the board of directors finds that the assets of the Association in any account exceed the liabilities of that account as estimated by the board of directors for the coming year.

(7) Be designated or may contract as a servicing facility for any entity which may be recommended by the Association's board of directors and approved by the Commissioner of Insurance. (1971, c. 670, s. 1; 1977, c. 343; 1979, c. 295,

s. 1; 1985, c. 613, ss. 5, 6; 1989, c. 206, s. 3; 1991 (Reg. Sess., 1992), c. 802, s. 4; 1999-132, s. 9.1; 2009-130, s. 1.)

§ 58-48-40. Plan of operation.

(a) The Association shall submit to the Commissioner a plan of operation and any amendment thereto necessary or suitable to assure the fair, reasonable, and equitable administration of the Association. The plan of operation and any amendments thereto shall become effective upon approval in writing by the Commissioner.

If the Association fails to submit a suitable plan of operation within 90 days following June 25, 1971, or if at any time thereafter the Association fails to submit suitable amendments to the plan, the Commissioner shall, after notice and hearing, adopt and promulgate such reasonable rules as are necessary or advisable to effectuate the provisions of this Article. Such rules shall continue in force until modified by the Commissioner or superseded by a plan submitted by the Association and approved by the Commissioner.

(b) All member insurers shall comply with the plan of operation.

(c) The plan of operation shall:

(1) Establish the procedures whereby all the powers and duties of the Association under G.S. 58-48-35 will be performed.

(2) Establish procedures for handling assets of the Association.

(3) Establish the amount and method of reimbursing members of the board of directors under G.S. 58-48-30.

(4) Establish procedures by which claims may be filed with the Association and establish acceptable forms of proof of covered claims. Notice of claims to the receiver or liquidator of the insolvent insurer shall be deemed notice to the Association or its agent and a list of such claims shall be periodically submitted to the Association or similar organization in another state by the receiver or liquidator.

(5) Establish regular places and times for meetings of the board of directors.

(6) Establish procedures for records to be kept of all financial transactions of the Association, its agents, and the board of directors.

(7) Provide that any member insurer aggrieved by any final action or decision of the Association may appeal to the Commissioner within 30 days after the action or decision.

(8) Establish the procedures whereby selections for the board of directors will be submitted to the Commissioner.

(9) Contain additional provisions necessary or proper for the execution of the powers and duties of the Association.

(d) The plan of operation may provide that any or all powers and duties of the Association, except those under G.S. 58-48-35(a)(3) and G.S. 58-48-35(b)(2), are delegated to a corporation, association, or other organization which performs or will perform functions similar to those of this Association, or its equivalent, in two or more states. Such a corporation, association or organization shall be reimbursed as a servicing facility would be reimbursed and shall be paid for its performance of any other functions of the Association. A delegation under this subsection shall take effect only with the approval of both the board of directors and the Commissioner, and may be made only to a corporation, association, or organization which extends protection not substantially less favorable and effective than that provided by this Article. (1971, c. 670, s. 1; 1973, c. 1446, s. 2.)

§ 58-48-42. Procedure for appeal to Commissioner from decision of Association.

In any hearing called by the Commissioner for an appeal made pursuant to G.S. 58-48-40(c)(7), no later than 20 days before the hearing the appellant shall file with the Commissioner or the Commissioner's designated hearing officer and shall serve on the appellee a written statement of the appellant's case and any evidence the appellant intends to offer at the hearing. No later than five days before the hearing, the appellee shall file with the Commissioner or the Commissioner's designated hearing officer and shall serve on the appellant a written statement of the appellee's case and any evidence the appellee intends to offer at the hearing. Each hearing shall be recorded and transcribed. The cost of the recording and transcribing shall be borne equally by the appellant and the appellee. However, upon any final adjudication the prevailing party shall be reimbursed for that party's share of the costs by the other party. Each party shall, on a date determined by the Commissioner or the Commissioner's designated hearing officer, but not sooner than 15 days after delivery of the completed transcript to the party, submit to the Commissioner or the Commissioner's designated hearing officer and serve on the other party, a proposed order. The Commissioner or the Commissioner's designated hearing officer shall then issue an order. (1991, c. 644, s. 31; 1993, c. 504, s. 42.)

§ 58-48-45. Duties and powers of the Commissioner.

(a) The Commissioner shall:

(1) Notify the Association of the existence of an insolvent insurer not later than three days after he receives notice of the determination of the insolvency.

(2) Upon request of the board of directors, provide the Association with a statement of the net direct written premiums of each member insurer.

(b) The Commissioner may:

(1) Require that the Association notify the insureds of the insolvent insurer and any other interested parties of the determination of insolvency and of their rights under this Article. Such notification shall be by mail at their last known address, where available, but if sufficient information for notification by mail is not available, notice by publication in a newspaper of general circulation shall be sufficient.

(2) Suspend or revoke, after notice and hearing, the license to transact insurance in this State of any member insurer which fails to pay an assessment when due or fails to comply with the plan of operation. As an alternative, the Commissioner may levy a fine on any member insurer which fails to pay an assessment when due. Such fine shall not exceed five percent (5%) of the unpaid assessment per month, except that no fine shall be less than one hundred dollars ($100.00) per month.

(3)   Revoke the designation of any servicing facility if he finds claims are being handled unsatisfactorily.

(c)   Any final action or order of the Commissioner under this Article shall be subject to judicial review in accordance with the provisions of G.S. 58-2-75. (1971, c. 670, s. 1; 1999-132, s. 9.1.)

§ 58-48-50. Effect of paid claims.

(a)   Any person recovering under this Article shall be deemed to have assigned his rights under the policy or at law to the Association to the extent of his recovery from the Association. Every insured or claimant seeking the protection of this Article shall cooperate with the Association to the same extent as such person would have been required to cooperate with the insolvent insurer. The Association shall have no cause of action against the insured of the insolvent insurer for any sums it has paid out except such causes of action as the insolvent insurer would have had if such sums had been paid by the insolvent insurer. In the case of an insolvent insurer operating on a plan with assessment liability, payments of claims of the Association shall not operate to reduce the liability of insureds to the receiver, liquidator, or statutory successor for unpaid assessments.

(a1)   The Association shall have the right to recover from the following persons the amount of any "covered claim" paid and any and all expenses incurred, including attorneys' fees and costs of defense, in connection with any claim against the person or the person's affiliate pursuant to this Article:

(1)   Any insured whose net worth on December 31 of the year next preceding the date the insurer becomes insolvent exceeds fifty million dollars ($50,000,000) and whose liability obligations to other persons are satisfied in whole or in part by payments under this Article; or

(2)   Any person who is an affiliate of the insolvent insurer and whose liability obligations to other persons are satisfied in whole or in part by payments made under this Article.

(b)   The receiver, liquidator, or statutory successor of an insolvent insurer shall be bound by settlements of covered claims by the Association or a similar organization in another state. The court having jurisdiction shall grant such claims priority equal to that to which the claimant would have been entitled in the absence of this Article against the assets of the insolvent insurer. The expenses of the Association or similar organization in handling claims shall be accorded the same priority as the liquidator's expenses.

(c)   The Association shall periodically file with the receiver or liquidator of the insolvent insurer statements of the covered claims paid by the Association and estimates of anticipated claims on the Association which shall preserve the rights of the Association against the assets of the insolvent insurer. (1971, c. 670, s. 1; 1989, c. 206, ss. 4, 5; 2003-167, s. 2.)

§ 58-48-55. Nonduplication of recovery.

(a)   Any person having a right to a defense or a claim against an insurer under any provision in an insurance policy other than a policy of an insolvent insurer which is also a covered claim, shall be required to exhaust first his rights under such policy. Any amount payable on a covered claim under this Article shall be reduced by the amount of any recovery under that insurance policy. For purposes of this section, a claim under an insurance policy shall include a claim under or covered by any kind of insurance, whether it is a first-party or a third-party claim, and whether it is a policy covering the policyholder or another person liable to the claimant, and shall include, without limitation, policies of accident and health insurance, workers' compensation insurance, medical expense coverage, and all other coverage except for policies of an insolvent insurer.

(a1)   Any person having a claim or legal right of recovery under any governmental insurance or guaranty program which is also a covered claim shall be required to exhaust first his right under such program. Any amount payable on a covered claim under this Article shall be reduced by the amount of any recovery under such program.

(b)   Any person having a claim which may be recovered under more than one insurance guaranty association or its equivalent shall seek recovery first from the association of the place of residence of the policyholder except that if it is a first party claim for damage to property with a permanent location, he shall seek recovery first from the association of the location of the property, and if it is a workers' compensation claim, he shall seek recovery first from the association of the residence of the claimant. Any recovery under this Article shall be reduced by the amount of recovery from any other insurance guaranty association or its equivalent.

(c)   No claim held by an insurer, reinsurer, insurance pool, or underwriting association, whether the claim is:

(1)   based on an assignment, or

(2)   based on rights of subrogation or contribution, or

(3)   based on any other grounds,

nor any claim of lien, may be asserted in any legal action against a person insured under a policy issued by an insolvent insurer except to the extent the amount of such claim exceeds the obligation of the Association under G.S. 58-48-35(a)(1).

(d)   Any person that has liquidated by settlement or judgment a claim against an insured under a policy issued by an insolvent insurer, which claim is a covered claim and is also a claim within the coverage of any policy issued by a solvent insurer, shall be required to exhaust first his rights under such policy issued by the solvent insurer before execution, levy, or any other proceedings are commenced to enforce any judgment obtained against or the settlement with the insured of the insolvent insurer. Any amount so recovered from a solvent insurer shall be credited against the amount of the judgment or settlement. (1971, c. 670, s. 1; 1985, c. 613, ss. 7, 8; 1989, c. 206, s. 6; 1991 (Reg. Sess., 1992), c. 802, s. 5; 2003-167, s. 3.)

§ 58-48-60. Prevention of insolvencies.

(a)   Repealed by Session Laws 1989, c. 206, s. 7.

(b)   To aid in the detection and prevention of insurer insolvencies, the board of directors may, upon majority vote, request that the Commissioner order an examination of any member insurer which the board in good faith believes may be in a financial condition hazardous to the policyholders or the public. Within 30 days of the receipt of such request, the Commissioner shall begin such examination. The examination may be conducted as an NAIC examination or may be conducted by such persons as the Commissioner designates. The examination report shall be treated as are other examination reports. In no event shall such examination report be released to the board of directors prior to its release to the public, but this shall not preclude the Commissioner from complying with subsection (c) below. The Commissioner shall notify the board of directors when the examination is completed. The request for an examination shall be kept on file by the Commissioner but it shall not be open to public inspection prior to the release of the examination report to the public.

(c)   It shall be the duty of the Commissioner to report to the board of directors when he has reasonable cause to believe that any member insurer examined or being examined at the request of the board of directors may be insolvent or in a financial condition hazardous to the policyholders or the public.

(d)   The board of directors may, upon majority vote, make reports and recommendations to the Commissioner upon any matter germane to the solvency, liquidation, rehabilitation or conservation of any member insurer. Such reports and recommendations shall not be considered public documents.

(e)   The board of directors may, upon majority vote, make recommendations to the Commissioner for the detection and prevention of insurer insolvencies.

(f)   The board of directors may, at the conclusion of any domestic insurer insolvency in which the Association was obligated to pay covered claims, prepare a report on the history and causes of such insolvency, based on the information available to the Association, and submit such report to the Commissioner. (1971, c. 670, s. 1; 1989, c. 206, s. 7; 1991, c. 720, s. 27; 1995, c. 360, s. 2(j).)

§ 58-48-65. Examination of the Association.

The Association shall be subject to examination and regulation by the Commissioner. The board of directors shall submit, not later than March 30 of each year, a financial report for the preceding calendar year in a form approved by the Commissioner. (1971, c. 670, s. 1.)

§ 58-48-70. Tax exemption.

The Association shall be exempt from payment of all fees and all taxes levied by this State or any of its subdivisions except taxes levied by its subdivisions on real or personal property. (1971, c. 670, s. 1.)

§ 58-48-75: Repealed by Session Laws 1991, c. 689, s. 299.

§ 58-48-80. Immunity.

There shall be no liability on the part of and no cause of action of any nature shall arise against any member insurer, the Association or its agents or employees, the board of directors, or the Commissioner or his representatives for any action taken by them in the performance of their powers and duties under this Article. (1971, c. 670, s. 1.)

§ 58-48-85. Stay of proceedings; reopening of default judgments.

All proceedings in which the insolvent insurer is a party or is obligated to defend a party in any court or before any administrative agency or the North Carolina Industrial Commission shall be stayed automatically for 120 days and such additional time thereafter as may be determined by the court from the date the insolvency is determined or any ancillary proceedings are initiated in this State, whichever is later, to permit proper defense by the Association of all pending causes of action. Any party to any proceeding which is stayed pursuant to this section shall have the right, upon application and notice, to seek a vacation or modification of such stay. Any covered claims arising from any judgment under any decision, verdict or finding based on the default of the insolvent insurer or its failure to defend an insured, shall, upon application and notice by the Association be vacated and set aside by the same court in which such judgment, order, decision, verdict, or finding is entered and the Association either on its own behalf or on behalf of any insured or an insolvent insurer, shall be permitted to defend against such claim on the merits. Any party who has obtained any such judgment or order shall have the right, upon application and notice, to have the judgment or order restored if within 90 days following the entry of the judgment or order the Association has not notified such party and the court that it intends to defend the matter on the merits. (1971, c. 670, s. 1; 1989, c. 206, s. 8; 2003-167, s. 4.)

§ 58-48-90. Termination; distribution of funds.

(a) The Commissioner shall by order terminate the operation of the North Carolina Insurance Guaranty Association as to any kind of insurance covered by this Article with respect to which he has found, after hearing, that there is in effect a statutory or voluntary plan which:

(1) Is a permanent plan which is adequately funded or for which adequate funding is provided; and

(2) Extends, or will extend to the North Carolina policyholders and residents protection and benefits with respect to insolvent insurers not substantially less favorable and effective to such policyholders and residents than the protection and benefits provided with respect to such kinds of insurance under this Article.

(b) The Commissioner shall by the same such order authorize discontinuance of future payments by insurers to the North Carolina Insurance Guaranty Association with respect to the same kinds of insurance; provided, the assessments and payments shall continue, as necessary, to liquidate covered claims of insurers adjudged insolvent prior to said order and the related expenses not covered by such other plan.

(c) In the event the operation of the North Carolina Insurance Guaranty Association shall be so terminated as to all kinds of insurance otherwise within its scope, the Association as soon as possible thereafter shall distribute the balance of moneys and assets remaining (after discharge of the functions of the Association with respect to prior insurer insolvencies not covered by such other plan, together with related expenses) to the insurers which are then writing in this State policies of the kinds of insurance covered by this Article and which had made payments to the Association, pro rata upon the basis of the aggregate of such payments made by the respective insurers during the period of five years next preceding the date of such order. Upon completion of such distribution with respect to all of the kinds of insurance covered by this Article, this Article shall be deemed to have expired. (1971, c. 670, s. 1.)

§ 58-48-95. Use of deposits made by insolvent insurer.

(a) Notwithstanding any other provision of this Chapter pertaining to the use of deposits made by insurance companies for the protection of policyholders, the Association shall receive, upon its request, from the Commissioner and may expend, any deposit or deposits made, whether or not required by statute, by an insolvent insurer to the extent those deposits are needed by the Association first to pay the covered claims as required by this Article and then to the extent those deposits are needed to pay all expenses of the Association relating to the insurer: Provided that the Commissioner may retain and use an amount of the deposit up to ten thousand dollars ($10,000) to defray administrative costs to be incurred by the Commissioner in carrying out his powers and duties with respect to the insolvent insurer, notwithstanding G.S. 58-5-70.

(b) In, however the case of a deposit made by an insolvent domestic insurer, the Association shall receive, upon its request, from the Commissioner, the portions of the deposit made for the protection of policyholders having covered claims. As for the general deposit, those portions shall be in the proportions that the insolvent domestic insurer's domestic net direct written premiums for the preceding calendar year on the kinds of insurance in the account bears to its total net direct written premiums for the preceding calendar year on the kinds of insurance in the account.

(c) The Association shall account to the Commissioner and the insolvent insurer for all deposits received from the Commissioner under this section. After the deposits of the insolvent insurer received by the Association under this section have been expended by the Association for the purposes set out in this section, the member insurers shall be assessed as provided by this Article to pay any remaining liabilities of the Association arising under this Article. (1979, c. 628; 1985, c. 613, s. 10; c. 666, s. 41; 1987, c. 864, s. 6; 1989, c. 206, s. 9; c. 452, s. 5; 1993 (Reg. Sess., 1994), c. 678, s. 23; 2001-223, s. 24.4; 2001-487, s. 103(a).)

§ 58-48-100. Statute of repose; guardians ad litem; notice.

(a) Notwithstanding any other provision of law, a covered claim with respect to which settlement is not effected with the Association, or suit is not instituted against the insured of an insolvent insurer or the Association, within five years after the date of entry of the order by a court of competent jurisdiction determining the insurer to be insolvent, shall thenceforth be barred forever as a claim against the Association.

(b) As to any person under a disability described in G.S. 1-17, the Association may not invoke the bar of the period of repose provided in subsection (a) of this section unless the Association has petitioned for the appointment of a guardian ad litem for such person and the disposition of that petition has become final. If a guardian ad litem is appointed pursuant to this subsection more than four years after the date of entry of the order by a court of competent jurisdiction determining the insurer to be insolvent, the period of repose under subsection (a) of this section shall be extended for such person one year after the date of the appointment.

(c) Within six months after the Association has been activated as to an insolvent insurer, the Commissioner may request that the Association submit an amendment to the plan of operation in accordance with G.S. 58-48-40, which amendment shall be applicable only to that insolvent insurer and shall prescribe a fair, reasonable, and equitable procedure for notice to insureds and to the public. (1985, c. 613, s. 9.)

§ 58-48-105. Transfer of balance of security funds.

(a) All moneys received and paid into the Stock Workers' Compensation Security Fund under former G.S. 97-107, together with all property and securities acquired by and through the use of moneys belonging to this Fund, including interest earned upon moneys in this Fund, shall be transferred and deposited into a new account with the Association created pursuant to G.S. 58-48-115. This account shall be separate and apart from any other accounts similarly created and from all other Association funds. The Association shall be the custodian of the account, and shall administer the account in accordance with the provisions of this Article.

(b) All moneys received and paid into the Mutual Workers' Compensation Security Fund under former G.S. 97-114, together with all property and securities acquired by and through the use of moneys belonging to this Fund, including interest earned upon moneys in this Fund, shall be transferred and deposited into a new account with the Association created pursuant to G.S. 58-48-120. This account shall be separate and apart from any other accounts similarly created and from all other Association accounts. The Association shall be the custodian of the account, and shall administer the account in accordance with the provisions of this Article. (1991 (Reg. Sess., 1992), c. 802, s. 6.)

§ 58-48-110. Purpose of the accounts.

The purpose of the accounts created in the Association pursuant to G.S. 58-48-115 and G.S. 58-48-120 of this Article shall be solely to:

(1)   Receive the balance from the accounts created under former G.S. 97-107 and G.S. 97-114;

(2)   Receive assessment moneys from member companies as provided in G.S. 58-48-115(a)(3), 58-48-120(b), and 58-48-120(c);

(3)   Receive interest on moneys in the accounts;

(4)   Pay stock or mutual carrier claims made against the security funds established under G.S. 97-107 and G.S. 97-114, but only for claims existing before January 1, 1993; and

(5)   Refund to the contributing stock companies in accordance with G.S. 58-48-115 the excess moneys in the stock fund account as set forth in G.S. 58-48-115(a)(2). (1991 (Reg. Sess., 1992), c. 802, s. 7.)

§ 58-48-115. Creation of Stock Fund Account; maintenance of Stock Fund Account; and distribution of Stock Fund.

(a)   The moneys received by the Association pursuant to G.S. 58-48-105(a) shall be distributed as follows:

(1)   An amount equivalent to one and one-half times the contingent liabilities of the Stock Workers' Compensation Security Fund created pursuant to former G.S. 97-107 existing on December 31, 1992, shall be deposited in a separate reserve account to be maintained by the Association which shall be designated as the "Stock Reserve Account." The amount of the Fund's contingent liabilities

and the amount to be deposited in this Stock Reserve Account shall be determined and approved by the Department.

(2) The balance of the moneys received from the Stock Workers' Compensation Security Fund created pursuant to former G.S. 97-107 shall be refunded by the Association to member insurers that were contributing stock carriers during calendar year 1989 in accordance with the determination of the Department under this subdivision. The amount to be refunded to each stock carrier shall be in proportion to the contributions paid in by each stock carrier. The Department shall, as nearly as practicable, determine this amount under generally accepted accounting principles and the determination of the Department shall be final and not subject to appeal.

(3) Should the balance of the moneys in the Stock Reserve Account be reduced to less than one and one-half times the contingent liabilities of the account, the Association shall assess all member insurers that are stock carriers writing workers' compensation in this State at the time of the assessment in an amount equivalent to one and one-half times the contingent liabilities of said account. The assessment under this subdivision shall be made in accordance with the provisions of G.S. 58-48-35(a)(3). (1991 (Reg. Sess., 1992), c. 802, s. 8.)

§ 58-48-120. Creation of Mutual Fund Account; maintenance of Mutual Fund Account.

(a) The moneys received by the Association pursuant to G.S. 58-48-105(b) shall be deposited in a separate reserve account to be maintained by the Association which shall be designated as the Mutual Reserve Account. The amount in this account shall be equivalent to one and one-half times the contingent liabilities of the Mutual Workers' Compensation Security Fund created pursuant to former G.S. 97-114 existing on December 31, 1992. The amount of this Fund's contingent liabilities and the amount to be deposited into this Mutual Reserve Account shall be determined and approved by the Department.

(b) If the amount received by the Association from the former Mutual Workers' Compensation Security Fund created pursuant to G.S. 97-114 and received by the Association pursuant to G.S. 58-48-105(b) is insufficient to equal one and one-half times the contingent liabilities of the Fund existing on

December 31, 1992, the Association shall, over the five years following January 1, 1993, assess the member insurers that are mutual carriers writing workers' compensation insurance in this State at the time of the assessment in the amount it determines necessary to make up the difference between the money received by the Association pursuant to G.S. 58-48-105(b) and one and one-half times the contingent liabilities of the Fund as determined by the Department of Insurance pursuant to G.S. 58-48-120(a). The assessment under this subsection shall be made in accordance with the provisions of G.S. 58-48-35(a)(3).

(c)   After December 31, 1997, should the balance of the moneys in the Mutual Reserve Account be reduced to less than one and one-half times the contingent liabilities of the account, the Association shall assess all member insurers that are mutual carriers writing workers' compensation insurance in this State at the time of the assessment in an amount necessary to raise the account to an amount equivalent to one and one-half times the contingent liabilities of said account. The assessment under this subsection shall be made in accordance with the provisions of G.S. 58-48-35(a)(3). (1991 (Reg. Sess., 1992), c. 802, s. 9.)

§ 58-48-125. Payments by the Association.

The accounts created in G.S. 58-48-115 and G.S. 58-48-120 shall be used to pay the claims against insolvent stock workers' compensation insurers and insolvent mutual workers' compensation insurers, respectively, pursuant to G.S. 58-48-110(4) where the insolvency occurred prior to January 1, 1993. The expenses of administering these accounts, including loss adjustment expenses, shall be paid out of the respective accounts. (1991 (Reg. Sess., 1992), c. 802, s. 10; 1993, c. 504, s. 30.)

§ 58-48-130. Termination.

The account created in G.S. 58-48-115 shall be dissolved when all liabilities of the Stock Workers' Compensation Security Fund, under former G.S. 97-107 have been satisfied. Any excess moneys in the Stock Reserve Account shall be refunded to the member insurers that were stock workers' compensation carriers during the preceding calendar year. The amount to be refunded to each stock carrier shall be in proportion to the assessments paid by each stock carrier. The account created in G.S. 58-48-120 shall be dissolved when the liabilities of the Mutual Workers' Compensation Security Fund, under former G.S. 97-114, have been satisfied. Any excess moneys in the mutual reserve account shall be refunded to the member insurers that were mutual workers' compensation carriers during the preceding calendar year. The amount to be refunded to each mutual carrier shall be in proportion to the assessments paid by each mutual carrier. (1991 (Reg. Sess., 1992), c. 802, s. 11.)

Article 49.

Determination of Jurisdiction Over Providers of Health Care Benefits; Regulation of Multiple Employer Welfare Arrangements.

§ 58-49-1. Purposes.

The purposes of this section and G.S. 58-49-5 through G.S. 58-49-25 are: To give the State jurisdiction over providers of health care benefits; to indicate how each provider of health care benefits may show under what jurisdiction it falls; to allow for examinations by the State if the provider of health care benefits is unable to show it is subject to the exclusive jurisdiction of another governmental agency; to make such a provider of health care benefits subject to the laws of the State if it cannot show that it is subject to the exclusive jurisdiction of another governmental agency; and to disclose the purchasers of such health care benefits whether or not the plans are fully insured. As used in G.S. 58-49-5 through G.S. 58-49-20, "person" does not mean the State of North Carolina or any county, city, or other political subdivision of the State of North Carolina. (1985, c. 304, s. 1; 1993 (Reg. Sess., 1994), c. 569, s. 1; 2001-334, s. 18.1.)

§ 58-49-5. Authority and jurisdiction of Commissioner.

Notwithstanding any other provision of law, and except as provided in this Article, any person that provides coverage in this State for medical, surgical, chiropractic, physical therapy, speech pathology, audiology, professional mental health, dental, hospital, or optometric expenses, whether the coverage is by direct payment, reimbursement, or otherwise, shall be presumed to be subject to the jurisdiction of the Commissioner, unless the person shows that while providing the services it is subject to the exclusive jurisdiction of another agency or subdivision of this State or of the federal government. (1985, c. 304, s. 1; 1993 (Reg. Sess., 1994), c. 569, s. 2; 1995, c. 193, s. 40.)

§ 58-49-10. How to show jurisdiction.

A person may show that it is subject to the exclusive jurisdiction of another agency or subdivision of this State or the federal government, by providing to the Commissioner the appropriate certificate, license, or other document issued by the other governmental agency that permits or qualifies it to provide those services. If no documentation is issued by that other agency, the person may provide a certification by an official of that agency that states that the person is under the exclusive jurisdiction of that agency. (1985, c. 304, s. 1; 1993 (Reg. Sess., 1994), c. 569, s. 3.)

§ 58-49-12. Exceptions to jurisdiction; health care sharing organizations.

A health care sharing organization shall not be subject to the jurisdiction of the Commissioner and shall not be considered to be engaging in the business of providing health care benefits as long as the health care sharing organization does the following:

(1) Maintains nonprofit entity status under the Internal Revenue Code.

(2) Limits its participants to those who share similar interests as defined by the organization.

(3) Provides for the financial or medical needs of a participant through contributions from one participant to another in accordance with criteria established by the health care sharing organization.

(4) Provides amounts that participants may contribute with no assumption of risk or promise to pay among the participants and no assumption of risk or promise to pay by the health care sharing organization to the participants.

(5) Publishes a written monthly statement to all participants that lists the total dollar amount of qualified needs submitted to the health care sharing organization, as well as the amount published or assigned to participants for their contribution.

(6) Provides a written disclaimer on or accompanying all applications and guideline materials distributed by or on behalf of the organization that reads, in substance, as follows:

"NOTICE: The organization facilitating the sharing of medical expenses is not an insurance company and neither its guidelines nor its plan of operation is an insurance policy. Whether anyone chooses to assist you with your medical bills will be voluntary. No other participant will be compelled by law to contribute toward your medical bills. As such, participation in the organization or a subscription to any of its documents should never be considered to be insurance. Regardless of whether you receive any payment for medical expenses or whether this organization continues to operate, you are always personally liable for the payment of your own medical bills." (2011-103, s. 1.)

§ 58-49-15. Examination.

Any person that is unable to show under G.S. 58-49-10 that it is subject to the exclusive jurisdiction of another agency or subdivision of this State or of the federal government, shall submit to an examination by the Commissioner to determine the organization and solvency of the person, and to determine whether or not such person complies with the applicable provisions of this Chapter. (1985, c. 304, s. 1; 1993 (Reg. Sess., 1994), c. 569, s. 4.)

§ 58-49-20. Subject to State laws.

Any person unable to show that it is subject to the exclusive jurisdiction of another agency or subdivision of this State or the federal government, shall be subject to all appropriate provisions of this Chapter regarding the conduct of its business. (1985, c. 304, s. 1; 1993 (Reg. Sess., 1994), c. 569, s. 5.)

§ 58-49-25. Disclosure.

(a) Any production agency or administrator that advertises, sells, transacts, or administers the coverage in this State described in G.S. 58-49-5 and that is required to submit to an examination by the Commissioner under G.S. 58-49-15, shall, if said coverage is not fully insured or otherwise fully covered by an admitted life, accident, health, accident and health, or disability insurer, nonprofit hospital, medical, or dental service plan, or nonprofit health care plan, clearly and distinctly advise every purchaser, prospective purchaser, and covered person of such lack of insurance or other coverage.

(b) Any administrator that advertises or administers the coverage in this State described in G.S. 58-49-5 and that is required to submit to an examination by the Commissioner under G.S. 58-49-15, shall advise any production agency of the elements of the coverage, including the amount of "stop-loss" insurance in effect. (1985, c. 304, s. 1.)

§ 58-49-30. Multiple employer welfare arrangements; definition; administrators.

(a) As used in this section, the term "multiple employer welfare arrangement" or "MEWA" means that term as defined in Section 3 of the Employee Retirement Income Security Act of 1974, 29 U.S.C. § 1002(40)(A), as amended, that meets either or both of the following criteria:

(1) One or more of the employer members of the MEWA is either domiciled in this State or has its principal headquarters or principal administrative office in this State.

(2) The MEWA solicits an employer that is domiciled in this State or that has its principal headquarters or principal administrative office in this State.

(b) Repealed by Session Laws 1991, c. 611, s. 3.

(c) Each insurer licensed to do business in this State that administers a MEWA shall, at the request of the Commissioner, provide the Commissioner with such information regarding the insurer's administrative services contract or contracts with such MEWA or MEWAs that the Commissioner requires. No unlicensed insurer shall administer any MEWA.

(d), (e) Repealed by Session Laws 1991, c. 611, s. 3. (1989 (Reg. Sess., 1990), c. 1055, s. 1; 1991, c. 611, s. 3.)

§ 58-49-35. Multiple employer welfare arrangements; license required; penalty.

(a) It is unlawful to operate, maintain, or establish a MEWA unless the MEWA has a valid license issued by the Commissioner. Any MEWA operating in this State without a valid license is an unauthorized insurer.

(b) G.S. 58-49-30 through 58-49-65 do not apply to a MEWA that offers or provides benefits that are fully insured by an authorized insurer or to a MEWA that is exempt from state insurance regulation in accordance with the Employee Retirement Income Security Act of 1974, Public Law Number 43-406. (1991, c. 611, s. 1.)

§ 58-49-40. Qualifications for licensure.

(a) To meet the requirements for issuance of a license and to maintain a MEWA, a MEWA must be:

(1) Nonprofit;

(2) Established by a trade association, industry association, or professional association of employers or professionals that has a constitution or bylaws and that has been organized and maintained in good faith for a continuous period of five years for purposes other than that of obtaining or providing insurance;

(3) Operated pursuant to a trust agreement by a board of trustees that has complete fiscal control over the MEWA and that is responsible for all operations of the MEWA. Except as provided in this subdivision, the trustees must be owners, partners, officers, directors, or employees of one or more employers in the MEWA. With the Commissioner's approval, a person who is not such an owner, partner, officer, director, or employee may serve as a trustee if that person possesses the expertise required for such service. A trustee may not be an owner, officer or employee of the administrator or service company of the MEWA. The trustees have the authority to approve applications of association

members for participation in the MEWA and to contract with an authorized administrator or service company to administer the operations of the MEWA;

(4)   Neither offered nor advertised to the public generally; and

(5)   Operated in accordance with sound actuarial principles.

(b)   The MEWA shall issue to each covered employee a policy, contract, certificate, summary plan description, or other evidence of the benefits and coverages provided. The evidence of benefits and coverages provided shall contain, in boldface print in a conspicuous location, the following statement: "THE BENEFITS AND COVERAGES DESCRIBED HEREIN ARE PROVIDED THROUGH A TRUST FUND ESTABLISHED BY A GROUP OF EMPLOYERS [name of MEWA]. EXCESS INSURANCE IS PROVIDED BY A LICENSED INSURANCE COMPANY TO COVER HIGH AMOUNT MEDICAL CLAIMS. THE TRUST FUND IS NOT SUBJECT TO ANY INSURANCE GUARANTY ASSOCIATION, ALTHOUGH THE TRUST FUND IS MONITORED BY THE NORTH CAROLINA DEPARTMENT OF INSURANCE. OTHER RELATED FINANCIAL INFORMATION IS AVAILABLE FROM YOUR EMPLOYER OR FROM THE [name of MEWA]." If applicable, the same documents shall contain, in boldface print in a conspicuous location, the following statement: "PARTICIPATING EMPLOYERS WILL BE RESPONSIBLE FOR FUNDING ALL CLAIMS INCURRED BY EMPLOYEES COVERED UNDER THE TRUST." Any statement required by this subsection is not required on identification cards issued to covered employees or other insureds.

(c)   Each MEWA shall maintain excess insurance written by an insurer authorized to do business in this State with a retention level determined in accordance with sound actuarial principles. Such contracts must be filed with the Commissioner and contain notification provisions requiring at least 60 days' notice to the Commissioner from the insurer issuing such coverage prior to the termination or modification of such coverage. The Commissioner may by rule prescribe net retentions levels for MEWAs in accordance with the number of risks insured.

(d)   Each MEWA shall establish and maintain appropriate loss reserves determined in accordance with sound actuarial principles.

(e)   The Commissioner shall not grant or continue a license to any MEWA if the Commissioner deems that any trustee, manager, or administrator is incompetent, untrustworthy, or so lacking in insurance expertise as to make the operations of the MEWA hazardous to the potential and existing insureds; that any trustee, manager, or administrator has been found guilty of or has pled guilty or no contest to a felony, a crime involving moral turpitude, or a crime punishable by imprisonment of one year or more under the law of any state or country, whether or not a judgment or conviction has been entered; that any trustee, manager, or administrator has had any type of insurance license revoked in this or any other state; or that the business operations of the MEWA are or have been characterized, to the detriment of the employers participating in the MEWA, of persons receiving benefits from the MEWA, or of creditors or the public, by the improper manipulation of assets, accounts, or excess insurance or by bad faith.

(f) To qualify for and retain a license, a MEWA shall file all contracts with administrators or service companies with the Commissioner, and report any changes to such contracts to the Commissioner in advance of their implementation.

(g) Failure to maintain compliance with the eligibility requirements established by this section is a ground for denial, suspension, or revocation of the license of a MEWA. (1991, c. 611, s. 1.)

§ 58-49-45. Certain words prohibited in name of MEWA.

No licensed MEWA shall use in its name, contracts, literature, advertising in any medium, or any other printed matter the words "insurance", "casualty", "surety", "mutual", or any other words descriptive of the insurance business or deceptively similar to the name or description of any insurer doing business in this State. (1991, c. 611, s. 1.)

Vision Books Order Form

Fax Orders: 1-980-299-5965

Phone Orders: 1-704-898-0770

E-mail Orders: www.visionbooks.org

Mail Orders: Vision Books, LLC
P.O. Box 42406
Charlotte, NC 28215

Shipp To:
Name_____
Address_____
City_____State_____Zip_____
Phone_____Fax_____
Email_____@_____

Bill To: We can bill a third party on your behalf.
Name_____
Address_____
City_____State_____Zip_____
Phone____(   )_____Fax_____
Email_____@_____

Pamphlet Number ($15.00 Each)	Qty	Total Cost
_____	_____	_____
_____	_____	_____
_____	_____	_____
_____	_____	_____
_____	_____	_____
_____	_____	_____
_____	_____	_____
_____	_____	_____
_____	_____	_____
Full Volume Set 1-92	92 Pamphlets	1,380.00

Free Shipping Shipping & Handling on Full Volume Orders
Add $1.00 Shipping & Handling per pamphlet $_____

Total Cost $_____

Thank you for your support. Management!

DID YOU ENJOY THIS BOOK?

Vision Books, LLC would like to hear from you! If you or someone you know has been fasely imprisoned, we would like to hear your story. If the 'North Carolina Criminal Law and Procedure' has had an effect in your life or if you have suggestions, we would like to hear from you. Send your letters to:

Vision Books, LLC
Attn: Staff Writers
P.O. Box 42406
Charlotte, NC 28215
Email: staff@visionbooks.org

Order Additional Copies:

Fax Orders: 1-980-299-5965

Phone Orders: 1-704-898-0770

E-mail Orders: www.visionbooks.org

Mail Orders: Vision Books, LLC
                      P.O. Box 42406
                      Charlotte, NC 28215

www.ingramcontent.com/pod-product-compliance
Lightning Source LLC
Chambersburg PA
CBHW051627170526
45167CB00001B/89